Down With Power

L. Neil Smith at Phoenix Pick

Tom Paine Maru–Special Author's Edition
The Venus Belt
The Crystal Palace
Sweeter Than Wine

Pallas
Ceres

Hope (with Aaron Zelman)

Robert A. Heinlein
Take Back Your Government

www.PhoenixPick.com

Down With Power

LIBERTARIAN POLICY IN A TIME OF CRISIS

L. Neil Smith

an imprint of

ARC
MANOR
Rockville, Maryland

ISBN: 978-1-61242-055-4

www.PhoenixPick.com
Sign Up for Free Ebooks

Library of Congress Cataloging-in-Publication Data

Smith, L. Neil.
 Down with power : libertarian policy in a time of crisis / L. Neil Smith; introduction by Dr. Sean Gabb.
    p. cm.
 Includes index.
 ISBN 978-1-61242-055-4 (alk. paper) -- ISBN 978-1-61242-056-1 (ebook)
 1. Libertarianism--United States. I. Title.
JC599.U5S558 2012
320.51'2--dc23

                            2011050899

Published by Phoenix Pick
an imprint of Arc Manor, LLC
P. O. Box 10339
Rockville, MD 20849-0339
www.ArcManor.com

This book is dedicated, with love and gratitude, to the great Ernest Hancock, who knows why, and two others, who know who they are.

Portions of this book appeared originally in my online journal *The Libertarian Enterprise*, http://www.NCC-1776.org, and on the website of Jews for the Preservation of Firearms Ownership at http://www.JPFO.org. Special thanks to my friend, editor, and right arm, Ken Holder, and to my lovely and talented wife, Cathy L.Z. Smith.

Contents

Introduction by Dr. Sean Gabb

I discovered L. Neil Smith on the second Thursday in March 1985. I was on a railway train somewhere between King's Cross in London and York, and I found a copy of his novel *The Probability Broach* in one of the luggage racks.

This is a great novel. It has a main plot that both grips the reader and is seamlessly integrated with the alternative history background. Under any circumstances, the book would have been a lucky find. But if it depends mainly on inherent quality, the appreciation of any text depends also on the mood of the reader. And I was in just the right mood for Neil.

I was depressed. I was very depressed, and for various reasons. I was depressed that the Thatcher government, in which I had placed so much faith, was turning England into a police state. I was depressed that none of my libertarian friends were able to see what I could, and were even muttering behind my back that I was "rather unsound." I was depressed because I had no money. I was depressed that, after such heroic efforts in 1981 and 1982, I was fat again, and that I had none of the willpower needed to stop being fat. I was depressed because, perhaps for associated reasons, it was hard to find anyone I actually fancied who wanted to sleep with me.

Now, I will not say that reading *The Probability Broach* helped me lose four stone of ugly fat and make my first million. But it did let me see the world more clearly and my own place within it as a libertarian. Back in those days, I must explain, the British free market movement was not really that libertarian. Alone, we used to read great slabs of Hayek and von Mises, or commentaries on them, or imitations of them. If we gathered in public, it was usually to listen to some Tory MP or businessman on the make, talking about the need to stuff the trade unions or see off the Russians. Chris Tame was always the great exception to the rule. But it was to be years before I became his closest friend. Otherwise, our movement was remarkably parasitic on the success—whatever that might amount to—of the Thatcher government. Unless Chris was in the room, when I did start talking about civil liberties, the best I usually got was a brief silence, followed by an impatient "Oh yes, we believe in all that as well."

What I got from *The Probability Broach* was my clearest perception yet of what libertarianism should be about. Yes, we believe in free markets, and in enterprise, and, so long as there must be a government, in certain constitutional safeguards. But this is all supportive of the true argument for liberty—which is that it allows us to have a really good time for a very long time. The alternative America that Neil shows us is a place where people say and do whatever they please. They smoke. They drink. They fly about in rockets. They have the bodies they want. I seem to recall that they sometimes change sex. They certainly control what age they appear.

If I have just said anything that seems disparaging of Hayek and von Mises, I do apologise. But it was only by reading Neil that I was fully able to understand the world that their flat and colourless sentences had been written to help bring into being. It no longer mattered what everyone else thought about me; and, though we were still eight years away from my discovery of the Internet, I felt inspired to start writing up what I thought was so awful about the world and how it might be made a better place.

Having mentioned the Internet, I suppose I should remind everyone born since about 1975 how difficult it was in the olden days to find anything at all outside the mainstream. I had found Neil by accident. It was days before I could hunt down any of his other fiction in the big London bookshops. It was a waste of time even to try looking for any of his political writings. When everything was on paper—and often put there by a duplicator, or at best by a photocopier—laying hands on fringe material was a hit-or-miss business. And it was that even when published in your own country. Nowadays, whatever you want—bizarre and possibly illegal porn, the alleged utterances of Osama bin Laden, tomorrow's weather forecast for Provo in Utah—is never more than a few clicks away. Back in 1985, it would not have been absolutely impossible in London to get access to the newsletters Neil was writing in America. But it was far beyond my abilities.

Eventually, though, I did get myself on-line; and there, on liber-net, Neil was waiting. If it was still several years before I found the courage to send him fan mail, Neil was, from 1993, part of my favourite regular on-line reading. His essays were models of lucidity and contempt. We were living in different countries. Many of the things he was writing about had little relevance for me in England. But I could admire the lucidity of his style. And I could admire the depths and force of his contempt.

This was not contempt, mind you, of what is most conveniently, though perhaps misleadingly, called "the left." That was easily found in our movement on both sides of the Atlantic. No, what I admired was his contempt for our supposed allies. In England and in America, libertarians had been listening for decades, at least, to promises that such-and-such a "conservative" politician was on our side, and that, when he spoke vaguely to the masses about free markets and constitutional limits on the State, he was not saying the tenth of what he really meant. Well, we had listened to these rogues and liars—Nixon and Heath and Thatcher and Reagan, and John Redwood and Newt Gingrich, and all the others—and it was time for those of us who had now finally got ourselves a big audience on-line to say exactly what we thought of them, of them and of the lesser rogues and liars who were still crying them up as closet libertarians.

And here, eighteen years later, we still are. Much has changed since then. I can now boast that, while we have never met in the physical sense, Neil is now a dear and valued friend. But he is still writing, still turning the literary equivalent of a flame thrower on enemies of our civilisation. And it is a very great honour that he has now asked me to introduce this latest volume of his writings.

I could stop here. It is, after all, the job of an introduction writer to say something nice about the main contents, and then to shut up. But I do have in mind one further observation about Neil that I might not otherwise find the opportunity to make, or to make in one place. This is that, once you leave aside his inspirational fiction, he is a very angry man.

You will find, for example, that every essay in this book is, in one way or another, a masterpiece of denunciatory rhetoric, and you will not take from it very much that is positive. Oh, you will, every so often, read about his cure for the toilet that America has become—which is a strict enforcement of the Bill of Rights. But how do you assemble the coalition needed to get the right sort of President elected? How do you scale back not only the claims of a kleptocratic elite, but also the expectations of ordinary people that may not be entirely legitimate, but are not unreasonable when you bear in mind that the free-market solutions to which they ought to be looking have been regulated out of existence, or simply crowded out? What about old age pensions? What about healthcare subsidies—subsidies that even Ayn Rand was in the end not too proud to claim?

But this is not a criticism. You do not go to Neil for these things. There are policy institutes all over America with millions of dollars to spend on long and worthy, and sometimes honest and disinterested, prescriptions. You go to Neil for the anger of righteousness.

Have you ever seen a friend or a loved one die? Have you ever lain awake at night, wondering how long before it will be you lying unconscious in that hospital bed, with tubes sticking out of you? You might tell yourself that these are the inevitable misfortunes of life, and that we are lucky to be alive now, in an age where we and our friends and loved ones have some chance of getting near to the end of our normal life spans, or even somewhat beyond. We could say that. We do say that. But we are now living in the fifth century of an exponential growth of human control over nature. Why is it that we have so many bombs that, if we let them all off at once, we might turn our planet into a ball of rock as dead as all the others in our solar system—and why is it that making it to ninety is very nearly as remarkable for us as it was to the Ancient Greeks?

The answer is because every step in the progress of our knowledge has been impeded or perverted or at least largely to the advantage of a parasitic ruling class. Every English child—and perhaps every American child too—learns the mediaeval rhyme:

Baa, baa, black sheep,
Have you any wool?
Yes sir, yes sir,
Three bags full.
One for the master,
One for the dame,
And one for the little boy
Who lives down the lane.

That is how—the century before last partially excepted—it has always been. Everything created by the people has been shared with the military and propagandistic wings of the ruling class. In mediaeval times, it was a third of the wool to the King and a third to the Church, and a third left to us. The only difference today is that, as we have become more productive, the third left to us has shrivelled to a sixth or a tenth or a fiftieth. The rest is taken by men with guns, or to feed armies of smiling and utterly malign intellectuals.

Just imagine a world in which those two big wars of the last century had not been fought, and in which the ruling class had been kept under the same semi-limitation as it was until 1914. Or let us write off the millions shot or blown apart or gassed or starved in those meaningless slaughters. We doubtless lost a few Newtons and Mozarts, but these wars were a long time ago, and mentioning their utter worthlessness upsets too many people who ought to know better but do not.

Suppose only that America and England and Western Europe had, after 1945, been taxed and regulated half as much as they were. We might not by now have indefinite life extension and prospecting colonies in the Asteroid Belt. But do you really think we would still be facing our pathetically short life spans, and a last few months or years rotten with cancer and taking mostly ineffective pills from which the commercial wing of our ruling class does very nicely?

No, forget a scaling back of the ruling class after 1945. Instead, let us only suppose that "victory" against Soviet Russia had really been followed by the "peace dividend" we were promised. Even then, things could so easily have been better than they are. Even twenty years of reduced parasitism would have left us richer, and therefore healthier, and therefore happier. But, in place of these very pale approximations to a free society, we are now where we are now. In England and America, we struggle to pay our taxes. We are sprayed with lies about villainous foreigners in funny clothes whose only wish is to kill us. We worry that our children will say something out of place, and bring social workers knocking on our doors. We are left with just enough of what we produce to divert ourselves—with flat-screen television sets and industrialised holidays—from the knowledge that we are serfs.

That is what I find in the non-fiction of L. Neil Smith—denunciations of the current order of things, and the burning and clearly-expressed conviction that it could so easily be different.

If you are leafing through this introduction and wondering whether to buy the book—do buy it. If you have bought it already and have started with my introduction—you are in for a treat. If you want some pious explanation of what a good idea it might be to privatise the cracks between the paving stones, you have not been a perfectly rational consumer. If, on the other hand, you want chapter and verse on how your country is owned by pigs and run by wolves, and on how glorious it would be if we stopped being sheep—in this case, ladies and gentlemen, fasten your belts and enjoy the ride!

Down With Power: Author's Preface

9/11 changed nothing. Politicians still lie, cheat, and steal for money and power. Ordinary people still struggle every day to defend rights that were supposed to have been guaranteed.

—L. NEIL SMITH

In his 1992 film *Freejack*, which is concerned, in part, with an unusual kind of virtual reality, Anthony Hopkins, whose reality it is, invites the protagonists to explore it with the words "Welcome to my mind." In a way, that's the invitation that I'm offering here, except that, unlike my novels, there is considerably more than one mind involved.

You may encounter some today who call themselves libertarians, yet reject the positions I lay out in this book. This is an unfortunate result, in part, of the Libertarian Party's maniacal attempt to build a "bigger tent," over the past couple of decades, by the simple, if self-defeatingly stupid, tactic of watering down what libertarians have always believed until they deemed it acceptable to those who are not libertarians. Yet there remains within the movement—as opposed to the party—a core of strong individualists who value principle over expedience, understanding that their way will lead to eventual victory, while in the long run, the other is a recipe for political suicide.

When somebody tells you that he or she is a libertarian, and asks you for your vote (because that, above all, is what the waterers-down are all about, and to hell with any other consideration) ask him or her where he or she stands on the issue of private gun ownership, on children's rights, on ending the War on Drugs, on putting an end to the policy of dropping bombs on pregnant widows and 10-year-old goatherds in the Third World, or on the absolute moral obligation of any party that calls itself libertarian to abolish all taxation, forever.

Their answers, or the lack thereof, will tell you whether these are real libertarians that you've talking to or merely "LINOs"—libertarians in name only. Their destructive presence—the Libertarian Party's 2008 presidential candidate is one such specimen—is one of the reasons I believed it was necessary to write this book.

But I have digressed, as you will find I do from time to time.

No two individuals can ever agree on 100 percent of anything 100 percent of the time. The old saying is, get any two libertarians together and you'll instantly have a debate on your hands. But what I have written here represents the views of most genuine libertarians over the past half century. I should know; I've been a libertarian since 1962 when I was 15. So in that sense, welcome to their minds, too.

I am not saying, of the measures proposed here, that this is what some future libertarian society or government will do (although I have said it, often, in the 30-odd novels I've written). What I am saying here is that this is what must be done now, by anyone in the position to do it, if we truly want our culture—Western Civilization—to survive. As I write these words, its continued survival is by no means certain.

For going on a quarter of a century, I have striven to be the electronic equivalent—one of the first—of a newspaper columnist. I began posting articles I'd written on my "Lever Action BBS." (Before that, I'd had them printed on colored paper, to make them stand out, and hand-distributed them at places like gun shows; I also published a broadside called TANSTAAFL!, which stands for "There ain't no such thing as a free lunch," a saying that we all learned at the knee of Robert A. Heinlein.) My cyberjournal *The Libertarian Enterprise* was first published in 1995, and it still appears online every Saturday night.

http://www.NCC-1776.org

Like an old-time newspaper columnist (and apparently unlike today's J-school grads), I often research what I write about, but, as with a newspaper column, you won't find my work strewn with footnotes. I see my job, for the most part, as taking facts "everybody knows" and putting them together in a way that nobody else has ever thought of before.

If readers doubt my facts, or my interpretation of them, or if I mention something that they've never heard about before—like the ancient city of Çatalhöyük, which I refer to in the chapter on cities, for example—they have an historically unprecedented ability to check the facts themselves, simply by typing a few words in a search engine.

Over four hundred years of newspaper columns, no columnist has ever had to contend with such a thing as readers who have their own information sources—which is probably how we got into this mess. Having spent a lifetime of suffering their lies of commission and omission, listening to establishment "journalists" in the traditional "Old Media" whimper about the Internet (which is in the historical process of eating them all alive) is nothing but sweet music to my ears.

As it should be to yours.

I have named and arranged the chapters of this book so it will be easy to discover what libertarians think about any given issue of the day. This is intended to help those who are new to the movement to educate themselves, and to encourage candidates to position themselves as real libertarians in their campaigns. If what I've written embarrasses the LINOs until they depart our movement in outrage or frustration, then this modest effort will have proven worthwhile for that reason alone.

Have fun,
L. NEIL SMITH
Fort Collins, Colorado
July 2011

The Zero Aggression Principle

A libertarian is a person who believes that no one has the right, under any circumstances, to initiate force against another human being for any reason whatever...

—L. NEIL SMITH,
The Libertarian Enterprise

This is not a book about libertarian philosophy (there are plenty of those already), but about the way libertarian philosophy applies to the making of libertarian policy.

Libertarians are often accused—by their political opponents, and even worse, by a few within the movement, who would destroy it in a misguided attempt to make it more "palatable" to a general public they apparently don't know very well—of being too impractical, too unpragmatic, too unaware of the real world around them, too lost to fantasy.

Scott Adams, for example, creator of the famous Dilbert cartoons, proclaims himself "a libertarian minus the crazy stuff," which makes me wonder exactly what "crazy stuff" he means. Not destroying people's lives because they choose to smoke a politically incorrect vegetable? Not persecuting them for doing ordinary things that were perfectly legal 50 years ago—like raising what crops they want, or draining a pond on their own land? Not stealing half of everything people work hard for, in order to spend it violating their rights, spying on them, messing with their lives, or starving or bombing millions of children overseas?

Is that what you mean by the "crazy stuff," Scott?

With 9/11 as an excuse, many in government today appear to regard the ancient, time-honored right of *habeas corpus* as "the crazy stuff." And our confidence in Scott's claim that he's a libertarian isn't exactly strengthened by his bizarre support—as reported in Wikipedia—of New York's fascistic mayor, Michael Bloomberg, for President in 2008. Clearly, there is a severe need for some objective criterion—a definition—regarding what it means to be a libertarian.

Happily, such a definition already exists.

If there is a central tenet, or a key belief that all libertarians share, it is that each and every individual is the owner—the "sole proprietor"—of his or her own life and of "all the products of that life."

Historically, people have come to the libertarian movement from many different directions. In any given group of them, you are likely to encounter atheists (many of them readers and students of Ayn Rand), Christians, Buddhists, Muslims, pagans, and Wiccans. The all-important concept of self-ownership that they share can be logically derived from principles even more basic, or simply accepted as a self-evident truth.

Most libertarians will agree that all human rights are, in effect, property rights, beginning with the most fundamental right of all, to self-ownership and control of one's own life. That's what Thomas Jefferson and his fellow Founding Fathers meant by "life, liberty, and the pursuit of happiness." As owners of their own lives, individuals are completely free to do absolutely anything they wish with them—provided, of course, it doesn't violate the identical right of others—whether the people around them happen to approve of what they do or not.

Libertarians believe (and in this, they are also in agreement with America's Founding Fathers) that all human rights are negative in nature and boil down, in the end, to a single right: not to be molested or interfered with by government or anybody else. (Socialist politicians detest this idea; they want to create "positive rights"—to health care, for example, that they can magnanimously bestow upon their worshipful subjects, or take away if the slaves start getting uppity.) The only way that an individual's rights can be violated is through the use of physical force or the threat of physical force. Simple persuasion—nagging, "jaw-boning," or "browbeating"—doesn't count; the way to deal with that is through the exercise of character.

However since power, political or otherwise, consists of nothing more than the ability to alter the behavior of others in ways they wouldn't otherwise accept, through the use of physical force or the threat of physical force, libertarians embrace one and only one prohibition.

No matter what you may hear to the contrary—generally from certain political types who wish to derive some benefit from being called a libertarian, but who can't (or won't) make the cut ethically or politically—the one thing that sets genuine libertarians apart from other people is their strict adherence to the "Zero Aggression Principle." This is the way that principle has been defined in the online virtual pages of my weekly opinion journal *The Libertarian Enterprise*:

> A libertarian is a person who believes that no one has the right, under any circumstances, to initiate force against another human being for any reason whatever; nor will a libertarian advocate the initiation of force, or delegate it to anyone else.
>
> Those who act consistently with this principle are libertarians, whether they realize it or not. Those who fail to act consistently with it are not libertarians, regardless of what they may claim.

This has also been called the "Non-Aggression Principle," although we personally find the acronym "ZAP" much more appealing and dynamic than "NAP." In any case, that's all there is to libertarianism, nothing more, and certainly nothing less. Everything that libertarians believe, everything that they propose flows from the Zero Aggression Principle.

Although the Zero Aggression Principle seems to have a number of historical sources, it's unclear who first thought of this extremely simple yet revolutionary formula. Thomas Jefferson got it right—"No man has a natural right to commit aggression on the equal rights of another, and this is all from which the laws ought to restrain him"—consistent with the concept that rights are negative, and making the all-important distinction between initiated and defensive force. I first heard of it in an Ayn Rand essay; my daughter has grown up with it.

The basic notion underlying the Zero Aggression Principle is deeply embedded in the American value system, in Western Civilization, and possibly even in human nature itself. As Will Smith said his mother put it (playing the fighter pilot who makes "first contact" with an alien invader in *Independence Day*): "Don't start nothin', won't be nothin'." Reflexively, whenever we hear about a fight—or a war—the first thing that any of us demands to know is who started it. And we are generally inclined to choose sides, if we do, on that basis alone.

If you look the matter up, say, in Wikipedia, what you'll see, for the most part, are a lot of noble-sounding excuses for not living up to the demands this principle places on us. What they all boil down to, in the end, is sophistry, which, according to Dictionary.com, is nothing more than "a subtle, tricky, superficially plausible, but generally fallacious method of reasoning," in this case transparently aimed at getting around the principle without appearing to be unprincipled.

The problem—for the sophists, that is—is that, once the Zero Aggression Principle has been brought into the ethical discussion, nothing can ever be the same again. Anyone—including those who may fraudulently call themselves libertarians—who is aware of the Zero Aggression Principle and refuses to live by it, or promise to, is giving himself away. He is the badguy, at least potentially, reserving to himself a right that he mistakenly believes he has, to beat you up or even kill you, should he deem it necessary or simply convenient sometime in the future. What he's saying is that he cannot be trusted, not as a friend, not as a neighbor, not as a colleague, not as a comrade.

I have studied this extremely simple yet revolutionary concept all my adult life, almost half a century. I still discover ramifications and aspects I hadn't thought of before. Unlike other ethical systems, for example, the Zero Aggression Principle does not require us to turn the other cheek pacifically. Once an aggressor has revealed himself—by the initiation of force—he has crossed a morally qualitative boundary.

There can be no argument here about the specious, if ancient, doctrine of "degrees of force." You can be killed or maimed for life just as easily with a fist or a screwdriver as with a knife or a gun. The question isn't how much or what kind of force did your assailant initiate, but simply did your assailant initiate force. If the answer is yes, the degree of force you employ to stop him is up to your discretion.

Likewise, if he survives, it is up to those against whom he initiated force to decide what must be done with him. At the same time, the Zero Aggression Principle doesn't license any and all acts of violence toward others. The villain must meet highly stringent standards of villainy before anyone is ethically free to act against him.

There is more direct connection between fundamental libertarian philosophy and policy formation than is the case with many another political movement. Conventional politicians almost never think their philosophy through and set it down for everyone to examine. In most cases, they don't dare. Republicans would soon discover that they're actually socialists. Democrats would discover that they're actually fascists.

Socialism is the doctrine that the group is more important, has more rights, than the individual, who may be sacrificed—stolen from, restrained, kidnapped, even killed—to serve the interests of the group. As freedom writer and lecturer Robert LeFevre put it, to any extent that a society has a "public sector," to that extent, it's socialist.

I have never met a Republican who was opposed to taxation in principle or didn't favor military conscription during wartime. "Duty, Honor, Country" are all collectivist—which is to say socialist—preoccupations.

Socialism advertises itself as a system under which government owns the means of production. Fascism, a direct historical outgrowth of the failure of socialism, pretends to respect private property, while the "owners" bear all the liabilities and costs, and government controls the enterprise through regulation, skimming the profit off as taxes.

I have never met a Democrat who wasn't contemptuous of business owners, or who opposed massive increases in business taxation and regulation.

As a result, the policies of conventional politicians are a murky hodge-podge, either of positions randomly selected to win votes (in which case their underlying "philosophy" has to be tinkered with and "adjusted" continuously as political fashions come and go) or of positions that they're stuck with on account of their particular history.

By sorting out what they believe beforehand, and formulating a policy one hundred percent congruent with that, libertarians have a distinct advantage. They can demonstrate an honesty, integrity, rationality, and consistency sadly missing from American politics today.

When people say that they can tell a politician is lying because his mouth is moving, they will finally come to make an exception for libertarians, much as many libertarians make an exception for the nominally Republican Congressman Ron Paul. In my experience, many of the public will end up supporting libertarians, not so much because they agree with every aspect of libertarian policy or principle, but because they know they can count on complete libertarian openness and predictability.

As an example of that, I have tried to subject each chapter in this book, and whatever position I have taken on any given issue, to two very important tests. One will be to ensure that it's consistent with the Zero Aggression Principle, and the other with the Bill of Rights.

Which we'll discuss later.

So break out "the crazy stuff" and long may it wave. We are about to enter extremely dangerous times, in which we can allow no place for devious, "clever," and deceptive tactics. History shows that people cannot be tricked into becoming free. If liberty is to survive—if we are to survive—our only chance lies in directness and full disclosure.

And that is what this book is about.

The Curse of 1913

One of the sadder facts of human existence is that power
will get you through times of no brains better than brains
will get you through times of no power.

—L. NEIL SMITH

The next time anyone offers you a ration of excrement because you appear to believe in a conspiracy theory (despite the incontrovertible fact that these United States of America were founded by a band of conspirators) be sure to bring up the name "Jekyll Island." Jekyll Island lies off the coast of Georgia (the one in the American South, not in the former Soviet Union), and at one time was the location of a grand luxury resort—the Jekyll Island Club—whose membership was limited to the one hundred most wealthy and powerful men in the country.

These were the wealthy, powerful men who, in 1913, at the urging, and with the assistance, of New York Senator Nelson W. Aldrich, along with other protofascists, arrived at the island by a secret, private train to devise what would be advertised as a "scientific currency system"—the same system that is falling apart all around our ears today.

That system was (and remains) the Federal Reserve. Most Americans don't think about it very often. At some level, they assume that it's a part of the United States government. But it's no such thing. The Federal Reserve is a cartel (or a cabal, if you prefer the expression) of gigantic and powerful private banking institutions, the majority of which are not even American. From 1913 to this day, these foreigners—often malign foreigners—have largely controlled our monetary system.

They're the principal reason you're not encouraged to believe in conspiracies.

By any measure, 1913 was a very bad year. Mexico and China were both having revolutions. In the Philippine Islands, to which we had promised independence 15 years earlier after the Spanish-American War—and then reneged—the Moros were in rebellion, and US troops under John "Blackjack" Pershing massacred 2000 civilians. There was a war raging in the Balkans, the King of Greece was assassinated, the Romanovs in Russia were having their last good year, a trolley and its passengers were buried in garbage in Niagara Falls, New York, a freighter full of dynamite blew up in Baltimore harbor, and a women's suffragette was trampled to death by the King of England's carriage horses.

Richard Nixon was born.

On the other hand, the zipper was invented.

It was also, absolutely and without a doubt, the worst year for individual liberty and for private capitalism in America—and on that account for our entire species—since the War Between the States. Princeton professor, former New Jersey governor, and un-abashed racist Woodrow Wilson was elected President and, largely because of that, 1913 basically witnessed the rescission of every single precious economic and political principle ever established by the American Revolution. Huge strides were made toward turning the children of that Revolution back into the powerless serfs their ancestors were before 1776.

On February 3rd of that year, the 16th Amendment to the United States Constitution was declared to have been ratified (although some doubt among historians lingers, even to this day, over the legality of the procedure), allowing the federal government to overcome certain restrictions that had been established on it by the Founding Fathers and to impose and collect—from individuals—a graduated income tax.

From each according to his ability, to each according to their power.

On April 8th, the 17th Amendment mandated the direct election of United States Senators (who had originally been chosen by their state legislatures), removing yet another layer of insulation between the individual and the all-consuming, increasingly imperialistic federal government.

America had begun as a handful of small, independent republics, united for some—but certainly not for all—purposes, through the nexus of a virtually powerless central government. What we might refer to as the new nation's basic "operating system," the Articles of Confederation, was almost immediately flushed down the "Memory Hole" and the United States Constitution was adopted in its place, doing irreparable damage to the original concept the Founders had in mind, by establishing a strong, essentially unanswerable central government. The War Between the States wrecked the concept almost completely. The 17th Amendment rendered state governments essentially irrelevant and finished off the Founding Fathers' dream of a peacefully united confederation.

On October 3rd, the United States Revenue Act of 1913 was passed by Congress, reimposing the federal income tax spawned by the Abraham Lincoln administration—and later declared unconstitutional by the Supreme Court—first imposed to finance what was perhaps the first total war in human history. Now, backed up by the 16th Amendment, the new tax would soon be employed to finance the country's second total war.

Finally, on December 23rd, the Federal Reserve System, little more than an elaborate counterfeiting scheme that continues to this very day, was erected—without the consent of the governed—at the behest of President Woodrow Wilson and the Jekyll Island conspirators, ending an unprecedented and almost miraculous century and a half of ever-increasing, freely-generated and mutually-exchanged American wealth.

Early libertarian thinker Frank Chodorov wrote of the income tax, "...it gives the government a prior lien on all the property produced by its subjects. [Thus the government] unashamedly proclaims the doctrine of collectivized wealth...That which it does not take is a concession." Meaning that anything we slaves get to keep, out of what we've labored to create, is seen by the government as a charitable sacrifice.

Any discussion about whether the United States is being overcome by "creeping socialism" is ludicrous. The United States has operated as a socialist dictatorship—albeit, until recently, a dictatorship with velvet gloves on its iron fists—since that cursed year of 1913.

Almost immediately, there were dire consequences. Before 1913, Americans didn't allow themselves to be tagged, earmarked, tracked, traced, folded, spindled, or mutilated by government busybodies. They were free to live their lives, if they wished, in perfect privacy and anonymity. Thanks first and foremost to Wilson and his "Progressive" movement, this is no longer possible, and the results, for individual liberty as well as for the health and safety of the nation, have been disastrous.

It shouldn't have come as a surprise to anyone that the process was helped along, massively accelerated, in fact, only three years later, when Wilson's government tested its brand new shiny powers of taxation (and seized the "emergency" power to take over, control, and use every American's life) by involving the US—unnecessarily, and contrary to Wilson's campaign promises—in the First World War, at the eventual cost of 22,625,253,000 1914 dollars, and 117,465 American lives.

The cost today would be $319,611,416,417.56.

Altogether, fifteen million people were killed.

The fact that the British Cunard liner RMS *Lusitania*, whose innocent American passengers were the Wilson government's principal excuse for entering the conflict, was, in fact, a ship of war under international law—it had deck guns, under canvas cover, and carried a hold full of munitions—was a secret kept by both governments for decades. In the 1950s, the wreck was depth-bombed by the British navy in an attempt to destroy evidence that *Lusitania* was legally a warship.

Historian Barbara Tuchman devoted a whole book—among her best, *The Guns of August*—to trying to figure out what the hell caused World War I. Dismissing the popular theory that it was just a pissing contest over a dead Archduke, the best even she could do was guess that everybody in the vast incestuous extended family that European royalty consisted of, had all kinds of nifty new toys—tanks, machineguns, airplanes, poison gas—and were simply itching to try them. We got to play because our toys (paid for by Wilson's income tax) were even niftier, and we American "cowboys" were better at using them.

Philosopher and social commentator Bob Dylan put it this way: "World War I, it came and it went, the reason for fighting I never did get."*

---

* "With God On Our Side," copyright 1963, by Bob Dylan, from his album *The Times They Are A-Changin'*

The Crash of 1929 and the Great Depression became inevitable, caused directly by passage of the Federal Reserve Act of 1913, which allowed the private banking system (mostly a small handful of foreign crooks) to control a phenomenon—the price of borrowed money, which we call "interest"—that formerly had only been controlled by the "Invisible Hand" of the free-market system. Cheap money is always popular, especially politically, and people borrowed and spent money on things their common sense and better nature would have kept them from buying if the interest rate, kept artificially low, had been higher.

Nobody today seems to have learned a goddamned thing from that event.

The famous libertarian columnist and editor Vin Suprynowicz has frequently suggested that most of America's problems today could be solved simply by repealing every law passed in 1913 and afterwards. I find it very hard to disagree. Allowing for others who would place that date earlier—1860, 1794—or who, like the late Robert LeFevre would prefer a Constitution consisting only of five words, "Congress shall make no law," it would certainly represent a good beginning.

Life was unquestionably better (not necessarily easier, mind you, we do love our dishwashers, flat-screen televisions, and computers) when people had more freedom. The loss of significant amounts of that freedom occurred in 1913, when the Federal Reserve and income taxation were imposed on Americans, followed by endless volumes of so-called "Progressive Era" legislation that still has us bound hand and foot today.

Naturally, those nations that had not preceded America in its descent into tyranny were quick in their attempts to catch up with it. It is no coincidence that the 20th century featured the largest, most powerful governments in human history, and at the same time, the most deadly and devastating wars. The link is unprecedented control by governments of the money supply, and equally unprecedented powers of taxation.

Without a doubt, taxation is the fuel of war.

I'll say it again, so there's no mistake: taxation is the fuel of war.

Taxation is the fuel of war.

Doing something serious and permanent about that—beginning by auditing the Federal Reserve, declaring a tax amnesty retroactive to 1913, establishing a commission to investigate the Constitutionality of the Sixteenth Amendment and possible legal irregularities in its ratification—will do more to restore confidence in our civilization than anything else anyone can think of, end our economic problems, and lead America back to unprecedented peace, freedom, progress, and prosperity.

As popular lecturer and former Libertarian Presidential candidate Michael Badnarik (among others) often points out, America, "the best idea for a country anybody ever had," survived perfectly well for over a century without an income tax, chiefly by maintaining a much smaller government, which represented a much smaller threat to individual liberty.

In 1943, Austrian economist and philosopher Friedrich von Hayek described Western Civilization's seemingly inexorable descent into totalitarianism as *The Road to Serfdom*. We do not know, yet, whether that road can be traveled both directions, but we can only learn by trying.

At the moment we have a massive task before us, throwing off an openly socialist regime while trying to avoid electing a fascist government in its place. Many another nation has failed at this. On the other hand, we are better equipped to accomplish it, in terms of what we have learned, how much the public understands, and who we have to help us—more Americans are aware of their rights now, under the first ten amendments, and, if all else fails, are vastly better armed than ever before—than any previous generation in history since the Revolution.

Perhaps by 2013, we can be back again, on the road to freedom.

The Myth of "Animal Rights"

In my experience, those who profess to believe in animal rights usually don't believe in human rights.

—L. NEIL SMITH

It says here the governments of Bolivia and Ecuador have decided officially that the Earth is a living organism. And, even though it doesn't logically follow, they have declared on that account that animals and plants have rights, which must be respected by mere human beings.

Which leads me to wonder: (A) how do these criminal aggregations of pickpockets and head-thumpers expect the common people of their nations, largely dependent on herding and farming to feed their families, to earn a living, and (B) don't they have any pitchforks and torches down there in Bolivia and Ecuador? Don't they have any damned lampposts?

Turns out these "initiatives" are the work of the United Nations, whose members—more pickpockets and head-thumpers—fondly dream of imposing the same insanity on all of us, eventually reducing human population by 90 percent. But first they have to dispose of the idea—a very inconvenient and annoying idea—that human beings have rights.

Contrary to popular belief, the enemies of freedom understand the mechanics of inflation perfectly. (Stay with me, now, this is not a digression.) Nor is it a random natural phenomenon like the weather, as the media want us to think, or a result of conspiring capitalists, or consumers doing too much consuming. It is a process by which the value of a currency not backed by anything of intrinsic value (like

31

gold or silver) is systematically diluted by creation of additional un-backed currency. The more of it in circulation, the less value it has. If this calculated act of criminal fraud were perpetrated by anyone but the government, we'd call it counterfeiting. And that's exactly what it happens to be, no matter who is running the printing presses.

In a similarly systematic way, individual liberty is being diluted through a kind of moral inflation (in much the same way emotion, in our culture, is replacing reason), in which unsupportable asser-tions about "positive rights"—to a government education, to state healthcare, to a clean litterbox—are used to render valueless those negative rights that really do exist, principally, the individual right to life, liberty, and property utterly without interference or molestation. Animal rights are just another way socialism pursues its obsolete, discredited agenda. The goal is not to uphold the rights of animals (animals have no rights; nobody knows that better than the Left) but render trivial—and destroy—the very concept of human rights.

There are two kinds of animal rights advocates. Try arguing with rank-and-file environmentalists, or the fanatics of "People for the Ethical Treatment of Animals," and you'll discover that you're not dealing with a political subject, or even a philosophical one, but with a bizarre new religion, clung to despite every fact (like the complete discreditization of "Global Warming") discovered to the contrary.

I am reminded of an argument I once found myself in, about sea turtles. I'd suggested that laws prohibiting trade in certain ani-mal products be repealed; among other benefits, turtles might be farmed for profit and thereby kept from extinction—who ever heard of chickens or turkeys being endangered? Yet, from the hysteria my modest proposal engendered—by breathing the sacred phrase "ani-mal rights" and the vile epithet "profit" in one sentence—you'd have thought I'd demanded that the Virgin be depicted henceforth in mesh stockings and a merry widow like Frank N. Furter in *The Rocky Horror Picture Show*.

I became convinced of two things. First: that the animal rights movement would enthusiastically sacrifice its highest proclaimed value—the survival of an endangered species—if the only way to assure its survival was to let the moneylenders back into the temple. Animal rightists hate and fear free enterprise more than they adore sea turtles.

Where does it stop and on what principle? Is mere vegetarianism enough, or must we all wear masks, as some cults do in India, to avoid inhaling insects and killing them? And what of the right to life of plants? Are we morally obligated to keep those frozen lab vials that are all that remains of the once deadly scourge of smallpox, instead of incinerating them? Or perhaps even to let it out to roam free once again?

The second kind of animal rightists, who cynically constructed this religion in the first place, have no interest in the rights of animals, nor in the true believers at its gullible grassroots, but see it simply as a new way to pursue the same old objectives. But now they can use a single minnow, or a tiny weed, to stop construction of a factory.

Once again, inflation, in the economic sense, occurs whenever a government generates currency without intrinsic worth, watering down the value of currency already in circulation. There is also ethical inflation, the best example being when rights are arbitrarily bestowed upon something other than people—things like rocks, trees, birds, animals, or planets—watering down the meaning and value of human rights. In truth, there are only two kinds of entities in the vast ethical universe: (A) people, who have rights and who cannot be owned, and (B) property, which has no rights and can be owned. With every passing day, it becomes increasingly obvious that today's world leaders believe that most of the rest of us fall into that second category.

A friend of mine used to call environmentalists "watermelons: green on the outside, red on the inside." Never mind that the Earth got along perfectly well for four and a half billion years without any self-appointed saviors. As even Rush Limbaugh understands, animal rights are just a smokescreen, another excuse to abuse individualism and capitalism. And the sillier the situation created by their claims, the more surrealistic their guerilla theatrics, the better they like it.

What are rights, anyway? Where do they come from? Lions have claws and fangs, antelopes have swift legs, giraffes have long necks, birds have wings, rabbits breed like...well, rabbits. Human beings have rights.

Rights are humanity's primary—some would say only—means of survival. They arise from a characteristic unique to us (although it's politically incorrect these days to say so), a qualitative difference between human beings and animals so profound that the ramparts of the Himalayas are no more than a ripple in the linoleum by comparison. That difference—the very wellspring of human rights—is sapience.

(Note: I don't follow *Star Trek*'s flawed lexicon by using the word "sentience." Sentience is awareness, which many animals manifest to some degree. Some animals (like cats and dogs and pigs) can clearly think. Sapience—a primary product of our large and powerful brains—is awareness of that awareness. Only human beings can think about thinking.

I'm not saying anything new here. Pretending you can't see the monumental difference between people and animals (a difference any three-year-old can easily discern) is not just a shopworn, phony tactic—comparable to a majority of psychologists pretending the human mind doesn't exist—it's a confession that you can't see a difference between a fireplug and a flagpole—and that you're stupid.

Most animals are genetically programmed like computers. Although a few near the top of the evolutionary pyramid are capable of learning, they make no choices about what to do with their lives. By contrast, we employ our sapience to assess what we see, hear, smell, taste, and feel, then act on that assessment, not simply to ensure our survival, but to enhance its quality. The freedom to see, hear, smell, taste, feel, assess, and act—without impediments other than those imposed by the nature of reality—is what we are referring to when we say "rights."

More to the point: purpose, also a product of sapience, is an idea as unique to our species as rights. We are the only entities in tbe known universe with purpose. Purpose—regarding ourselves or anything else we lay our hands on in the environment—is whatever we say it is.

It was Robert LeFevre who observed that there are just two kinds of things in the universe, people and property. No matter how much you might wish it otherwise, animals are not people. Some—wild animals, for example—are unclaimed property whose species might be better off with owners. Animals are groceries. Animals are boot leather and briefcases. Animals are fiddle strings and fur coats. Animals are for medico-industrial experiments and riding to hounds. That's their purpose.

I, a human being, declare it.

Do what you like with your own animals.

If species are going extinct by the thousands—a claim, given the Left's historic disregard of the truth, we've no reason to believe—it's for the same reason the Soviets collapsed and there's never a cop when you need one. Socialism has been in charge, and socialism fails.

In any venue.

Basketball player Michael Vick was convicted some years ago under a law that could never have passed in a culturally diverse nation. No representative in a free country would have introduced it. No freedom-loving legislator would have given it a moment's regard. No judge would have let the prosecutor leave the court without fining him for contempt.

Mr. Vick was engaged with other dangerous criminals in the vile crime of breeding and training dogs to fight each other to the death. The sport has been going on for as long as men have had dogs. Money changed hands on the outcome and a good time was had by all, even the dogs who survived. I've seen exactly the same thing done with scorpions.

Is that any less a crime?

Is dog-fighting a sport I would cross the street to see? It is not. Do I harbor a secret dislike for animals? Not at all. I've had kitties and doggies and bunnies and parrots and hamsters and tortoises all my life. Even a magpie. I once kept a jar of pet paramecia until my mother made me throw it out—it did smell pretty bad.

Speaking of dogs, I have nothing but sneers for some Asians today trying to impress the West by putting an end to the ancient practice of cooking and eating them. Just because some of us have other uses for—and feelings about—canines doesn't make their culinary use illegitimate.

My current alpha-feline sometimes thinks he's my boss. Sometimes I let him. He sits beside me all day, every day, as I write. We are, both of us, lifelong, dedicated, unapologetic predators. He loves me, but that wouldn't keep him from eating me if I were dead. I love him, but that wouldn't stop me from cooking him if my family would starve otherwise.

I often wonder if they failed to catch Osama bin Laden for so long because the authorities were obsessed with items like railroading Vick. That mob of sanctimonious, inorgasmic, hypocritical lowlives know nothing about the real world and shouldn't have had anything to say about what happened to this remarkable athlete until they gave up wearing leather shoes and eating meat they'd bought packaged in a store.

And even then, to hell with them.

Here's another painful but undeniable truth: "progressives" love nonsapient animals for the same reason conservatives love fetuses: both are incapable of speaking for themselves, telling their self-appointed "protectors" to stick it where the sun don't shine. We treat animals humanely, not for the animals' sake, but for our own, so that we can think better of ourselves. Is that worth sending anyone to jail for?

Science fiction writers seem to be expected to predict the future whether it's appropriate or not. I've made some successful predictions myself, but my tinfoil beanie is off to Philip K. Dick, who nailed it when he wrote of America's deeply pathological attitude toward animals in "Do Androids Dream of Electric Sheep?," a subtheme conspicuously blue-penciled when the movie *Blade Runner* was adapted from the novel.

In the story, in a manner that reminded me of the masturbatory sequences in Ray Bradbury's *Fahrenheit 451*, people lavished more love and attention on pets than they did on each other, from whom they seemed hopelessly estranged. Possessing an animal of your own was so socially important that people were willing to settle for electromechanical sheep, rather than be without an infrahuman life companion.

I suppose this was meant to point up the guilt everyone felt for having destroyed all but a diminishing strip of the planet in a nuclear war. Shrinks adore Dick's work, as do the shrinkly inclined. Guilt alienated people from one another. Guilt toward the natural world made them yearn to cuddle the nearest squirrel or raccoon incapable of defending itself, begging for a forgiveness animals could neither comprehend nor deliver. The whole bizarre proposition rested on the irrational phenomenon of collective guilt. No surviving human had pushed the button. They'd had it pushed on them. They were victims, as legitimately as all the bears and the birds on Wolverton Mountain.

But along the trail, however tortuous, Dick put his finger on an American weakness precisely as Walt Disney had, accidentally, in a different way a generation earlier. Take them away from forest and farm, mountain and prairie for a few decades, and they turn into something so pathetic, so contempt-worthy, that words fail even someone who has written three million of them in the cause of self-defense and self-reliance.

They turn into...Europeans.

I grew up in the Air Force, a Scout from Bear to Eagle. My dad grew up fatherless, so he brought me up as best he could without a role model, hunting, fishing, gutting and skinning our kill, cooking and eating it all through the winter, or as long as it lasted. (The trout never seemed to last long.) Thanks to the Scouts, my dad, the many Strategic Air Command and Northeast Air Command survival schools he attended, there's hardly a furry or scaly critter moving across the continent, nor a green plant or fungus I haven't tasted once. Most are absolutely delicious, a quality I attribute to having evolved as an omnivore.

On the other paw, no matter how appealingly cartoon animals were drawn, no matter how cutely they were voiced, at no time did I ever confuse them with the real thing. Like any 1950s kid, I loved Bambi and Thumper and Flower (especially Flower, that's probably just me) still, they were only drawings, generated in the mind of a man—I could have learned to do it myself, with enough practice; thanks to the same guy, I spent a whole year drawing Victorian submarines and giant squid—and living a very different life than their real-world counterparts in a much crueler real world. In the real world, they could think, after a fashion (I'd had dogs and cats all my life, so I was pretty sure of that), but they couldn't reason and they couldn't talk.

Real animals, as I said earlier, were property, unclaimed, stolen, lost, or owned. They weren't people; they didn't have rights. We loved them as we loved our stuffed koalas and '56 Impala coupes, but they were property. Any 4H kid in McQueeney, Texas, knew that. Or in Salina, Kansas; Gifford, Illinois; St. John's, Newfoundland; or the grapevines of Sacramento, California, all places where this Air Force brat grew up.

A farm kid might keep a pig, sheep, or calf as a pet for a while, but eventually off it went for conversion into ribs, chops, or steaks. It seemed heartless at the time, but it was real. Chickens, turkeys, and nasty geese they took care of themselves. Also rabbits. There may be tears the first couple of times, but everyone looked forward to Sunday dinner.

And if need be, they could all shoot their own dog.

Don't get me wrong, I love animals. I've owned dozens and eat as many as I can every day. But my experience is that those who argue most fervently for animal rights generally don't believe in human rights, certainly not in the sense intended by the Dead White European Males who founded this civilization. Human rights are what civilization is supposed to be all about. The idea of animal rights is a disease festering in the shriveled cortices of sociopolitical parasites who, for reasons known best to them, abominate their own kind almost as much as they abominate themselves. This conceptual virus is then communicated, by the wretched creatures infected with it, to a greater number of hapless idiots too clueless to challenge it.

But since all animals are property, properly claimed or as yet unclaimed, necessary to the survival, well-being, and amusement of their evolutionary superiors, it follows that animal rights advocates are self-announced enemies of their own kind and should be treated as such. If everyone refrained from selling them food for six months, some of them would get the point and come around. The rest would starve to death. In either case, the animal rights problem would be solved.

In summary, a great deal is always made of Republicans versus Democrats or "progressives" versus conservatives. Some of it may even mean something. But these days, everywhere you look, it's becoming more a matter of the Lace-Panties Killjoy Party (the same pasty-faced, troglodytic flock of frilly-dillies, droolers, and mouthbreathers who also despise automobiles, firearms, industry, smoking, and, as I've pointed out elsewhere, everything that's come along during the past 90,000 years as a result of the discovery of fire) versus the rest of us.

Allow me to be the first in what I hereby declare to be a new, post-psychotic era of rationality and enlightenment to state that, despite decades of philosophically and scientifically absurd TV and newspaper propaganda to the contrary, animals serve only three purposes.

First, they are for Productive Class guys and their buddies in silly clothing to trudge out at some ridiculous hour of the morning and stomp through the snow, climb into trees, or stand around in freezing water with a bunch of smelly dogs and shoot. Believe me, I'm not knocking it, I'm only describing it. I'm a hunter and shooter myself.

Second, in combination with as many other tasty ingredients as possible, animals are for cooking, preferably by Chinese or Texican folks, who in my opinion are the ones (rather than guys with smelly dogs, or their wives) who do it best, and for eating among friends and family. They're also handy for seatcovers, pistol belts, and umbrella stands.

Third, animals are for the innocent heart-warming delight of tiny children and their parents who enjoy feeding them at the park or the zoo.

As for the UN, it must be obliterated, to paraphrase Cato the Elder, its New York City compound emptied and razed to the ground so that not one stone is left standing on another, and salt sown on the ruins.

The Age of Authority

Those who lead through authority have rivals on whom
they must expend as much energy and attention as they
do on their enemies. Those who lead by example have
enemies, but no rivals.

—L. NEIL SMITH

The Age of Authority is drawing to a close.

Most of us—the human species, that is—had no idea we were in any Age of Authority. A social order maintained by Authority was the very water in which all of us swam, of which most of us were generally unaware, and even when it injured or killed us, even when we boiled in it or froze, even when it took our rights, our property, or our lives, even when it took our children, we had no idea what was happening to us (or that there might be some alternative), except that things like that had been happening to us for as long as anybody could remember anything.

Throughout human history, society had been organized vertically, hierarchically: King, prince, baron, squire, peasant; Pope, cardinal, archbishop, bishop, monsignor, priest, parishioner; General, colonel, major, captain, lieutenant, sergeant, corporal, private; President, senator, congressman, governor, legislator, commissioner, mayor, taxpayer; not to forget Justice, judge, lawyer, clerk, bailiff, and jailer.

In a vertical hierarchy, each level of authority, under command of the level above it, is responsible for controlling the level directly below it, especially for controlling the flow of information up and down the line. The military call it the "chain of command." Commercial enterprises (corporations, nominally private, but commonly in a form of mercantilist partnership with government) mindlessly follow this form as well. It has been asserted that the happiest human being in the world is a mid-level bureaucrat with people above him to tell him what to do, and people beneath he can tell what to do. (This is also a pretty fair definition of the authoritarian personality.) For a period that has lasted at least eight thousand years, this has been the only way that anybody could conceive of organizing and running human affairs.

But the times, as Bob Dylan told us, they are a-changin'.

It seems that every human institution today is in some stage of collapse. Most of the nation's great social organizations—once useful and constructive groups like the Boy Scouts of America, the American Civil Liberties Union, the National Rifle Association, the Anti-Defamation League, the Republican Party, the Democratic Party, the Libertarian Party—over the years, over the decades, have grown tired, lazy, unimaginative, and seem to have lost the meaning of what they were doing, of why they were created in the first place. They strive only to continue to exist—directed for the most part by mere place-holders who don't give a damn about the mission and whose only interest is retaining their jobs—whether their existence is still justified or not. In many cases, they have been drowned in political correctness until it hangs off them like some thick, sticky, noxious semiliquid.

It isn't so much that our leaders have all suddenly become more dull-witted, more corrupt, and crazier than they were before. Not at all. Read history: their stupidity, dishonesty, and insanity are clearly visible in hindsight, given the perspective of a few decades or centuries. They've been this way all along. It's just a lot easier to discover now, and broadcast the news to the farthest reaches of civilization.

Even as short a time as fifty years ago, the ragtag, genetically depleted royalty of European socialist monarchies could cavort as they wished at their exclusive spas and resorts and hideaways without fear of public exposure. Today, paparazzi have done us all a favor, showing them as the unglamorous, ungainly, inbred culls they really were all along.

An otherwise respected parish priest might have lived his whole life through, spent his entire career, doing "good works," preaching to slowly dwindling congregations, and molesting altar boys who were too frightened or ashamed, even when they grew up afterward, to say anything.

From Wounded Knee to My Lai, and perhaps even well beyond that, a crazed military officer might order the wholesale execution of enemy civilians, and the soldiers who carried out his vile order never spoke of it, knowing they'd be the ones who were court-martialled if they did.

An aide might watch the politician he worked for accepting bribes—being plied by lobbyists and special-interest fixers with women, travel, liquor, or drugs, then voting on measures that were profitable for lawyers, mercantilists, and other politicians, but that often destroyed everything clean and decent—and have no hope that justice would ever be done, only that he, too, in time, might take part in the depravity.

The keepers of the "justice system"—judges, prosecutors, and defense attorneys whose principal occupation appears to consist of informing you, taxpayer and client, that your unalienable individual, civil, Constitutional, and human rights aren't quite what you thought they are, and never were—are among the most despised of this society's bottom-feeders, where once they were held in the highest esteem.

That age, the Age of Authority, is over and it's never coming back.

Two powerful philosophical and social trends are responsible for what is about to happen—what has already begun to happen—to Authority. Political egalitarianism made its modern appearance in the French and American revolutions, but has taken two centuries to have a full and measurable effect. Few believe any longer—as they did as recently as the Second World War—that there are older, wiser heads somewhere above us in society who know better than we do what is going on, and what to do with our own lives and the products of our lives. No Authority remains today that is unquestionable and unresisted by somebody.

The other agent of change is more recent, but has roots even further back in history than egalitarianism. Although few individuals realized it, the day the first page was struck by Gutenberg's printing press, Authority was doomed to wither. With almost every generation since then, unimpeded communication between individuals—without the assistance, permission, scrutiny, or censorship of Authority—has improved.

At one time, communications between different levels of power were essentially a one-way proposition. The great church bell, an extremely narrow-bandwidth device, imperious and unanswerable, demanded our attention and attendance. We lowly peasants were preached down to from a pulpit or were delivered promulgations from a palace balcony. Even well into the twentieth century, you couldn't talk back to the radio, or to the movies, or to the television. Letters written to newspaper editors—or to Congressmen, for that matter—were only grudgingly tolerated.

Today, except in morally backward countries that are soon to be overwhelmed by liberty no matter how they struggle to avoid it, communications flow freely, instantaneously, back and forth (rather than from top to bottom) and individuals can share their opinions and life experience with other individuals all the way around the world. Constructive information, intellectual discourse, smalltalk, gossip, and scandal all zip through cyberspace. Our world, the conditions that we live in, are either immeasurably better for it, or they soon will be.

Following the path of communications (and almost certainly because of it), our entire civilization has begun to remodel itself, as well. As the great libertarian author and lecturer, Robert LeFevre was fond of pointing out, there are basically only three ways for human beings to organize themselves. We have more experience with two than with the third.

Under the first system, one guy tells everybody what to do. For as long as anyone can tell, from the earliest dawn of humankind until the popular uprisings of the eighteenth century, with very few exceptions, that's exactly how it was done. He might be a village bully, a local boss, a petty baron, a duke, king, or an emperor. Or maybe a regent, a dictator, or a lord protector. Somebody who was better at beating up and killing other people—or whose ancestors had been—ruled the day.

The church, of course, had its part to play. Instead of supplying the long-suffering peasantry with comfort and consolation—which was supposed to have been their mission—or interceding for them with the armored class, theologians provided the monarchy instead with a labor-saving device: the "divine right of kings." Now, if you opposed the king, you were opposing God. That is, until Thomas Jefferson asserted to the world that "Resistance to tyranny is obedience to God."

After several ugly millennia, the Pennsylvania rifle and the guillotine finally put an end to all that (in fairness, it began with a Swiss crossbow) and it was time to try to figure out what to do next.

The second way, according to LeFevre, for human beings to organize themselves is for everybody to tell everybody else what to do. Let me say that again: everybody tells everybody else what to do. The best known example of this is democracy, and to some folks it sounds absolutely peachy, until, as Alexis de Tocqueville or somebody noted, one of them figures out that he can vote himself a nice, thick, juicy slice of you. Kind of the way our grandparents—the Government Generation—did with us, under their God-Emperor Franklin Delano Roosevelt (the Barack H. Obama of his day) and his Social Security scam.

And that, as LeFevre observed, is the real problem, with democracy in particular, and all forms of majoritarianism in general. They're unstable. Fragile. Everybody can't tell everybody else what to do forever, without consequences. Sooner or later, someone has to step in to stop the screaming arguments, the fistfights, and the gun battles, and that someone is the guy who winds up telling everybody what to do again.

The third way that LeFevre describes is by far the least explored—nobody tells anybody what to do—and yet it seems to be the only model of the three that suits the direction in which society appears to be evolving, from the vertical hierarchy it was for thousands upon thousands of years, into a more horizontal, politically egalitarian order.

The once mighty dinosaur of Authority is mortally wounded. Its days are clearly numbered. The great danger today is being killed by its thrashing tail before the monster finally realizes that it's dead. America's recent epidemic of savage police violence is a symptom of grave cultural disorientation and an hysterical fear of the loss of power.

And yet the beat goes on.

In movies and on TV, teachers are all fools, politicians are all crooks, the military and police (except for the occasional forensics expert) are all simpletons, and religious figures are all grifters or perverts. All corporations are evil, and everybody hates the mass media.

Right-wing commentators might perceive this as part of a left-wing Hollywood conspiracy to undermine Western Civilization (although the left is every bit as authority-bound, and I might add, frightened at the moment, as the right). I believe libertarians should see it as a good thing, in general. It reflects an underlying truth that none of these players is any longer necessary in the great scheme of things, at least in their traditional roles, and their continuing tenure is a fraud.

And they know it.

The question before us now is what are we going to do about it?

Many years ago, I wrote about something I called "Reconstitutive Unanimous Consent." Under ordinary unanimous consent, no group can do anything unless every last member of it approves. People—especially Republicans and Democrats—often complain that, under such a system, "nothing will ever get done." Aside from asking them, in a political context, what the hell is wrong with that, I'll point out that the Declaration of Independence "got things done" and it was adopted by a process of unanimous consent. It's also the way that juries—the one and only part of the so-called justice system that still works—operate.

Under Reconstitutive Unanimous Consent, the group is free to re-form itself after a vote, and those who opposed whatever was being voted on don't have to participate. That's basically the way a family, or people at a party, order a pizza. In fact, I used to call it "pizzacracy."

I also wrote about a concept called "Live As You Vote." For example, in Congress, those members who vote for victim disarmament—incorrectly called "gun control"—would be perfectly free never to have a gun. So would their unfortunate constituents. Everybody else would be at liberty to ignore what amounts to a ban on self-defense. Those who vote for a new tax pay it. Those who vote for war go off to fight.

Getting from here to there is relatively easy. As we now know, in the United States Senate, one vote over half doesn't cut it in every circumstance. You have to convince two-thirds—what's being called a "supermajority"—first. Our initial step would be to extend that rule to every other legislative body across the land, from the U.S. Congress, to every state assembly, to county commissions, to city councils.

It will call for amendments to the United States Constitution, fifty state constitutions, over three thousand county documents, city charters, everything—a worthy objective and one that doesn't have to wait for an election or depend on some dull-witted and embarrassing candidate. It will drastically reduce the number of new laws that get passed.

Not to mention new taxes.

And then the freedom movement must aim for a three-quarters supermajority.

And then seven eighths.

And then…well, you get the picture.

Unanimous consent must become the unstoppable wave of the future.

"Question Authority," you tell me? To hell with that nonsense—hang Authority up by its thumbs, cut off its toes, and let it drip dry!

Banks and Bankers

Banks are the means by which European aristocracy regained control of America once again following what we thought had been our Revolution.

—L. NEIL SMITH

I have been saying for years that, exactly like lawyers and literary agents, bankers somehow seem to have forgotten who's the boss.

I'm not an economist (a fact I could wake up every morning and thank the gods for, if I were religious, which I'm decidedly not), but I've been dealing with banks since I was a little kid in the 1950s, and I have never liked the "cut of their jib" or the way they do business.

As I say, I'm not an economist and although I am, in nearly every sense of the expression, a "student of Ayn Rand," my interest in the subject is pretty severely limited. I have never bothered to learn the ins and outs of formal economics, of "M-1," "M-2," "M-23," and so forth, nor do I care to do it now. Money is money is money, or—in the case of the worthless slips of paper issued by governments—it's not.

I am, however, sufficiently educated in physics to understand perfectly well that you can't make something out of nothing. It's too damned bad that most politicians and voters seem to lack that simple understanding. Money today literally isn't worth the paper it's been printed on because it's been spoiled by smearing all that ink all over it.

In any case, economics is not nearly as complicated a discipline as many—especially academics and politicians—would prefer you to believe. At the dawn of modern civilization, back when individuals like Galileo Galilei began peering upward through their newly-invented telescopes, they discovered that the mechanics of the sky were not exactly as they had been described by the authorities of the day.

Instead of every visible celestial body circling around the Earth, they found that the Earth—along with several other planets—was circling around the sun. One of those planets, Jupiter, had four small worlds circling around it the way the Moon circles around us. And the stars were so remote that they didn't seem to be circling anything at all.

We learned better later.

Supporters of the old theory, including the Church, fought back, threatening the life, liberty, and physical well-being of supporters of the new theory. As for those they couldn't reach, they argued that the old theory needed revising slightly. The Sun, Moon, and planets didn't circle directly around the Earth, but around a line around the Earth, "explaining" why Mars appeared to travel backwards from time to time.

They called these extra circles "epicycles," and each time some modern astronomer shot their theory down, they added another layer of epicycles to the one that had preceded it, until the planets were doing circles around the circles around the circles, and so on, each iteration postponing the eventual, inevitable collapse of their position. Much more importantly, however, the contrived complexity discouraged ordinary individuals from studying the situation and seeing through the smoke and past the mirrors to a simpler and grander truth.

Economics today is in much the same state as astronomy was in the Renaissance, its complicated vocabulary and complex theorizing meant mostly to keep non-economists from seeing certain simple truths about it.

Take banks, for instance.

People seem always to have had trouble, one way or another, with banks. And, one way or another, banks seem always to have had trouble with people. It's always been an uneasy relationship which bankers and their symbiotes, the politicians, have never hesitated to exploit to the hilt. The first bank records appear to have been written on clay tablets in cuneiform. In their primeval beginning, banks were little more than fortified warehouses in which, for a reasonable fee, you could store your valuable assets—usually consisting of gold, silver, jewelry, and grain—a bit more securely than you could at home.

After a while, somebody realized—maybe it was the bankers, maybe it was their customers, tired of paying that "reasonable fee" which slowly ate away at their savings—that nobody was getting any richer with all that wealth just sitting there in the warehouse. There ought to be some way to put it to work, preferably making even more wealth.

Bankers began lending their customers' wealth, for which borrowers paid a "reasonable fee" (now we call it "interest") which the bankers split with their customers. When cultural and religious taboos didn't interfere with the process, everybody made out, and capitalism was born.

It was at this point, however, somewhere around the Middle Ages, that everybody made a couple of really tragic mistakes. The first one occurred because people are basically lazy. Most of the time, this is a wonderful thing, the primary source of all human progress. The great Thomas Edison, for example, invented the electric light bulb because, as a kid, he'd detested cleaning kerosene lamp chimneys for his mother.

Apparently people got tired of carrying all those heavy gold and silver coins around in the little leather bags you see in paintings of the times and in the movies (although a little gold and silver went a long way back then, and the real bags couldn't have been all that big and heavy). There was also considerable physical risk involved: Sam Colt wouldn't come along to make men equal for another five or six hundred years. And women, although they often carried little daggers themselves—and really intimidating pairs of scissors—unless they were accompanied by a competent bodyguard, were at the mercy of the first thug who ran across them, especially if he happened to have a sword.

Instead of lugging all those big, nasty, heavy coins around, folks took up pen and parchment instead, and started writing instructions, of a kind. If they happened to owe their local apothecary a silver florin for his sovereign remedy against tansy or gleet (which don't seem to be quite the problem today that they apparently were in times past), they would dash off a short note to their bank, saying "Please give this apothecary guy one of the silver florins from my personal hoard, [signed] Luigiano the Fairly Resplendent, Gonfaloniere of Podunchio."

History would come to call it a "bank draft" or "check."

Later on, the bank began to write such letters for their lazy customers to carry around instead of all those nasty old heavy coins. (Observe that this innovation left bodyguards fully employed.) These were called "bank notes" and they represented real wealth, for which they could be exchanged whenever someone who had them wanted coins. They were the first paper money, and later would lead to nothing but trouble.

The invention of paper money made inflation possible. The tragic, life-destroying process of inflation is often dealt with by the media—as well as by government officials—as something natural and unpredictable, like the weather, but nothing could be further from the truth.

Inflation happens whenever the amount of stuff—printed paper, for example—people use instead of real money increases, without an increase in the real money—gold, silver, etc.—it claims to represent.

One of the fundamental laws of economics (okay, so I have studied it a little bit) and of human psychology as well, observes that the more there is of anything, the less any single bit of it is worth. If there's a trillion paper dollars in circulation, and the government suddenly prints another trillion, then the paper money we've saved up is halved in value—although if the government and their pet banks spend it quickly, they can enjoy the full benefit of it before that effect gets noticed. By the time it gets to us, however, it takes twice as much money to obtain the things we need or want. In effect, half our savings have been taken away by what amounts to an invisible tax.

Interestingly, the first inflating wasn't done with paper money. I have handled a good many ancient Roman coins that were polygonal in shape instead of round, because, whenever they passed through the hands of an unscrupulous banker or merchant, their edges were clipped off, to be added to a horde of such clippings which could then be melted down to make more coins. (That's why coins today have "milled" or decorated edges, to prevent such a practice.) The coins left dishonest hands at face value, although they were actually smaller, lighter, and worth less. Thus was the Roman money supply "watered down."

The great libertarian teacher Robert LeFevre told the story of England's King Henry VIII, who loved fighting foreign wars more than anything else, and was always looking for money to pay for them. All the historic fuss over his divorce, his various wives, and the Church of England was a smokescreen, according to LeFevre. What he really wanted to do—and did—was loot the holdings of the Roman Catholic Church.

Even that money soon ran out, however, and to pay for his men and horses and golden armor, he finally instructed the treasury to make coins out of junk metal (just as we do today), give them a gold or silver wash, and get them out into the marketplace. Henry's advisors were aghast, and fearful that such a fraud would cause rioting and revolution.

Yet when the advisers checked the marketplace, after a little while, they noticed two things: first, that the phony coins were being exchanged quite briskly, even when the coating had worn off and the dull gray of their base metal could be seen clearly; and second, that there were no real gold or silver coins in sight. These were being hoarded, not circulated. Hence the observation, which came to be known as "Gresham's Law" that "bad money drives out the good" from the marketplace.

In Germany, before World War II, and in Hungary, immediately afterward, inflation with paper currency became so extreme that it's said people took their wages home in wheelbarrows, that the money would hardly pay for a loaf of bread, and that workers were paid twice a day and immediately went out and bought food before prices rose even higher.

When I was young, a common thing for kids born in the shadow of World War II to trade back and forth were fifty million Deutschmark bills their G.I. dads had brought back from Germany. A few years later, a gold Hungarian pengo was worth thirteen trillion paper pengoes.

A possibly apocryphal story holds that the great economist Ludwig von Mises was walking with some officials past a building where the money presses were rumbling day and night. Asked what they could do to stop the terrible storm of inflation that was tearing their country apart, Von Mises simply pointed at the building and said, "Stop that noise."

Today, government and its symbiotic banks don't need printing presses. Thanks to a shady practice called "fractional reserve banking," they can lend out many times the amount of money they actually have, creating what I've called "air credit." During the Carter Administration, and then again during the Clinton Administration, banks were encouraged—even compelled—to lend non-existent money to would-be homeowners who had no way of paying it back.

Eventually, the banks, which had been promised that the government would back them up with regard to these rotten loans, got into serious trouble and had to be bailed out—with trillions more in air credit—which was the beginning of the economic mess we find ourselves in today. When other businesses began to fail—the automobile industry comes to mind—they had to be "rescued," too, with even more funny money.

Today, the dollar is worth only a small fraction of what it was just a few years ago, affecting trade and our relative position in the world.

What can be done?

From the time you are a little child with pennies, they stop at nothing to keep your money out of your hands. First, they make sure that half of it disappears in taxes. Then they convert what remains into paper and make half of that evaporate as inflation. Next, they convert what paper you have left into entries in a ledger. Finally, they convert those ledger entries into electrons, scattered into space.

There's only one way to stop them, with copper, silver, and gold, and platinum, with wealth that can't be counterfeited and that won't evaporate.

Banks and bankers must be put back in their proper place as simple guardians of the wealth of individuals. Exactly like government, they must forever be kept small and weak. There must be no special laws, no special powers or privileges for banks. Government commissions, state oversight committees, and so on soon become packed with former bankers or future bankers working overtime to make sure their businesses enjoy every government advantage possible—always to the detriment of their customers—while preventing the entry of potential marketplace competition.

Whether it's a simple burglary, mugging, rape—or fractional reserve banking—theft is theft, and fraud is fraud. Nor are any special laws required to deal with such crimes when they're committed by banks, which shouldn't be regulated any differently than, say, a filling station or a grocery store, which shouldn't be regulated at all. Certain common sense reforms are called for.

At present, it costs a bank customer twenty or thirty or forty or fifty dollars whenever he or she bounces a check. (Retailers often add their own fees, as well.) This amounts to kicking an individual when he or she is already down, since the person didn't have enough money to begin with to cover the check. It can end up costing him or her ten or twenty times the amount of the check they bounced, simply to feed the bank's insatiable, greedy maw. Add the factor of hard times, like those we all happen to be going through at present, and these fees become a major profit item. The bank's position as a bottom-feeding scavenger on human misfortune quickly becomes clearer—and more nauseating.

Another dirty banker's trick is what might be termed the "serial overdraft" scam, in which they invariably post charges against your account before they count your deposits, resulting in a cascade of fees.

I have asked several computer-savvy individuals who have worked for banks what the actual cost of processing a draft on insufficient funds amounts to, and in no case has that amount exceeded a couple of dollars. The rest of what they charge is illegitimate, punitive, and paternalistic. It is not now, nor has it ever been, a bank's place in the scheme of things to fine their customers or punish them. They have a choice: they can lecture them or collect a reasonable fee, but not both.

Yet another corrupt practice that needs a closer examination is the way that banks will happily accept a deposit—but then deny you the use of your own money until they have "confirmed" that it's really there.

In the electronic age we live in, when data flash straight across the country and around the world at the speed of light, the practice of holding a customer's transferred funds for "confirmation" for a week, for a day, for a minute, or even for a nanosecond is nothing more than bald-faced crooked larceny. During the period when you can't enjoy free access to your money, they feel free to lend it out to others, collecting interest on it that they don't share with you. It's a scam called "the float": your money, multiplied times the money of tens of millions of other suckers being worked over the same way, amounts to millions in ill-gotten gain for the bankers every single day.

Billions every year.

And what ever happened to interest-bearing savings accounts?

Lately banks have been finding ways to force employers to deposit their employees' salaries electronically. In some situations, having a bank account has become compulsory, a condition of employment. The banks' highest objective is that you never get to see your own money. Government, of course, loves this idea, because it feeds their sick, perverse obsession with monitoring everything that individuals do, every penny they earn, everything they spend it on, everything they eat.

And every time they go to the bathroom.

At the same time banks gleefully cooperate in violating their customers' natural and Constitutional right to privacy, dignity, and individual sovereignty, fundamental concepts that appear to have disappeared altogether from both the corporate and the governmental universes.

If banks were truly private enterprises, then they would be free to do as they liked in many of these respects. Facing competition, it would pay them well to defend their customers' interests from the predations of the lawless state. Unfortunately, however, they are not private enterprises, but merely another tentacle of government, twice over: they are organized as corporations, and specially chartered as banks.

As long as they remain tentacles of government, banks must be bound, as government is supposed to be, by the Bill of Rights, and regulated within an inch of their corporate lives to prevent the abuses, petty and otherwise, that they regard as doing business as usual.

I have half-jokingly considered advocating that bank officers be compelled to get themselves tonsured, their tellers to wear monkish robes or nuns' habits, if I believed that it would improve their general attitude and encourage some humility. But clearly that would violate the Zero Aggression Principle, and it would probably only make banks and bankers even more self-righteous than they are already. Hats that were once silly in Europe are now the stuff of pomp and circumstance.

Although I invariably favor laissez-faire economic policies, and wouldn't interfere with or limit any genuinely private enterprise, I do remember a time when it seemed much nicer to do business with banks, a time when branch banking was forbidden here in the state of Colorado. The battle for individual freedom against the state must be a battle against its corporate symbiotes—especially banks—as well.

Huge, impersonal, international banking conglomerates must be broken up—within principle—and a business model much more customer-oriented substituted, instead, mostly through the process of open competition, which banks have assiduously avoided for something like 300 years. As institutions of trust, banks must be discouraged from automatically taking government's side against their customers in matters such as private records disclosure and lockbox searches, and encouraged, whenever any doubt arises, to take their customers' side, instead.

The power to create money must be taken from the government-backed banking cartel called the Federal Reserve. Lawful money, as mandated by the Constitution—precious metal coins and nothing else—must be substituted for the wastebasket trash that we've become accustomed to.

Putting an end to limited liability—and the pernicious doctrine of the corporation as a person in and of itself—will aid us in this fight. Banks will be smaller, more local, and more respectful of their customers.

That means you and me.

From Çatalhöyük to Podunk: It's Time to Abolish City Government

The fact that nobody asks you to sing is not an indication that you should sing louder. This sounds obvious until it's applied to matters like mass transportation. There are virtually no private mass transit companies. This does not represent the failure of the market to provide a needed service, it represents the failure of an unneeded service to go away!

—L. NEIL SMITH

On the desk at my elbow that morning lay a blaze-orange sticker that some municipal parasite had slapped on my front door. It ordered me to cut my lawn to the city's specifications—which seem to change each and every year—upon pain of various punishments of dubious legality.

Never mind that my wife was recovering from a serious illness, or that I was wearing a cast on my broken right foot, or that it had been raining for days, making lawn cutting difficult and dangerous. Never mind that I had paid a friend to cut the lawn for me the previous week and the lawn Nazi had driven right by my front yard while he was doing it.

This all followed some incredibly rude, intrusive correspondence I had received at the beginning of the episode, making the same demands, offering lame excuses about public health the local commissars didn't really give a rat's ass were valid or not, or if anyone believed them. Given a different day, they'd have been ordering us not to alter the natural landscape lest we disturb the Holy greenicity of our Mother Gaia.

In the past, I've had similar problems with the municipal soviet socialists. At one point, the compost commissars even summoned me to court, where I defeated them easily by demonstrating that the damning photos taken by the lawn Nazi in question had been made by lying on the sidewalk so that my grass and weeds looked as tall as my front porch.

On another occasion, one of them came to my door accompanied by a young female police officer whose gun-side elbow positively quivered for an excuse to shoot me. The same city lamprey also sent a slovenly thug to cut my lawn at an outrageously inflated rate—and whether I wanted it cut or not—who threatened to "kick my ass" because I'd published a couple articles on the Internet criticizing his glorious benefactress.

I told him he would *try* to kick my ass, and he ran away.

If there's a good side to any of this, it's that dealing with these subcreatures has caused me to consider whether there's any real need for city government at all, or if it's just another deep, flowing trough where otherwise unemployable hogs can gorge themselves at our expense.

Our involuntary expense.

My conclusion? Given today's technology, and the temper of the times, there is no longer any justification for the existence of city government.

There. I said it, and I'm glad.

For maybe as long as 10,000 years, cities, constructed on or near the sites of valuable resources such as obsidian (in what may be mankind's earliest city, mentioned in the title, above), metals, fuel, and water, or located on rivers or other transportation routes, have served human beings as gathering and trading places, refuges of mutual defense, and focal-points for the arts and sciences as they began to develop.

Without a doubt, these were all extremely desirable things, and for all those dozens of centuries, ordinary individuals have proven themselves willing to put up with almost any kind of nonsense, any political larceny, any personal inconvenience, any regimentation, or nearly any other form of oppression from typical city rulers in order to obtain them. However, thanks primarily to the last two centuries of rapid progress in fields like transportation and communication, that time is happily over, and along with it, any remaining necessity for cities.

Today, however, thanks to the lawn Nazis—I hope history will remember them for it—and after nearly half a century of studying, thinking, and writing on this topic, it occurs to me that activities of city government fall into two, and only two, categories, neither of which could be said to be legitimate: those things that can be done better, more cheaply, and far more safely by individuals and the private market; and those things that shouldn't be done by anybody, ever.

For example, since I've already mentioned the long, trigger-happy arm of the law, it's significant that municipal police departments are not, and never have been, directly accountable to the population they commonly brutalize, oppress, and terrorize. (If you have a moment's thought that I might be exaggerating, look up Philadelphia, and a group of people who called themselves "MOVE.") They are accessible only through a complicated chain of city council members, mayors, city managers, and bureaucrats in numbers expressible only in scientific notation, with countless lawyers, union mouthpieces, and drooling sycophants among the round-heeled mass media to run interference for them.

As we've seen over and over again, the cops can execute an unarmed private individual in the streets, shooting him multiple dozens of times, and nothing significant ever comes of it. As bad as Waco and Ruby Ridge were, this sort of thing happens far more often and claims many more lives. The uniformed murderers are far more likely to be given medals of valor—exactly as they were at Ruby Ridge—than to get fired or imprisoned for their crimes, because their departments' pretenses at self-investigation and internal discipline are a sick joke so threadbare and dirty that nobody bothers to laugh at it anymore.

Or maybe I'm just fed up seeing four police cars idling at the curb, having pulled over a single, dangerous bicycle rider. On slow nights when I was a police reservist, we used to sit up on a hill overlooking the last remaining drive-in theater within the city limits, and watch whatever was playing. I don't want to date myself, but I saw most of Sam Peckinpah's *Straw Dogs* that way one summer night.

The drive-in is long gone, now, and the cops can only entertain themselves by bullying whatever unfortunate comes to their attention. Unquestionably, Chicago was a safer, saner, happier place when the greatest political power there was Alphonse Capone, than later, when it fell into the hands of corrupt authoritarian politicians like the Daleys.

Papa Dick and Baby Dick.

Among the latter is interfering with "acts of capitalism between consenting adults," dictating to people how they may use their own property, attempting to regulate or forbid purely personal conduct, and, perhaps worst of all, providing job security—and a power fix—for parasites, politicians, bureaucrats, and policemen, who are unable or unwilling to work for an honest living in the uncoerced marketplace. Another is wasting the energies and talents of genuinely productive individuals who would be much better off in the uncoerced market.

Give it a little thought: how much would you personally be willing to pay, out of your own pocket, to dragoon your neighbor at gunpoint into cutting his lawn to your personal specifications, or to keep him from growing and smoking whatever vegetable you happen to disapprove of?

Wouldn't you much rather spend it on a movie?

Mostly what city governments do today (and perhaps have always done, one way or another) is to violate as many of their constituents' unalienable individual, civil, Constitutional, and human rights as they possibly can, to spy on folks and order them around, telling them what they can do with their own lives, liberty, property, and to help county, state, and federal governments drain the Productive Class dry. What city governments represent, then, is simply another layer of oppression—and taxation—for hardworking people to try to live with.

Is a golf course, skating rink, or orchestra worth the price of liberty?

Or the braces on your children's teeth?

In doing away with this expensive and burdensome relic of the past, the highest priority should be given to abolishing city police departments whose policies and leadership are only accessible to voters and taxpayers through several layers of mostly unresponsive bureaucracy. Instead, to the extent that the task of keeping the peace should be handed over to anyone, it is the county sheriff, who serves at the pleasure of the people, and with whom they can usually interact directly.

Traditionally, city governments clean and repair streets, alleys, sidewalks, and drainage and sewer systems, provide a clean and healthy supply of water, collect garbage, fight fires, furnish emergency medical services, and in some cases a reliable and inexpensive supply of electricity and gas. In some jurisdictions they operate the public schools.

Equally, in various parts of the country, each of these functions—including police patrols—is provided by private individuals and businesses, almost invariably at lower prices and with higher quality standards than government offers, and without the social cost of its snooping into the private details of our lives as it pretends to serve us. Moreover, if we become dissatisfied, we can always hire somebody else.

It is time, now—well past time—to put it all together, and to abolish this dangerous, unnecessary, undesirable, archaic, and obsolete institution, "and to provide new guards" for our future security.

City governments should be relegated to the trash heap of history if for no other reason than their contemptible and embarrassing greed—the best definition of which is an inordinate desire for the wealth of other people, wealth which the greedy could never hope to earn themselves.

If attempting to raise taxes, as most cities are doing, during a Depression is nothing else, it is the absolute height of stupidity, evil, and insanity. When a culture's economy turns downward, it is almost always the fault of government, and government should have the decency (but seldom does, of course) to skulk off and lie low for a while.

The longer the better.

How about forever?

This Depression is no different than any other that came before it. Our battered civilization desperately needs three things to repair what George Bush and Barack Obama have gleefully demolished: (1) a comprehensive tax amnesty, (2) a universal tax holiday for at least a year, immediately followed by (3) across-the-board tax cuts in the 99 percent range. On expectations alone, the economy would recover instantaneously.

If government can't support itself on voluntary contributions, on charity, lotteries, and bake sales—it has more than enough resources to auction or raffle off—then it doesn't deserve to exist.

Politically, none of this will be particularly easy, but then real progress never has been. Many vested interests will leap up to support and defend the unnecessary and expensive structure of city government. In this state, for example, you can't simply vote, even unanimously, to disincorporate a municipality. Under state law, it will be declared an "abandoned city," and will be seized and controlled by the state government.

And so will you.

Tremendous amounts of money are involved, of course, salaries, contracts, and so on. But it isn't just the money. Too many sick individuals in our culture derive what amounts to a sexual thrill from ordering others around. If you threaten their fetish, they will fight back.

It's worth the effort, though, in terms of individual liberty, as well as the retention of wealth stolen to support these obsolescent excrescences. There are something like 30,000 towns and cities in America today. It is not suggested that they be done away with. As cultural artifacts and conveniences, they will continue to exist for centuries to come, many of them ultimately serving as large scale museums.

But the parasitic political structures that have been built on top of these social entities have to be eliminated, once and for all, if only because they serve as incubators and nurseries for the political class, feeding the epidemic power sickness that plagues our country today.

Cities are essentially a neolithic invention no longer necessary to human survival or well-being. They have not been necessary since the invention of the telephone and the internal combustion engine which their operators hate and fear. Like other obsolete vestiges that our species has outgrown—opera, ballet, railroads—they could not continue to exist without massive volumes of stolen wealth from the federal and state governments. Cities are machines that exist now only to drain the Productive Class and violate the rights of individuals, bottomless cesspool sources of unending bribery, corruption, and extortion.

Incremental reforms, if we are to tolerate them, should begin with the abolition of municipal police departments in favor of sheriff's departments, which are directly correctable by the public. Even then, stringent limits must be applied to the officer/population ratio, in order to eliminate the "standing army" the Founding Fathers worried about, and which has manifested itself in our time as the "thin blue line" that is all that stands between the American people—and their freedom.

In my hometown, city government is like *The Blob* in that old Steve McQueen movie, ever-expanding, all-devouring. Businesses come and go—often because of things the city government does to them—and when the Productive Class gives up and closes its doors, the city parasites move in, and suddenly there's another office, this time for the administration of left elbows or the preservation of the Norway rat.

It might be a good idea to limit the ratio of city floorspace to commercial floorspace the same way as the officer/population ratio. Whatever else we do, city governments must be strictly forbidden to own real property of any kind, and they must be forced to divest themselves of whatever real property they hold now. Moreover, if they can't keep the streets—all streets—clear of trash and snow, and maintain them in good repair, they should be allowed to do nothing else.

The plain truth is that such measures only put off the inevitable. Three decades ago, the *Reason* magazine crowd demonstrated beyond a shadow of a doubt that both volunteer and commercial fire departments (just as an example) are superior in every respect to what cities provide at the involuntary expense of the Productive Class. It would clearly be better to organize water and sewer service as private corporations than as arms of the city government. And anybody could construct, maintain, and service roads and streets better and more safely.

The same three decades have also shown that self-defense is an individual bodily function, exactly like breathing, eating, making love, or going to the bathroom, that can't be safely or sanely delegated to anybody else. If you try, you end up with a gang of uncontrollable uniformed bullies doing things to your life, liberty, and property—depriving people of the means to defend themselves comes to mind—that you'd hoped to avoid by hiring them in the first place.

There are no benign functions of city government. It "provides" recreational facilities underwritten by people who probably had better use for the money that was extorted from them. Each note played by the city symphony is a harsh cry of innocent people being robbed—most often to benefit their richer concert-going neighbors—and who will have just that much more trouble putting food on the table, a roof over their heads, shoes on their children's feet, and braces on their teeth.

It's time to dissolve city governments and let them go. One less layer of bullying and threatening means one more layer of individual happiness.

And that's really what it's all about.

Political Poison

Let the other guy offer compromises. Think of them as rungs on the ladder you're climbing. Keep your own goals fixed firmly in your mind and make sure you never move any direction but upward. That's how the other side got where they are. It works.

—L. NEIL SMITH

As American kids grow up, authority figures all around them—public school teachers, local and national political leaders, the broadcast and print media, ministers and priests, and other useless busybodies—are always very enthusiastic about the idea of compromise.

Compromise, these judas goats and stable ponies always proclaim in the most glowing terms, is the one absolutely indispensable, magical key to living and working within that best of all possible political worlds, a democracy. If everybody takes a stance and won't budge, if nobody is willing to give at least an inch (if not a mile), why, then nothing will ever get done! This, of course, overlooks the obvious fact that there are a great many circumstances—almost all of which involve government in some way—in which nothing ever should get done.

Somewhere around the fourth grade, if we have anything like half a brain left after all the indoctrination, we begin to notice certain things about this compromise bonnet-bee that make it clear that it's something less than the wonderful notion its proponents always say it is.

The first is that, since neither side can reasonably expect to get what it really wants, the best that anyone can ever hope for, from a properly engineered compromise, is that both sides will wind up equally dissatisfied. This is not, we submit, an acceptable way to run a civilization. It is a recipe to guarantee the perpetuation of bitter conflict, creating the ideal breeding ground for politicians (like puddles for mosquitos), for whom solved problems are a threat to their livelihood.

The second thing one notices, thanks to the left-wing politicians in Congress who are usually the principal advocates of compromise, is that it always seems to be the other guy who's supposed to be willing to give way. (Sort of the same way you never get to be "others" when "others" are the entities we're all supposed to live to serve.) It's the leftists' opponents who are always accused—usually at big press conferences and in newspaper columns—of being stiff-necked and unwilling to accept even the most reasonable, "common-sense" amount of legislation.

Somehow, it always turns out to be reasonable, "common-sense" legislation that will tear another bleeding chunk out of the Bill of Rights. (You may also have observed that the only time the Left ever gives a rat's ass about the Bill of Rights is when the Right is in power.)

The third thing that even a nine-year-old kid notices is that, having finally been badgered and brow-beaten into accepting a compromise of some kind, whoever has been sucker enough to do it will be expected to do it all over again, the next time the subject comes up.

"What's mine is mine," goes the saying, "and what's yours is negotiable."

Which is exactly how we ended up in the mess we're in now.

For example, many of us are old enough to remember clearly, as children, watching and listening to the American Medical Association cravenly give way, one step at a time, to slimy leftist politicians—of course they would have called it "compromise"—until today, even if Americans succeed in repealing "Obamacare," they will still be afflicted with a situation (it never deserved to be called a "system") that is neither free-market nor socialist, but combines the worst aspects of both—which is why we need separation of medicine and state.

Now I ask you: if a fourth grader could see all of that clearly, what's wrong with the people—the glorious leadership of the National Rifle Association comes to mind—who still can't see it as adults?

Time and time again, the NRA has allowed itself to get beaten and bloodied—along with us and our rights—because its leaders dull-wittedly believe they can negotiate with the enemies of freedom. The badguys know what they want—absolute elimination of private weapons ownership in America, almost certainly, history warns us, as a prelude to the kind of mass killing called "demicide"—while the NRA doesn't have a clue what it's supposed to be fighting for, and never did.

I guess we'll eventually see whether the Tea Parties and the next two elections can manage to teach them anything. Somebody badly needs to knock them down, sit on their chests, and scream down their hairy nostrils that any compromise at all with evil is—guess what—evil!

Don't believe it? Let's try a simple thought experiment. Suppose a crazed serial killer invades your home, gets the drop on you (you did have your carry-piece on you, didn't you?) and ties you to a kitchen chair. You see that he's done the same with each member of your family—for present purposes, let's say that you have a spouse and three kids. The killer tells you that he's looking forward to eviscerating your spouse and three kids while you watch, and then doing the same to you.

Clearly, this is an evil idea.

You reply that you would rather see your family and yourself unharmed.

This is a good idea.

The killer admits that he can see your point. He'll offer you a compromise. He'll only kill two of your family, and you get to choose which.

Okay, is this compromise a good idea or a bad one? While it allows two members of your family to stay alive (provided the killer keeps his word—and we haven't gotten around to discussing your life, yet), it implicitly demands that you go along with the deaths of the other two, and even requires that you seal the deal by doing the choosing.

So much for "the lesser of two evils"—there ain't no such animal.

But if you still think it's a good idea, then you belong in the NRA, which let our enemies pass the National Firearms Acts in the 30s, the 1968 Gun Control Act, the "cop-killer bullet" ban that lets government tell us what kind of ammunition we can purchase in order to defend ourselves from it, the Brady Bill and Ugly Gun and Adequate Magazine Ban in the 90s, and recently, HR 2640, the "NICS Improvement Act" which tightens the noose around our necks just a little bit more—all because, reportedly, they were afraid something worse might pass.

So they compromised.

Ain't compromise swell?

But the NRA is far from alone in its idiotic eagerness to make compromises with evil. In 1977, when I was a member of the National Platform Committee of no less freedom-oriented an organization than the Libertarian Party, I warned my colleagues and compatriots that the insufferable violations of everybody's unalienable individual, civil, Constitutional, and human rights most of them had just experienced in the process of flying to the convention city of San Francisco—"security measures" were just getting started at the nation's airports and seem mild, today, by comparison—represented the beginning of a fascist regime that would eventually spread out to engulf the entire country.

I was laughed at, and exactly the same excuses were mouthed—by "leading thinkers" of the freedom movement—that you now hear from "useful idiots" in "man in the street" interviews on television. In the thirty-something years that followed, not one of those former committee members ever thought to acknowledge that I was ahead of my time.

Some activists in the general freedom movement suggest that, in a broader sense, it is all of us, to one degree or another, who are to blame for advancing tyranny, simply by being willing to make deals with it. We're always too polite with individuals who are evil, crazy, or just plain stupid, meekly going along with their outrageous nonsense instead of dealing with it—and them—appropriately. How would Thomas Jefferson have responded to a demand that he provide urine and other intimate bodily substances before he was allowed to have a job, an idea that would have had our ancestors priming their flintlocks?

Without pausing to read the damned thing, the Congress passed the USA Patriot Act—which, for all intents and purposes, cancelled out the Bill of Rights—and scarcely anybody so much as whimpered. But this kind of travesty was hardly unprecedented. Before that, it was warrantless wiretapping, no-knock raids, RICO (designed specifically to deny legal representation to the accused), and legalized black bag jobs of the kind the Watergate burglars went to jail for. Of course now they can enter and search your house and never even tell you about it.

All because most of us are just too bloody polite.

In a matter of less than twenty years, our campuses, the media, and then our places of business were taken over by a kind of social disease we now call "political correctness" in which it's considered unacceptable to call a thing by its true name, to want to know who started the fight, to judge individuals by their actual abilities or virtues, or to enjoy anything that might make the most hypchondriacal lunatic among us whimper or sniffle that he's allergic to anyone who smokes tobacco, wears perfume, or even thinks about consuming peanut butter.

What we should have done is laugh in our correctors' fascistic faces, gone right ahead telling ethnic jokes about each other, and sent the hypochondriacal loonies off to their bins. Our moral sword and shield should have been the Bill of Rights. Instead—because we were too dadblasted polite again—we allowed them to walk all over us.

There are, in fact, two kinds of compromise, trivial and moral. A trivial compromise concerns issues unrelated to questions of good and evil. "What shall we have on our pizza?" is an excellent example. (Yes, I know some people think anchovies are evil—more for me.) So are "What movie shall we see tonight?" and "Where shall we take our next vacation?"

There's nothing bad with this trivial kind of compromise. It's how marriages and friendships manage to last. Knowing that, the enemies of freedom try to make the other kind of compromising they want you to do—a compromise between good and evil—seem just as ordinary and trivial.

So let me offer you this simple pair of moral and political guidelines.

First, if a political proposal is made that weakens or destroys the Bill of Rights—you must never accept the other guy's word about this—or if it generally threatens to limit or damage individual liberty, then it's evil. It cannot be compromised with. It can only be opposed and ultimately obliterated by any and all of the means at our disposal.

Second, as libertarians know, if a proposal calls for government (or any other) use of force against anyone who hasn't initiated force first, or plainly offered to, it's evil, and it cannot be compromised with.

If you try, all you'll end up with is more evil.

A final thought. There are some freedoms that are so fundamental, so vitally important, that they must never be subjected to voting, to the passage of legislation, or to the latest whims or fads of judges at whatever level. That's why the Founding Fathers (some of them, anyway) insisted upon a Bill of Rights, so that some individual rights would be sacrosanct, set above politics—among those rights, freedom of speech, freedom of the press, freedom from search and seizure, freedom from drumhead and kangaroo courts, freedom of religion, freedom to assemble, and most notably, the freedom to own and carry weapons.

Obviously, it didn't work out that way in the end, and the primary reason it didn't was compromise. Now, if we want any of our freedoms back, what we have to give up is compromise. We need a Constitutional amendment, just as an example, that puts real teeth in the Bill of Rights, severely punishing anybody—any politician, any bureaucrat, or any policeman—who attempts to violate, eliminate, or get around it.

And there can be no compromise about that.

Corporations, Mercantilism, and Capitalism

When you boil it down, all group behavior is about
eating, and all individual behavior is about sex.

—L. NEIL SMITH

People tend to have mixed feelings about corporations.
Just as it's said that "Everybody wants to go to heaven, but
nobody wants to die," it's equally true that everybody would
like to have a secure job with good pay and generous benefits, but
nobody really wants to spend their lives in an office cubicle, or on
an assembly line. Likewise, everybody prefers to have inexpensive
goods and services of a reliable and predictable quality, but nobody
wants to surrender their freedom of personal choice or their individual sovereignty.

Today, these ideas, new to many parts of the world, are springing up even in Japan where cradle-to-grave corporate socialism
has broken down and individuals no longer feel the loyalty—some
would call it fealty—to gigantic corporations that no longer express
loyalty to them.

Unfortunately, corporations, especially when they're controlled
by individuals who don't take the long view, often seem to find it
more convenient or profitable to override or ignore decent values—
as well as laws written to protect them—than observe and respect
them. In this, they are not unlike government. If we seek freedom,
they must be opposed and resisted, whenever necessary, exactly like
government. Clearly, it is no better to be oppressed by corporations
than it is by government.

Corporations are properly associated with mercantilism, rather than capitalism. Mercantilism is a system under which government grants special status to one or more companies at the expense of their competitors. The British East India Company, for example, possessed an exclusive, royally-granted "right" to conduct trade between India and China, on the one hand, and the British Empire, for more than 250 years.

No others need apply.

Private capitalism, by contrast, is a system under which, without asking anybody's permission, various enterprises compete with each other in the market by offering the highest quality goods and services they can, at the lowest possible prices. Progress occurs as companies and individuals strive continuously to raise quality and lower their prices.

The infamous 1773 Boston Tea Party was as much a revolt against mercantilism (an illegitimate partnership between government and its favored businesses—the same thing that we now call "fascism"), and the monopolistic British East India Company, as it was against the latest British government tax on tea. Scottish moral philosopher Adam Smith's famous *Wealth of Nations* was published in 1776 specifically to complain about mercantilism and make a powerful case for private capitalism.

A corporation is a group of individuals who create or acquire an organization to which they want government to grant special powers and immunities. One of these immunities is "limited liability." Whenever someone sues the corporation successfully, all they can ever hope to recover is whatever wealth has been set aside in the name of the corporation.

Meanwhile, the corporation's owners—those who are responsible for whatever the corporation does—are otherwise immune. The accepted "legal fiction" is that the corporation is a person, in and of itself, an individual with rights, whose responsibilities do not extend beyond its corporate boundaries, and are not the same as its owners'.

When economic circumstances permit it, corporations make periodic payments to their owners, called "dividends," sharing the company's profits and allowing money to slip through the corporate boundary into private hands where it is immune to whatever demands may be made on the company, a formula for acquiring enormous wealth at little or no risk.

In other words, if my dog bites you, you can sue me. But if I incorporate my dog, he becomes his own person, and I can't be held responsible for what he does. (I'm not absolutely sure of this theory with regard to dogs, but it's what seems to happen with corporations.) I can be fabulously wealthy, but if my dog has no assets, you's out of luck.

It is said that this "legal fiction"—which I always had a vague impression had arisen around the time of the 14th century Hanseatic League or the Bronze Age Beaker culture or something—is necessary to encourage business, and that without it the free enterprise system couldn't function properly. It's highly educational to observe that the free enterprise system seemed to function perfectly well until the middle of the 19th century, around the time of the War Between The States, which some cynical historians believe was fought mostly to benefit the corporate sponsors of Abraham Lincoln and the Republican Party.

Historian Gabriel Kolko—no friend to free-market capitalism, but a canny and accurate observer—has written that toward the end of the 19th century, corporations had grown so large and unwieldy that they needed government help to protect them from fresh new competition entering the market. Limited liability was an outright gift to them, as were so-called "antitrust laws," like the Sherman Act, which large institutions could deal with easily through their legal departments, but which put smaller, newer starter enterprises at a very serious disadvantage.

Thus corporations are founded on a lie, and they often represent at least as grave a danger to individual life, liberty, and property as governments do. The political left, which generally despises all business enterprises, whether mercantilistic or capitalistic, often exposes corporations for their inhumane and irresponsible policies—in hundreds of offerings from Upton Sinclair's *The Jungle* to *Silkwood* to *Erin Brockovich*. The protective legislation they have advocated and pushed through, supposedly on the behalf of the victims of corporations, has retarded competition (driving prices higher than they would otherwise be), stifled progress (corporations already have a reputation for intimidating or buying out innovators in order to stay in control and retain their "share" of the market), and allowed big corporations to become the bloated, clumsy monstrosities they are today.

72

In the long run, genuine advocates of liberty must strive to be neither pro-corporate nor anti-corporate, but should consistently act to defend and expand individual rights. The following measures are intended to benefit the individual by removing the results of decades of government interference in the market system in its support of corporations:

First and foremost, limited liability must be abolished, along with the "legal fiction" that the corporation is a person in its own right. Limited liability unjustly allows the owners of corporations to escape the consequences of the harmful acts of their "agent," the corporation.

On the other hand, as long as that "legal fiction"—or lie—is allowed to stand as a privilege granted by government, to that extent, the corporation is a creature of the government, and must be as fully restrained by the Bill of Rights as the government is supposed to be. This means that corporate strictures on free speech, or the carrying of personal weapons must be stricken down, as they might not be if the corporation were truly private property, and not an extension of the state.

In a society without limited liability, advocacy groups could be sued, if certain damaging measures they support become law. A recent example is the National Rifle Association, which has cynically and despicably endorsed what would amount to a new Alien and Sedition Act—legislation that would officially muzzle corporate criticism of the government by its rival organizations—in exchange for being granted immunity to it themselves. At the same time, environmental groups would have to calculate cost versus benefit for everything they propose.

Corporations are often criticized for being interested only in profit and loss. And yet, that is exactly how it should be; these entities are not charities, nor are they employment agencies; the first and only obligation of a corporation is to its shareholders. It is up to the rest of us to create and maintain a civilization in which profit can be achieved more easily and loss is less likely if they just behave like the decent adult human beings they falsely pretend to be.

Second only to abolishing the lie of limited liability, serious and meaningful tort reform—in the form of the British "loser pays all" model—must be given the highest possible priority, trial lawyers be damned, in order to discourage frivolous or mercenary lawsuits.

Next, all corporate taxes must be repealed. This is not intended as any kind of favor to corporations. The left seems chronically unable to learn that corporations do not pay taxes, but pass them on to customers who, as a result, get taxed twice. Eliminating corporate taxes would make goods and services cheaper, raising living standards, and enabling companies to offer more employment than is presently the case.

At the same time that we get rid of limited liability, abolish sovereign immunity (the doctrine that "the King can do no wrong") as well as fractional reserve banking, another business lie encouraged by government. This would mean smaller government and much smaller corporations.

Another thing that has to go is the capital gains tax. Americans are frequently criticized for having little or no savings. Clearly, if a society taxes something—people's savings or the interest they earn, for example—there will be less and less of it. This reform would change all of that, help stabilize the economy, and underwrite progress, as the savings were used to finance new and innovative business.

Along with the freedom to succeed, the equal right of individuals and corporations to fail must be energetically protected. If certain industrial processes and procedures become obsolete, then they must be replaced, or there can be no progress and resulting prosperity. Not only is protecting bloated and inefficient corporations—General Motors comes to mind—from bankruptcy illegal (look up Article I, Section 8 of the Constitution and tell me where it mentions bailing out car companies), it wastes precious time and resources, and also prevents newer, better companies and products from springing into existence.

As this chapter is being written, a particularly evil corporate scam is being exposed in which homeowners, hundreds of thousands of them, trying to avoid foreclosure in a government-wrecked economy, have renegotiated their loans under federal relief programs, only to discover that their homes have been sold out from under them by the bank, often to itself, without proper notice. Could this happen in a society where corporate shareholders and directors can be sued, not just for their corporate holdings, but for their personal assets, as well—or possibly arrested and jailed—for perpetrating such a fraud?

Also at the moment, most of the short-span attention of the news media is focused on the oil well disaster off America's Gulf

Coast. The well in question is located under a mile of water where it could only be discovered and extracted with a great deal of very expensive technology.

Drilling that far out at sea was made necessary because petroleum producers are currently forbidden by federal and state governments—usually driven by environmental pressure groups who hate, loathe, and despise all human progress and prosperity—to drill any closer, or on the land itself. That's one of several reasons gasoline prices remain high. To some extent, high gas prices may also represent a frightened attempt on the part of oil companies to "cash out" before what they see as the inevitable disaster, not of "peak oil" (one of the more idiotic hoaxes of our times) but the final collapse of a calamitously mismanaged economy, a phenomenon we might term "peak mercantilism."

There are alternatives—I am not speaking here of wind or solar power which are mostly hoaxes, subsidized by government—which could have made this disaster unnecessary. Those in control of the oil corporations are well aware of all of the new information emerging in their field: the abiotic (non-biological) origin of petroleum, the gradual replenishment from below of old "exhausted" oil fields, and the development of oil recovery and regeneration by means of thermal depolymerization.

In an economically healthy regime, unburdened by dinosauroid corporations, and filled with new, fresh, "free range" enterprises, these facts—and perhaps other developments, like catalytic or "cold" fusion—could be working for us now, to cure the economic mess we're in and set our feet back on the road to a better, brighter tomorrow.

Rational Defense in a World Gone Mad

Always attack in perpendicular fashion, from an unconventional and unexpected (but relevant!) direction. The enemy will be unprepared; you can strike him with your full strength while he finds nothing to attack effectively.

—L. NEIL SMITH

Sooner or later, libertarians are going to get stuck with the leftovers.

Just as a long and dismal history of repressive, unconstitutional legislation once threatened to leave potential libertarian office holders with an enormous crime rate to deal with—until the highly libertarian solution of simply letting everyone be armed who wishes to be changed everything, by reducing violent crime rates in double digits—so another unbroken record of incompetence on the part of Democrats and Republicans has created a necessity to assure onlookers with regard to libertarian views on the maintenance of national security.

No other issue—with the possible exception of abortion—has so continuously absorbed libertarian intellectual efforts (not to mention rhetorical energies), nor so frequently threatened to divide us.

Until its 1977 national convention, the Libertarian Party's policies could have been described as "quasi-conservative," suspicious toward the Soviet Union and other nations, reluctantly supportive of a massive deterrent machinery. In 1977, however, led by the LP national platform committee, the party line switched to "quasi-leftist," holding communism as a paper tiger and the United

States the principal villain of recent world history. Neither line, derivative as they were of established (and establishment) opinions, satisfied rank-and-file libertarians.

Compare this mess with the LP's treatment, at the time, of the issue of forced busing for racial balance in the nation's schools. Here, the LP took a principled stance against both racism and bayonet-backed social experimentation, demanding abolition at the root of the problem: collective ownership of the public school system, an entirely new slant that no other political philosophy was capable of taking. Nor was there discernable controversy within the party about it.

Unfortunately, through a series of extremely bad choices, the LP has since rendered itself irrelevant, but the movement continues. Any libertarian national defense plan needs to be exactly as singularly appropriate as the busing solution. As a philosophical anarchist, I'm more than willing to substitute the term "territorial defense," meaning nothing more (and nothing less) than individual self-defense cooperatively facilitated. I am not particularly concerned with the survival of the nation-state itself, but with the lives, property, rights, and culture of its inhabitants. I do not concede that other nations are no threat. If anything, I'm even more paranoid in this regard than most, as I hate and fear every government on the planet, and wouldn't trust the least of them to leave a defenseless neighbor unmolested.

However, a stateless order cannot be achieved overnight. The best we can realistically hope for is a "phased withdrawal" of government from our lives, during which the various arms of the octopus will wither away at varying rates. The sad truth is that the Pentagon will likely be among the last government agencies to evaporate, whatever we do.

Yet the present defense establishment is a far greater threat to Americans than it is to any potential foreign enemy, having repeatedly proven itself too massive and clumsy to deal well with human-scaled reality, but more than willing to "break things and kill people." The two million-odd individuals in uniform today must be regarded as a giant welfare scheme (never forgetting the corporate welfare lavished on the defense industry) or as a means of controlling an increasingly restive civil population should the need be perceived by those in power.

Any intelligent security plan must depend on libertarian virtues like individual enterprise, massive decentralization, and the technological superiority we can expect them to engender. In applying them to this problem, there are three basic categories to consider: (A) conventional warfare, the technical and tactical ambience that persists despite Hiroshima, Werner von Braun, and Robert S. McNamara; (B) strategic deterrence, generally taken to mean nuclear weaponry and its supporting hardware; and (C) so-called "asymmetrical warfare," including covert attack modes, until 9/11/01, a sort of garbage can for items which fit neither previous category, but which I have long believed will grow in urgency as we effectively dispose of the other two.

Conventional Warfare

From our Revolution through Vietnam, Iraq, and Afghanistan, history demonstrates beyond debate that there is only one practical method for purely defensive conventional warfare: the way of the guerrilla. Accordingly, the heart of this proposal is to reduce and fundamentally reorganize the present defense establishment, while increasing its legitimate efficiency. Understand that such an undertaking would occupy no more than a tiny portion of the ongoing business of America; it is by no means a "national priority" or a "crash program," but simply a gradually implemented series of common-sense practical adjustments.

The plan's principal elements are these:

1) An immediate end to American military presence in the Middle East.

2) Withdrawal of all American personnel from the more than 150 countries in which they're based, and closure of all overseas bases. This would enormously reduce current defense expenditures and also the risk of being drawn into a war over some irrelevant local dispute. Such bases serve no function in the guerrilla defense of the United States.

3) Combining all branches of military service into a single, cost-effective unit. This is clearly necessary, if only to reduce expensive redundancy. The Army, Navy, and Marines,

for example, each maintain their own air forces. Moreover, the traditional distinctions between these entities no longer operate as they once did, and the supposed efficiency that competition normally sparks is nowhere in evidence.

It's psychologically important here to discuss the elimination of all but a single, practical military uniform for the professional military, a consideration less trivial than it may seem. It would tend to reinforce the above-mentioned unification (traditions might well be preserved through distinctive hats or unit markings), and act as a constant reminder that our soldiers are performing a positive, market-oriented, division-of-labor service, exactly like beekeepers, UPS drivers, and filling-station mechanics, who also wear task-specific garb.

I first suggested decades ago the military work-clothes be simple fatigues without a hint of traditional military decoration, because police studies over the preceding decades in California and elsewhere had shown that preoccupation with spit-and-polish discipline, besides wasting valuable person-hours, actually undermines both the combat effectiveness of a unit and the survival chances of its individual members. Similarly, there is no rational excuse for military rituals like 4:00 A.M. bugle-blowing, obsessive bedmaking, aimless marching, sadistic shouting, hazing, and brainwashing. Twenty-first-century America needs intelligent specialists, capable of thinking for themselves.

The single element around which all training revolves should be weapons expertise. Over the last century, the number of rounds expended per enemy casualty has increased logarithmically. During World War I, Americans had a reputation among German troops as fiendishly accurate one-shot-one-kill sharpshooters. In Vietnam, American forces spent a million rounds per enemy casualty. Today, no organization trains people to handle guns as poorly as the American military, nor, in the opinion of this retired gunsmith and former ballistician, supplies its personnel with such miserably inadequate weapons.

4) Reduction in professional soldiery to training-cadre levels. Every nasty, difficult, and dangerous school in the current

military curriculum should be combined into a continuous program and all personnel, regardless of age, rank, or physical condition, be required to graduate or retire from service. Those who make it through Green Beret, Ranger, and paratroop training, qualify to use explosives, climb mountains, endure arctic, desert, and prisoner-of-war survival training—each with its own terrible attrition rate—would become charter members in the new American military. The primary effect would be a drastic reduction in forces to between 20,000 and 30,000 men and women, winnowed and toughened volunteers, intelligent professional killers further selected for their ability to teach their skills to others.

An integral and supremely important aspect of their training (fully as critical, in the end, as weapons expertise), would be their understanding and acceptance of the libertarian principle of non-aggression—as a substitute for the irrational mystiques which have been an important part of traditional military life. Philosophy or not, with their numbers limited to five figures, such a force could offer no threat to civil liberties or civilian government. Few, if any, among the present Pentagon-level command would make it through the selection process. The salaries of selectees could be increased tenfold or a hundredfold without affecting the current military budget.

5) Denationalization of the militia is the intermediate end which all the above is meant to serve. Defined in law as all able-bodied persons of arms-bearing age and physical ability, the militia under these principles would be limited to willing participants. Since the primary advantage of the guerrilla is intimate familiarity with his or her own territory, once the "National Guard" is taken out of federal hands, it must be reorganized, not on a state-by-state basis, but county-by-county, similar politically and socially to volunteer fire departments and mountain rescue units. It would also train for and perform purely civil tasks like emergency snow-removal and brushfire fighting.

The professional military cadre, on the other hand, would travel around the country singly or in extremely small groups, educating the local militia volunteers in the latest techniques of cooperative self-defense. The professionals would find serving 3130 counties, parishes, boroughs, and independent municipalities a stimulating full-time occupation.

6) The next step: liquidation of conventional capital-intensive military hardware. When it becomes possible to destroy a multi-million-dollar cruiser or aircraft carrier with a $20,000 missile, or a multi-hundred-thousand dollar tank with a three-dollar hand-held rocket, it's obviously time to stop cruising and tanking. Small mortars proved far more mobile and effective in Vietnam than clumsy, crew-served gunnery, and could usually be carried by a single individual on a bicycle.

   The sale of military white elephants to other countries might help capitalize our newly-forged system, based on cheaper, smaller, more effective weapons suitable for guerrilla use. The largest item might be armed hovercraft—a 250-mile-per-hour navy and cavalry combined against which submarines and tanks would be so much helpless scrap metal.

7) Domestic military bases should be eliminated except for one in each of four or five major ecological zones. Even these would be severely reduced, serving only to maintain the combat-effectiveness of the professional cadre. Present military reserves should be sold to support the program or turned over to their rightful owners where possible.

8) All gun control laws must be repealed, official weapons-registries at all levels of government destroyed, and currently warehoused weapons distributed throughout the populace. Historically, the first places taken over during an invasion or a coup are local police stations, so that lists may be obtained of those who own weapons.

   Assuming a still functioning Department of Defense (collecting and spending money), arming the citizenry might require a hundred billion dollars—enough to make even non-libertarians gasp in protest. On the other hand, limited-government libertarians consider it a legitimate function of the State to provide for the physical security of

the country. Arming individuals is by far the most efficacious means of achieving that end. These weapons would be
handed over permanently (returning some fraction of what
the government has stolen from taxpayers) and would be a
one-time effort, stretching out over at least a decade, replacing vastly more expensive and less-efficient programs.

The government already holds vast arsenals of weapons,
some dating back to the Spanish-American War. (We recently learned of 850,000 Korean War pieces—presumably
M-1 Carbines, M-3 submachine guns, and Garand rifles—
excellent weapons that the White House refuses to release
to the public that paid for them.) Many of these guns would
have little or no application to a guerrilla-style defense system, but their sale to collectors would help fund a more effective distribution plan.

Furthermore, the 11% excise tax on every gun sold in
this country (the National Rifle Association's not-so-bright
idea to ingratiate itself with establishment media by supporting wildlife conservation, as if hunting were the only
reason for buying a gun) would be eliminated. If uniform
hardware could be agreed on by a majority of militia units,
the resulting production volume would greatly lower costs.

Before going further, it is important to note some differences between this proposal and the defense system of
Switzerland which it may seem to resemble. Although
participation would presuppose personal ownership of adequate weapons, membership itself would by no means be
compulsory. Nor would it be limited to males. Nor would
I consider (as Robert Heinlein once proposed) membership
to be a condition for the franchise or any other civil right.
There is one thing to admire about Switzerland's system
though: they haven't had to fight a war for 400 years.

Physical requirements would be less stringent for the
militias than for the professional cadre. Basically, if you
could roll your wheelchair up to the firing line and shoot,
there would be a place for you.

Some may be anxious to assure the ethical and informed
use of mass-distributed weapons. To any extent which it can
be assured, this would be a function of the training cadre—

another reason why their libertarian values must be deeply implanted. It is unfortunate that liberals—who have struggled so long to prove that the trouble with sex is not that we have the capacity, but that people must be educated in its exercise—cannot see that the same holds true for our violent capabilities.

Strategic Deterrence

Strategic defense, no less than conventional, is susceptible to the same principles of low-cost decentralized voluntarism. I have always opposed international disarmament treaties because, at whatever level, gun control never works. Medieval knights, forbidden by their Pope to use the newly-invented crossbow, simply ignored the Papal prohibition, establishing a thousand-year tradition in this area of legislation.

It is too late to control nuclear weapons because they are already obsolete. For decades, the U.S. military has possessed lasers capable of knocking down an airplane. If more powerful models do not already exist, they soon will, consigning bombers and missiles to the junk heap of military history. Linked with early-warning radar, they will, in effect, generate an "umbrella" against any merely mechanical method of attack.

Lasers suffer from atmospheric attenuation—air and water vapor dissipate the beam. Not so, however, at the midflight altitudes of intercontinental missiles. Under libertarian economic policies, a vastly richer private sector can place permanently inhabited structures in orbit for research, communications, manufacturing, recreation—and defense. Unlike ballistic missiles, lasers can be used over and over again (greatly lowering the number of necessary installations) and, in peacetime, would have numerous civilian applications.

Possibly including weather control.

Even lasers can be improved upon. "Particle beam weapons" employ heavier subatomic constituents and presumably suffer less atmospheric attenuation. Such energy weapons offer the hope of an effective, inexpensive, non-nuclear defense, an end to decades of the special kind of international terrorism that superpowers practice. Americans can take their entire atomic arsenal and dump it in the Philippine Trench.

Backyard SDI

The "Backyard Strategic Defense Initiative" is a notion first discussed in the 1980s by a certain science fiction writer—the one writing this book—and his friend Steve Heller, a software engineer, based on a World War I German artillery piece called "Big Bertha" or the "Paris Gun." The explanation below closely follows a dialogue written for the political novel *Hope* by yours truly and Aaron Zelman, founder and head of Jews for the Preservation of Firearms Ownership.

The Paris Guns—there were a pair of them, actually—were mounted on railroad flatcars, and could throw shells more than 75 miles by shooting them up into the stratosphere where there's less air resistance, drastically elongating the shape of their parabolic flight path. The Germans had meteorologists on their firing teams. The first shot, from German turf, destroyed a church full of people one Sunday in Paris. The French were terrified. They thought they were being bombed by a dirigible flying so high up that it couldn't be seen.

Unlike Big Bertha, however, Backyard SDI can only be employed defensively. It can't be used for aggression. Instead of 2000-pound bronze shells full of explosives, it will use lightweight fiberglass shell containers filled with 800 pounds of BBs—a million of them—and a tiny explosive charge, designed to reach about 100 miles above the Earth's surface and burst in front of oncoming intercontinental missiles, leaving about one BB per cubic meter, forming an effectively impenetrable—if very temporary—shield. Compared with the nuclear missiles coming in at about 18,000 miles an hour, each BB will be stationary.

When it strikes the missile (or when the missile strikes it) it'll make a BB-sized hole going into the weapon, and an incandescent Volkswagen-sized hole coming out. That's the end of a multi-million-dollar missile, for the price of a World War I cannon and a bushel of BBs. Or make that 3130 cannons, owned and operated by 3130 county militias.

A friend of mine and advisor is skeptical about Backyard SDI. He doesn't think the system could hit a missile hardened for re-entry, coming in at several times the speed of sound. I appreciate his doubts, but as I said, 800 pounds of BBs comes to a million stationary objects in a single shell, designed to deploy at the critical moment into half a million cubic yards in front of the missile, each occupied by a BB.

Make the cannon automatic, firing 60 to 100 rounds into space per minute.

Now imagine 3130 counties, parishes, boroughs, and independent municipalities, all shooting at the same time, directed by Cheyenne Mountain, or by manned satellites high above the fray (and armed with their own defense systems which may look a lot like the Navy's Phalanx guns).

If you build it, they won't come.

The Paris guns were makeshift, jury-rigged devices, consisting of a medium-bore barrel shoved through the stubbed-off breach of a larger gun and supported by cable truss; many improvements could be made on such a system, including polygonal progressive rifling that squeezes the projectile tighter and spins it faster the closer it comes to the muzzle, prolonging the peak pressure of the gases (which will require more modern metallurgy) and greatly increasing the velocity of the projectile.

When the remaining 999,999 BBs that didn't hit the missile come back down, their terminal velocity—the maximum speed that a .177" diameter sphere can achieve free-falling through the atmosphere—should be too low to hurt anything or anybody it hits. One of them might make an interesting souvenir, though, a BB that's been up in space.

The missile fragments should disperse and burn up on re-entry.

Although militias will own the big guns and be in charge, there will be some cooperation with government, which already maintains a missile early warning system. It can tell militias where to aim their cannons and when to fire. In time, cheap orbital technologies, developed by private corporations, will allow some giant BB guns to be based on manned space platforms. Meanwhile, the total cost of the Backyard SDI militia program will be roughly eight hundred million dollars, mostly not from the federal budget. Quite a difference from the $25 trillion that the Reagan "Star Wars" program was supposed to cost.

In the meantime—which is likely to be fairly long, because the American people need to be convinced, and then they will have to convince the Congress—America will have her missile submarine fleet and aircraft carriers to protect her. Backyard SDI will completely change the order of things where foreign policy and the military are concerned.

Covert Attack Modes

Viruses and toxins delivered by missile or plane can be taken care of by orbiting energy weapons or even the so-called "Phalanx" system of radar-guided Gatling guns that defend naval vessels from cruise missiles. But what about vials of horror brought into the country in a briefcase? It is even legendarily possible to create an atomic chain reaction by piling enough fissionables together. What if fanatics were to import components (in lead-lined briefcases) and assemble them by hand?

As unlikely as these contingencies may appear, the irony is that they may be employed precisely because a libertarian society's conventional and strategic defenses are so well taken care of. Nevertheless, we must should resist and ultimately eliminate the elaborate and repressive security measures that have been erected around us by a government taking full advantage of the attack of 9/11/01.

An ethical solution must be found to the problem. At present there is no adequate answer—one point: terrorism is most effective in large gatherings of strangers; it won't work in small communities where everyone knows everyone else—although a lot of time and money could be spent trying to devise one, and worse, a good many liberties could be trampled trying to implement it. In the end, simply getting our troops out of other people's countries should take care of the problem.

One difficulty remains. If you've read Heinlein's *The Moon Is a Harsh Mistress*, in which Lunar convicts win political independence by "throwing rocks" at the Earth, and if you're familiar with the idea, put forward by Luis and Walter Alvarez, that mass extinctions, notably that of the dinosaurs, are the result of other rocks—meteors and asteroids—hitting Earth, you can appreciate why, if it's up to current authorities, or successors of the same mindset, they'll never let ordinary folks into space. And you can bet that if they've thought of "throwing rocks" at others, they worry about others doing it to them.

Pax Americana

One final measure will virtually assure a total and permanent end to international hostilities: in time of declared war or invasion, the government must dissolve and disband, a provision that would guarantee nightmares and migraines to any potential enemy. With nobody empowered to surrender, the country would have to be taken square foot by square foot. We the people use up two billion (2,000,000,000) rounds of .22 rimfire ammunition every year. In the end, the enemies of freedom, foreign or domestic, will have to face a lethal wall of tiny, lethal bullets.

Capture Washington? Congratulations, pal, now you've got a swamp in Maryland. New York? Swell, you can take over the bankruptcy proceedings!

War is the consequence of bad statesmanship. If Congress faced mass unemployment as a punishment for such incompetence—and especially if they were the first to go fight—peace might eventually break out.

In summary, then: withdraw overseas troops; combine all branches of service; reduce the professional military to training-cadre status; denationalize the militia; liquidate all military white elephants; and arm the populace. For strategic security, rely on advanced non-nuclear technology.

The principal advantage of such a program is that it will allow us to change security from a continuous ongoing crisis and debate, within both the libertarian movement and the United States, into a simple job, a solved problem, that can be done with, taken care of once and for all.

Then we can move on to something more important.

Some Random Thoughts About the War on Drugs

*If you're not a little bit uncomfortable with your position,
it isn't radical enough. How can you be too principled?
Take the most extreme position you can—you're claiming
territory you won't have to fight for later, mostly against
your "allies."*

—L. NEIL SMITH

It is not my purpose in this essay to explore the merits or demerits of drug use, a question that should properly be left to the individual. It is irrelevant—and often a matter of sheer conjecture and unsupported opinion—whether drugs in general, or any drug in particular, may be good or bad for the individual or for society. In an era in which most of the world—especially government and the media—was hoaxed into believing in global warming, it would be wise to be suspicious of any "science" offered in support of government policies.

Even if drugs are fully as destructive as they are usually claimed to be, it is morally wrong—and demonstrably more destructive—for government to deprive people of their unalienable, individual, civil, Constitutional, and human right to make an utter mess of their own lives. Since human beings are generally inclined to learn more from the mistakes they make, rather than from their triumphs, the right to fail, for individuals and groups alike, may be even more important than the right to succeed; it must be fiercely protected at almost any cost.

Those who argue that an individual's drug use affects others—the drug user's family, for example, or his friends, his employers, his co-workers, his lodge brothers, or little children starving in India or

China—are merely attempting to deprive those people of personal choices that they should be free to make, concerning their association with the drug user. Even children should have the right to disassociate themselves from a parent whose drug use threatens their well-being.

Moreover, while we may love certain people in our lives, and they may love us, that doesn't make us their property any more than it makes them ours. Each and every individual is the owner and sole proprietor of his own life, and nobody who understands history and human nature wants to live in a society where that principle is not upheld.

While employers have an understandable interest in forbidding drug use on the job, they have no right to dictate what an employee does on his own time as long as it doesn't affect his or her performance at work. Current testing policies enforce company preferences off the job as well as on, and they must either be modified or discontinued altogether.

Exactly the same restrictions should apply to schools.

Importantly, there is nothing in the Constitution—by which, under Article VI, Section 2, officials at every level of government are obligated to abide—that authorizes the banning of any substance or enforcing that ban with the threat of injury, incarceration, or death. The lawful powers of the federal government are enumerated in Article I, Section 8, and they do not include prohibiting drugs or any other substance or establishing paramilitary police agencies to enforce such a prohibition. Politicians early in the 20th century understood this, and passed a Constitutional amendment allowing them to outlaw alcohol. No such amendment was ever passed, or even proposed, with regard to drugs.

Given the number of turf wars, drive-by shootings, compromised police and other officials, and invasions by uniformed thugs of the wrong address that are closely associated with the War on Drugs—and with special attention directed to the bloody open warfare between competing drug cartels and a putrescently corrupt Mexican government presently spilling over our southern border—it should be clear by now that drug laws and the attempt to enforce them cause vastly more destruction to individuals and society, and consume much more time, energy, and money, than the drugs in question ever did. We owe the existence and character of the police state which has sprung up all around us largely to government excesses in the name of the War on Drugs.

A new correspondent of mine recently asserted that the real reason that America never won the "war on drugs" is that "we never really made it a war. Terror and violence," he insisted, "can only be subdued through greater terror and greater violence. Systematically target the boss narcos with cruise missiles," he suggested, "and continue with their replacements, and the flow of drugs [will die] in less than a year."

I seriously doubt that, but I didn't debate it. Instead, I asked him what, precisely, gives anybody a right to do something like that? Show me that portion of the Constitution that specifically authorizes it.

I added, "Mention 'the children' once, and you'll be sent back to Start and lose all of your points. The only ones who should stop kids from using drugs are their parents—and the kids themselves, of course."

"It worked for mine."

"Terror and violence" against drug producers and dealers is no more permissible than terror and violence against grocery store owners or bicycle dealers. There are murderous morons in government who ache to do this same sort of thing to gun dealers and their customers. Know that, and you'll have a beginning at understanding how to handle the problem—to the extent that it really is one—in a sane, ethical way.

Remember, there was no drug problem until there were drug laws.

I confess I get heated on this issue, even if I have less than no interest in the drugs themselves. (I'm an alcohol and caffeine man.) But it is the worst kind of usurpation against individual sovereignty and self-ownership to point a gun and tell people what they can and cannot do with their own lives—"for their own good." I would far rather live with gangsters running things than with do-gooders who think they have a right to organize my life for me. The truth, now, wouldn't you really rather Chicago was run by Al Capone than Baby Dick Daley?

On top of that, government has wasted countless billions of our dollars since about 1900, and it's squandered millions of lives, worldwide, in a futile attempt to keep people from doing whatever politicians disapprove of. How stupid do you have to be to see that drug cartels are not empowered by drugs, they are empowered by drug laws?

How many diseases might have been cured with that money? How many trips to the Moon and other planets have we thrown away? If you want to know where your Picturephone, your flying car, and maybe even your interstellar drive went, they were devoured by the War on Drugs, a war whose "victories" are worse disasters than those of the drugs themselves.

And along the way, we have empowered and enriched, not just the drug lords, but countless scumbag politicians, bureaucrats, and cops, and given them permission to stick their fingers up our asses, demand blood and urine samples, and generally violate our privacy, dignity, and liberty. Ironically, the honest ones are worse than the corrupted ones.

The men who fought the American Revolution would have answered these foul usurpers with iron, fire, and lead. So forgive me for falling far short of that and getting a little exercised. Drug laws (and the myriad other usurpations that inevitably followed) have destroyed the America I once believed in and the future I expected to arrive. No one has a right to interfere with "acts of capitalism between consenting adults," no matter how high their moral dudgeon or how many useful idiots they drag along with them. It is that very interference, by two coercive states, that is at the heart of the violence on the border. It's the drug laws that have made this mess. The real enemies of life, liberty, and property are in Congress and our state legislatures.

In the first third of the 20th century, the Volstead Act and alcohol Prohibition brought unprecedented oppression and violence—both from criminals and "law enforcement"—into the lives of ordinary Americans, and nobody seems to have learned a damned thing from it. Drug Prohibition allows criminal scum to make obscene amounts of money because cheap agricultural products have been made illegal—and therefore massively profitable—for no logical or Constitutional reason. Equally loathsome politicians, bureaucrats, and jackbooted thugs scheme psychopathologically to accumulate power for its own sake by frightening the population and keeping them at one another's throats.

How many more incarcerations for possession of politically incorrect vegetable byproducts, how many more violent raids at the wrong addresses, how many more unjustifiable killings by militarily equipped policemen with too many guns and too much power, does this culture have to tolerate before somebody cries, "Enough!"? When will somebody with a tall enough soapbox point out that the cultivation, manufacture, distribution, sale, possession, and consumption of drugs are all normal human activities guaranteed protection under the Constitution?

The production, processing, transportation, sale, possession, and consumption of drugs is, in fact, a Ninth Amendment right, differing in no respect from the production, processing, transportation, sale, possession, and consumption of bread. All laws contravening the Ninth Amendment are unconstitutional and therefore illegal. Every government agency responsible for enforcing these laws is therefore a criminal conspiracy, and every individual who works for them is an unapprehended criminal.

America didn't have a drug problem before it passed drug laws. While drugs were consumed by large numbers of people—the number of women habituated to the opium found in laudanum is, no pun intended, staggering—they were, for the most part, easily able to live their lives, do their jobs, and raise their families pretty much the way we do today. None of that changed until legislation was passed generously handing the drug trade over to criminals and criminal organizations, removing commercial safeguards of uniformity and sanitation, cruelly endangering the lives and freedom of drug users, and generating all kinds of associated crimes of violence and the risk of disease and death.

Interestingly, the first turf wars, drive-by shootings, corrupt police and other officials, and invasions of the wrong address occurred, not in connection with drugs but with alcohol prohibition, an historic period that doesn't appear to have taught anybody anything.

Advocates for one drug or another often claim that their drug is less dangerous to individuals and less damaging to society than tobacco or alcohol. This "Do it to Julia" tactic—which George Orwell warned us about in 1984—is less than productive. What each of us must demand consistently is freedom for all to make important choices in our lives, rather than have them made for us by the government and the kind of sick, twisted, broken individuals who use it to control others because their own lives are so repulsive and unbearable.

Especially in this era where we can no longer trust science to be truthful, there is no reason tobacco and alcohol—or other drugs—should be regulated or taxed differently from any other product. The motivation to do so is punitive, essentially religious in character, and therefore forbidden under the First Amendment which states, in effect, that public policy is not to be made on the basis of religious beliefs.

Advocates for drugs like marijuana often point out that if it were legal, it could be taxed, as a sort of bribe offered to the government to leave its users alone. This is the submissive behavior of a slave mindset, and it has no place in the struggle for individual liberty. Taxation—of any kind—is theft, a far greater wrong than using drugs.

As an issue, I am less than enchanted with the concept of "medical marijuana" because I can't shake the impression that it was thought up by its advocates as a "clever" way to inch, sneakily, toward full "legalization."

On the other hand, what are we to believe about the character of any politician who would willingly watch innocent cancer victims starve and wither away under the ravages of chemotherapy, suffering prolonged deaths, writhing in indescribable agony, rather than allow Prohibition to slip backward a single political inch? Such a creature is a monster, a collectivist, willing to sacrifice any number of individuals to his dark, evil fantasy of control over the lives of others.

I oppose "legalization" with its implications of regulation and special taxation; I simply want to see all the drug laws repealed. There's no more reason to "legalize" marijuana—or anything else, for that matter—than there is to "legalize" bananas. Alcohol was "legalized"—meaning that Prohibition never really ended, it only changed in shape—and it staggers along today under a burden of discriminatory taxes and microscopic scrutiny inappropriate in a free country.

Criminals should be tried and punished on the basis of what they did, rather than how they were when they did it, or what they used to get that way. If we can outlaw drugs because they sometimes cause some people to injure or kill others, then, given the history of the last thousand years, between the violent and ugly excesses of Christianity and Islam alone, we should be able to outlaw religion for the same reason.

Many individuals in government don't seem to understand the laws of economics. Most of them—aside from those in Congress—seem to be concentrated in the area of "drug enforcement." They often brag at news conferences that their interception of drugs between producer and consumer has raised the "street value" of the drugs, meaning that the drugs are now scarcer than they were. What these statists stubbornly refuse to acknowledge is that this only increases the market incentive to cash in on those higher prices by making up for the artificial scarcity.

Can they really be that stupid? Or do they understand cynically that the livelihoods of thousands of police officers, administrators, bureaucrats, and politicians depend heavily on never actually ending the illegal traffic in drugs? The drug war, in fact, is a kind of corrupt, evil game played endlessly by so-called "law enforcement" and traffickers, in which both profit obscenely at the irreparable expense of the Productive Class in particular and Western Civilization in general.

Simply repealing drug laws at every level of government would save tens of billions of dollars every year, money that is badly needed now for America's economic recovery, money that shouldn't be wasted on an effort that has not only gone on for decades without positive results, but which has made the situation vastly worse than it was to begin with.

Repealing drug laws would remove the risks involved with producing and distributing drugs, bringing "street prices" crashing down (it's estimated that a "spoon" of heroin would cost about a quarter in the free market), thereby eradicating any incentive that criminals might have to compete with legitimate businesses, and greatly reducing—if not eliminating altogether—any economic reason to "push" drugs on children.

Choices about drugs and drug use must be left to the character of the individual, or, all choices having been made for them, we will inevitably end up with individuals who have no character at all. And concern for "the children," which is often an excuse for the most atrocious of authoritarian policies, must be left in the hands of their parents.

The alternative is chaos, insanity, and ruin.

How do you like it so far?

I don't use drugs myself, but it annoys me whenever I hear conservatives getting shirty about others using drugs because "it's against the law." The fact is, drug laws are against the law. Nothing in Article I, Section 8, of the Constitution permits their existence. The Ninth Amendment clearly protects the production, sale, purchase, and use of drugs. Article VI, Section 2, passes that protection on to lower jurisdictions. Those who pass and enforce drug laws are criminals themselves. If you're concerned about obeying the law, people involved with drugs must be left to direct their own lives, whether you approve or not.

One-Dollar Gas

Never soft-pedal the truth. It's seldom self-evident and almost never sells itself, because there's less sales resistance to a glib and comforting lie.

—L. NEIL SMITH

O f all the things to suffer a crisis about, by far the silliest is energy. There is no shortage of energy whatever in America or in the world.

What there is a shortage of—as usual, with 20th and 21st century problems—is individual liberty, exacerbated by a surplus, a hideous glut, of mercantilist interference with the free-market system. Energy corporations today are unanimous in grim determination that you and I—and those who provide our other goods and services—must be limited to purchasing our energy from them, and only from them.

That's what the wars in the Middle East are all about.

Unfortunately, their investment in yesterday's scientific ideas, obsolete technology, and gradually collapsing infrastructure make buying energy from them one of the worst bargains we could possibly strike.

Government has a hand in this, as well. Generally the more energy that is available to any given individual in any given society, the more individual liberty there is in that society. That is probably the reason why authoritarian, collectivist governments (if you'll pardon a redundancy) adopt mythologies that claim energy is scarce or will soon be.

Nor is the essentially fascistic environmentalist movement at all interested in cheaper, cleaner energy or greater human freedom. Their goal is to round up all of humanity in vertical concentration camps called "arcologies," forcibly reduce the population, mostly by lowering the quality and standard of living, clear the countryside (the way the British did in Scotland in the 18th and 19th centuries), and let it "return to nature"—except, of course, for the dachas of the nomenklatura and their more attractive and compliant peasant slaves.

If billions must die to achieve this Utopian dream, so much the better.

For those with different plans for our futures (and I emphasize the plural here), it's important to understand that existing known reserves of oil, natural gas, and coal in North America alone, are enough to meet our needs for centuries. That's why it's so important for the enemies of liberty to restrict or eliminate prospecting, extraction, and refining energy here, employing evil and inhumane rationalizations that rest on an assumption that animals, plants, and even naked dirt and rocks are more important than their fellow human beings.

Whom they plan to kill off anyway, in the long run. These are the moral cripples famous for saying that "What the world needs is a good plague."

Environmentalists, far from being friends of the Earth, are the enemies of humanity. They want you impoverished, enslaved, or dead. Nobody who actually cares about his fellow human beings—or for the future of his children—should ever feed them, house them, clothe them, transport them, protect them, or support them in any other manner.

Let the bastards freeze in the dark.

But I digress.

Just because there is still plenty of fuel—energy—left in the ground, that doesn't mean that we shouldn't look for more. The more of anything there is, the cheaper it gets. The cheaper it gets the more we can afford to use. The more we can afford to use, the faster our progress out of the War Century, the century of the biggest, most powerful, and most destructive governments in human history.

And upward, to the stars.

One of the most startling—and gratifying—discoveries in recent decades is that most petroleum is not derived from dead animals or plants, but was created by non-biological, or "abiotic" processes in the Earth's crust. These processes continue to this day, and, according to some experts, oil fields once thought to be depleted are presently filling up again, from underneath, with geologically newer oil.

There are those who say that anywhere you drill—provided you drill deeply enough—you'll strike oil. (Naturally, a shallow hole is cheaper to drill than a deeper hole, so some minimal forethought and exploration are called for.) The claim is controversial, and especially repugnant to those who have invested their lives and fortunes in conventional theories about the origin of oil, but the Russians, acting on it, went from being one of the world's largest importers of petroleum to one of the largest exporters, in only half a century.

Oil, in fact, is the second most abundant liquid on the planet, and, in a free market, should cost a mere fraction of what it does now.

There are a number of alternative cheap, clean energy sources to oil, gas, and coal, and I am not referring to diffuse and marginal technologies like solar power and windmills. These perennial favorites of the environmentalist movement have extremely limited small scale applications, such as lighting road signs far from civilization, or pumping well water into stock tanks (windmill-provided power to cities is very costly compared to conventional sources) and otherwise represent expensive and completely unnecessary diversions. The same goes for what I would term "fuel substitutes," such as hydrogen and ethanol.

What might be termed "conventional nuclear power"—atomic fission—is unsatisfactory only because it requires a government or large corporation to underwrite, build, and operate it. Otherwise, it is the cleanest, safest, most reliable source of energy on the planet and most of the complaints about it are hysterical or politically contrived.

A generation ago, it was common among the anti-nuclear activists to claim that fission is so unsafe that insurance can't be found to cover it. This is a lie. Insurance companies simply couldn't compete with the protection afforded by government under the Price-Anderson Nuclear Industries Indemnity Act, which limits a company's liability to an unrealistic and unjust figure in the case of a nuclear accident. We now see this same legal "philosophy" set aside by executive command in the case of the Obama-BP oil spill, and this may end offshore drilling entirely.

Although dozens of nuclear reactors provide some 19 percent of the electricity consumed in America (significantly higher than the world average, although 80 percent of France's electricity comes from nuclear power), that figure is in decline, and there have been no new reactors built for many years. The United States Navy maintains over a hundred reactors on its vessels with what is reported to be perfect safety, even on those rare occasions when ships have succumbed to some other disaster and been destroyed. The decline of the United States as a culture can almost be dated to its abandonment of nuclear power, not so much because nuclear power is a good thing, but because it betrays a psychological and emotional loss of the country's grip on the future.

More than anything, the future of nuclear power was killed off by federal construction regulations that seemed to be changed arbitrarily every day, slowing the building process to a crawl, greatly increasing its cost, forcing constant redesigns that might be reversed the next day.

Equally to blame were hundreds of frivolous nuisance lawsuits on the part of the anti-nuclear movement which genuine tort reform of the "loser pays" kind may have prevented. Interestingly, the anti-nuclear movement began with no actual concern about nuclear power itself; its founders, Jane Fonda and Tom Hayden among others, found themselves missing the "good old days" of the anti-Vietnam war movement, and began casting around cynically for something new that they could protest.

In the history of nuclear power, there have been two "accidents," one at Three Mile Island, near Harrisburg, Pennsylvania, in 1979, and one at Chernobyl, in the Ukraine (then a part of the Soviet Union) in 1986.

In the case of Three Mile Island, when a malfunction occurred, the emergency shut-down system worked exactly as it was supposed to, and the danger was grossly exaggerated by anti-nuclear activists and their propagandists in the news media. Edward Teller, the so-called "father of the H-bomb," visited the site and said afterward that he was the only casualty at Three Mile Island, having suffered a minor heart attack in the parking lot, which he blamed on Jane Fonda and Ralph Nader.

Chernobyl is another kettle of fish altogether. Like all communist technology, it was built on the cheap, the product of shoddy, possibly drunken workmanship, substandard materials, corrupt management, and questionable design. Its emergency containment system failed to meet world standards, and it was said, half-jokingly, by western engineers that the Soviets saved money on their reactors by not building an adequate containment vessel around the reactor until it was actually needed.

If anything, Chernobyl demonstrates the serious risks of allowing too much government control of, and interference with, any industry. The danger is only increased in the case of something like nuclear power.

The only legitimate technical objection to nuclear power is that it produces radioactive waste—spent fuel—that must be disposed of somehow, usually by storing it deep in abandoned mines where it will remain radioactive and dangerous for thousands of years. The answer to this problem is "rebreeding," a process by which this spent fuel is made useful once again by exposing it to radiation within a special reactor.

France routinely reprocesses a significant amount of its nuclear fuel, and is said to enjoy the cleanest air in Europe. Unfortunately, America has no more breeder reactors, having shut them all down years ago, supposedly, for fear that the end product, the nuclear fuel plutonium, could also be used to build atomic weapons. This is incredibly irrational and stupid, exactly like giving up the use of dynamite in road construction because it might be used for criminal purposes.

At least two technologies, currently suppressed, could each supply enough power to civilization, on their own, to run civilization for centuries. One of these sources is catalytic or "cold" fusion which, contrary to popular belief was never discredited after its discovery in Utah by Fleischmann and Pons, but is still being researched and developed enthusiastically in Europe by certain governments and corporations.

What seems like a dream to some—a footlocker-sized fusion reactor in everybody's basement, or under the hoods of their cars, that would supply all their energy needs with minimal attention and no nuclear waste or chemical exhaust—is a nightmare to others, chiefly those who generate energy now by burning coal or natural gas, or who string the wires across the countryside from powerplants to your house.

Regrettably, there isn't a single industrial ox in today's society that isn't gored by what they perceive as the threat of cheap, clean fusion. It is said that its discoverers fled America to Europe, and for a time, actually disappeared, out of fear that they would be killed. All governments hate and fear the individual—and corporate mercantilism isn't very far behind them—and wish to restrain him, because they're afraid that, unrestrained, he'll act just like they do.

Thermal depolymerization is a late-comer to the field of energy, but one that shows great promise and is already a proven technology. In this process, any organic garbage can be "cooked" into what amounts to "light, sweet crude," the most desirable variety of petroleum. Cast-off computer cabinets were mentioned in the first article about it, as a raw material source. Old automobile tires—of which there are huge mountains in America, some of them slowly smoldering—can be processed to produce oil, plus carbon black, a useful industrial product.

Environmentalists whine constantly about landfills. The process of thermal depolymerization will transform them into energy mines. The best part is that, having been demonstrated to work in a small proof-of-concept plant in New Jersey, the process's inventors believe they can produce oil for somewhere between fifteen and eight dollars a barrel, in a world market where conventional oil is several times that figure, and it doesn't have to be shipped here by pipeline or tanker. Nor does it have to be drilled for on land or at the bottom of the sea. It can even be produced locally, as a routine part of municipal sanitation.

What it means, at the pump, is one-dollar gas. "One-Dollar Gas"—that's a winning campaign slogan, for any political party intelligent enough to pick it up and run with it. Regrettably, when I offered it—and more than once—to the Libertarian Party, they declined to do so.

Unfortunately, those who provide our energy now, using outdated technology, at much higher prices, feel threatened by this invention—as well they should—and are doing their level best to suppress it. It is up to the new media—the Internet and talk radio—to expose this illicit activity, bring it to a halt, and promote the new technology.

When I was young—surprisingly so, perhaps as young as eleven or twelve—I realized more or less suddenly that the solutions to all of the world's problems had almost certainly been discovered already, quite possibly many times over, but that nobody else wanted to hear or think about them. If libertarians have a natural destiny, it is to think the unthinkable, speak the unspeakable, and get the world to listen.

In general, if we are to survive and advance, the energy industry must be detaxed and deregulated soon. Costs will plummet, and there will be no more reason to rely on unfriendly strangers for our well-being.

I Now Pronounce You Spouse and Spouse

America's historic misfortune is that her people, in aggregate, have never been quite equal to the ideals upon which she was established.

—L. NEIL SMITH

The black civil rights movement was just getting underway when I was starting junior high school in Fort Walton Beach in northeastern Florida.

It came as something of a surprise to me because I'd been out of the country the previous four years, and in those days, most methods of communication—even including the so-called news—were slower, more difficult to access, and under unimaginably tighter control than today.

One of the many civil rights issues involved schools that had been segregated, those in which only whites could be enrolled, and those built especially for blacks. This was before there were many Asians in our culture, and I seem to recall that Hispanics were classified as white (although I could be wrong about that—it's the way things were in the Air Force, in which I'd grown up). The catchphrase was "separate but equal" and the segregationists' assertion was that, if the facilities afforded to black people were of the same quality as those afforded to non-blacks, then equality, under the law, had been achieved.

For a number of reasons, some good, some bad, this was not looked upon as a satisfactory solution by a great many individuals. One example of a bad reason was the implication—not terribly subtle in most instances—that black children were somehow retarded (in the dictionary sense that they had been held back, even in schools of equal quality) and would benefit from attending school with white children.

This is the substitute for reasoning that resulted in the insanity of school busing for integration, when one of the principal objects, to begin with—for blacks—was simply the right to send their kids to the school nearest, that is, most convenient, to home. If I were a black person, I would regard anyone who wanted to "help" me for such a reason—invariably it was the Volvo-driving, wine-and-cheese-eating socialists who called themselves "liberals" in those days—as a mortal enemy, no better than any Ku Klux Klansman, and treat him accordingly.

Remember the phrase, "Mau-mauing the flak-catchers"?

A better reason to fight for integration was presented to me by my civics teacher (I apologize for not recalling his name), who was a friend and supporter of James Meredith and was photographed walking with him on his famous stroll across the University of Mississippi campus.

Black people pay taxes. They have no more choice about that than white people do. Their money is not regarded as "separate but equal" but gets dumped, instead, into the general trough along with everybody else's money for consumption by Boss Hogg and all the little Hoggs. Whatever the money of black people pays for entitles them to equal access.

It was on that basis (and quite a number of other things that I learned later—such as the difficulty of simply finding a place to eat or get a night's sleep when traveling across country) that I came to embrace the civil rights movement, even though, in the end, it wound up being co-opted and corrupted by socialists, exactly like the women's movement was, and the libertarian movement stands in danger of today. I did not support the "public accommodations" argument, which basically nationalized every mom and pop business in the country, although these days I would support the mandatory integration of corporations.

Now let's shift focus for a moment. Those whose sexual preference happens to be different from mine (I'm a flaming heterosexual—ahh, it feels so good to come out of the closet!) and possibly yours, the individuals who sometimes label themselves "GLBT" (for Gay, Lesbian, Bisexual, or Transgendered) pay exactly the same taxes as straight people.

You can probably see where I'm going with this.

The local county courthouse, the county clerk's office, the county clerk, and the judge, justice of the peace, and bailiff, are all paid for, using money extorted from their constituencies, under penalty of law, in full equality, without regard to race, creed, color, or sexual preference.

Anybody who pays for those things, especially in the same way—at the threat at government gunpoint of injury or death—has a civil right to equal access to them. The county clerk records deeds, and fluffs a lot of other duff, without regard to who or what the taxpayer involved has sex with. There is no reason—which is to say, it is unreasonable—to change that policy when it comes to registering marriages.

Civil marriage, as opposed to what happens in a church, synagogue, or mosque, mostly involves the formal disposition of property. The only possible alternatives are to extend to GLBT individuals exactly the same rights afforded to "normal" people, or—and it would still be petty and stupid—to exempt them from paying taxes altogether, since they are being denied services those taxes are supposed to pay for.

Arguments about the "sanctity of marriage" are both horrifying and laughable. When I was still in grade school, not living in the South, I had my first encounter with what you might call professional or hardcore racism, in the form of grubby pamphlets brought to school and handed around by a couple of other kids. I have no idea where they came from, originally, but if the same thing were to happen today, before they could have the politically incorrect children executed for it, the administrators and teachers would soil themselves and pass out.

I found the pamphlets fascinating, but not for the reasons their publishers had intended. Their contention was that white people are in some way genetically superior to everybody else (only they didn't use the word "genetically," not in the late 1950s). And at the same time, preaching against "race-mixing," they warned that a single drop of non-white "blood" was capable of corrupting the entire mighty Aryan genome.

What kind of "superiority" is it that can be destroyed so easily? If I were a white supremist, I would believe that my genes are capable of overwhelming everybody else's. I would believe that bestowing them upon non-whites was a way to raise the entire human race to near godhood.

Wouldn't you, if you truly believed you were superior?

At this writing, I have been married to my wife for nearly thirty years. Together, we have been richer and poorer, through sickness and in health. We have our daughter, our little home, and the cause of liberty to struggle for. In what possible way can any of that be weakened or damaged by recognizing the right of others to be married, too? Those who oppose gay marriage on the grounds that it somehow tarnishes traditional marriage are the same kind of wimps who believe their precious "blood" can be diluted by a single drop of non-white blood.

We are all aware of (many of us are old enough to remember) the "anti-miscegenation" laws passed by bigots—and not just in the South—who didn't want blacks and whites to sleep together, let alone marry; there are many bigots left out there, who still hate the idea of interracial marriages and relationships. It makes me wonder: what would people like this, falsely claiming to represent conservatism or Christianity, do to Jewish weddings, if they could?

The "inconvenient truth" (if Albert Gore hasn't spoiled that fine old phrase by now)—the proverbial "elephant in the parlor"—is that any legislation written to deny "GLBT" individuals their civil rights is based solely and necessarily on religious beliefs that have no legitimate place within the body of law of a republic mandating, as the First Amendment clearly does, the formal separation of church and state.

Conservatives contend that the First Amendment contains no such mandate, that, in fact, the words "separation of church and state" do not appear in the Constitution (which is true, as far as it goes), but only in the writings of Thomas Jefferson, whom many of them despise as America's first "liberal." The great problem with this contention is that the First Amendment—along with the remainder of the Bill of Rights—was written by his friend James Madison, specifically to allay Jefferson's suspicions, well-justified, as it turned out, that the new Constitution represented a threat to individual and states' rights.

When all else fails, although they always complain bitterly when so-called "progressives" do the same thing, opponents of gay marriage drag "the children" into the argument. Marriage, they maintain, is for the purpose of continuing the species, which "obviously" gays can't do.

This of course, overlooks the fact that many heterosexual couples don't have children, either because they are physically incapable of it, or because they simply don't want to be parents. Are conservatives suggesting that there be some kind of officially-mandated fertility test before a marriage license can be issued? After all, most states test for venereal disease, and have done so for a long time. Or maybe they'd like to organize a corps of procreation police who keep an eye on married couples to make sure they're doing their best to make babies.

The "go forth and multiply" argument also overlooks the fact that lesbian couples frequently have "turkey baster" babies, artificially inseminating themselves with sperm supplied by generous male friends. Ironically, GLBT people, many of whom are unable, or do not wish, to bear their own children, are sometimes denied the children they so desperately want by government adoption agencies. Instead, children who might have gone to a loving home with two fathers or two mothers sit childhood out in a shelter with no parents, no love, and no way out.

Anti-GLBT forces clearly believe (although they may not admit it) that GLBT couples who wish to adopt will corrupt their children by "turning them gay." Unfortunately, the GLBT community exacerbates the problem by resisting any scientific investigation into exactly what distinguishes them from "straight" people. What we do know, clearly, is that straight couples only create straight children—just look at the Dick Cheney's family, for example. We can also rest assured that teaching children acceptance, tolerance, and respect for GLBT people will not make those children themselves GLBT. It will merely make them realize that if they are GLBT, they don't have to hate themselves for it.

To be clear: just as a gay man is no more likely to rape you in the shower than your friendly neighborhood Senator, a gay parent is no more likely to abuse his children sexually than the average straight parent.

The conservative argument that legalizing gay marriage will lead to adults marrying minor children, or marrying property such as pets or inanimate objects, is a panicky last-resort. Neither minors nor property are able to sign legally-binding contracts such as marriage licenses. The right to marry multiple spouses, which is another thing they worry about, is already protected, not by Sharia law, which they also worry about, but by the First Amendment, which guarantees religious liberty. Laws against bigamy, as well as the longstanding federal persecution of polygamous Mormons, are almost self-evidently unconstitutional.

Conservatives claim that the drive for gay marriage is motivated primarily by economics, and that the millions of individuals who would be eligible to share in their spouses' Social Security or insurance benefits would "break the system." But they know that the system is already broken, and, in a truly free society, there wouldn't be any system to break. What's more, in such a free society, the insurance companies would be able to choose freely for themselves the couples they want to recognize as "legitimate," providing another basis for market competition, and eliminating the spurious insurance argument altogether.

The gay individual I know best informs me that the majority of GLBT folk don't want to be dismissed as "just another minority." They march to demand equal rights. As the black civil rights movement should have taught us, equal—but separate—is not truly equal. Those who contribute to civilization have a right to share fully in all of its benefits, something the anti-GLBT side never seems to appreciate, maybe because they've never seen that separation from the inside.

The 2008 platform of the Libertarian Party states: "Sexual orientation, preference, gender, or gender identity should have no impact on the rights of individuals by government, such as in current marriage, child custody, adoption, immigration, or military service laws."

The Right to Own and Carry Weapons

To be human is to live by means of the artifacts that humans devise. To build a home, and scorn a weapon, is hypocrisy. It's also a good way to lose the home.

—L. NEIL SMITH

This essay is not about numbers.

Numbers can be handy, sometimes, and at present, where the issue of weapons and self-defense is concerned, they are solidly on the side of individual liberty. But almost anyone can make numbers seem to prove anything he wants them to. They never seem to win arguments or change minds. If you want numbers pertinent to the private ownership of guns and other weapons, there are plenty of other places to find them.

This essay is about relationships—that is, about how one thing relates to another. For example, here's a relationship: people who have guns can tell people who don't have guns what to do, even if that includes—as it has at several ugly points in fairly recent history—kneeling down in a ditch and taking a bullet in the back of the head.

There's a reason we call it "victim disarmament" rather than "gun control." Don't ever let anybody attempt to persuade you that they are advocating such a policy for any other reason. The unpleasant fact is, there are those among us—it's no secret; they proclaim it proudly and with increasing volume and frequency—who desire to possess that power, who yearn to be the ones who can put a bullet in the head of a helpless captive, or better yet, to order some underling to do it for them.

Thus there are three reasons to have guns, each being of equal importance.

The highest law of the land, the first ten amendments to the Constitution, commonly known as the Bill of Rights, maintains—in one of the most carefully-worded phrases in political history—that the private ownership of guns is "necessary to the security of a free state."

Remember that, in those days, the word "state" meant (as it still does in most contexts today) "nation," and that each of the thirteen former colonies that, together, had violently and bloodily wrested their independence from England, was considered to be a nation unto itself.

Considered itself a nation unto itself.

Also, the word "state" could be taken to mean, as it can still be today, "condition," carrying unmistakable undertones of individual liberty, without reference to whatever polity one might happen to live in.

America's Founding Fathers didn't just mean fending off England again, or France, or the Lost Continent of Mu. They meant the free and independent states of Maine or Massachusetts or Maryland defending themselves from the central government (a stronger central government than many of them had intended under the Articles of Confederation) being imposed on them now by the new Constitution. And, by extension, they also meant individuals defending their lives, their property, and their rights from any government at all, be it local, state, or national.

This assertion of a right to own and carry weapons in order to maintain a condition of individual freedom must surely have been seen as a direct threat to English authority on their own home ground. America's Founding Fathers saw that right as deriving from the natural rights of all Englishmen, which in many ways they felt they were defending.

But as usual, I have digressed.

Most gun control laws are aimed specifically at illegally getting around that fundamental set of protections from government abuse. For example, Americans today are effectively (albeit, not explicitly) forbidden to own machineguns—the most useful weapon for keeping a government under control. The excise tax was prohibitive at the time of passage, during the Depression, and the required registration and approval by various levels of authority negate their Second Amendment usefulness—of what use can any weapon be that the government knows about?

This travesty occurred because that quivering coward Franklin Delano Roosevelt, and his cabinet of collectivists and Quislings were afraid (and rightfully so) that they were about to be overthrown in a coup d'état organized by businessmen—evil capitalists, including one of the nation's largest firearms and ammunition manufacturers—spooked by the President-elect's widely-advertised friendliness with communism and communist ideas. It would be carried out by veterans of World War I, betrayed, angry, and desperate to feed their families. Interestingly, both the Great War and the Great Depression were messes caused by Roosevelt's lying predecessor, the racist, elitist Woodrow Wilson.

Stop and think about it. If most Jews in Germany had been armed, would there have been a Holocaust? Jews certainly armed themselves in Warsaw—beginning with only a few pistols and revolvers—and they managed to take at least an entire Nazi division, several thousand hardened troops, "offline," out of combat, for three solid months, dying in the process, but saving an incalculable number of lives elsewhere.

It's obvious that our would-be rulers have taken a look at Warsaw, and at the Alamo—where 247 heroes armed with rifles, pistols, and large knives delayed the gold-braided megalomanic President General Antonio Lopez de Santa Anna and some 2,000-6,000 Mexican troops (depending on what revisionist you're reading) for two precious weeks, long enough for Sam Houston to build an army and humiliate him at San Jacinto.

They've considered Masada, the "Jewish Alamo"—actually, the Alamo was the Texican Masada—before that, where some 960 Jews, armed about as well as their Imperial Roman enemies, held the high ground for three months against the entire legion it took to defeat them.

And of course there is Mount Carmel, near Waco, where in 1993, a violent, publicity-hungry bureaucracy ran into a group who refused to be driven from their home, their church, to be arrested in front of TV cameras, and used to glorify—and justify—an unconstitutional agency. If the FBI were really all they claim to be, they would have come to Waco, to Mount Carmel, arrested each of the

ATF agents there, and gone away again, leaving their victims, the Branch Davidians, alone.

Our would-be rulers, however, have come to different views about how the right to own and carry weapons—an unalienable individual, civil, Constitutional, and human right not granted, but acknowledged and promised absolute protection by the Constitution—ought to be "handled." Many of them have good reason for concern. A well-armed populace stands in the way of their cherished ambitions—ambitions that by any sane, decent measure, are those of sociopaths and serial killers.

Bill and Melinda Gates, for example, through the foundation that bears their names, spend billions of dollars on vaccines for the third world. Yet according to Paul Joseph Watson and Alex Jones, writing for PrisonPlanet.com ("Eco-Fascists Call For Tyranny To Enforce Draconian Agenda," Thursday, September 16, 2010) Gates has given speeches openly advocating using such vaccines as a tool of forced sterilization, in order to lower global population in the name of combatting global warming.

Gates also advocates using death panels to deny healthcare to the elderly.

In a 1977 textbook, co-authored by population-fanatic Paul Erlich, the current White House "science" czar, John P. Holdren, called for an obscenely dictatorial, eco-fascist, and inhumane "planetary regime" to carry out policies like forced abortions and mandatory sterilization, as well as drugging the water supply in an effort to "cull the human surplus."

James Lovelock, perpetrator of the crackpot "Gaia Hypothesis" has demanded that democracy "be put on hold" and that "a few people with authority" should run the planet. Author Keith Farnish openly calls for acts of sabotage and environmental terrorism, including blowing up dams and demolishing cities to return the planet to an Agrarian Age and rid the world of Industrial Civilization. The disgraced and discredited NASA "scientist" Dr. James Hansen endorses Farnish's ideas.

Almost unbelievably, Watson and Jones report that a Dr. Eric R. Pianka, a biologist at the University of Texas in Austin, has expressed the "need" to exterminate 90% of the world's population through an airborne Ebola virus. "The reaction," they report in horror, "from...scientists and professors in attendance was not one of shock or revulsion; they stood and applauded Pianka's call for mass genocide."

These are the vile creatures in positions of leadership today in academia and government, and it's only the tip of a very big, very dirty iceberg. For Watson and Jones' whole Prison Planet story—and more motivation than you needed to keep your powder dry—go to: http://www.prisonplanet.com/eco-fascists-call-for-tyranny-to-enforce-draconian-agenda.html

If individuals were free to move onto land presently controlled by governments, and to employ technologies abhorred by the psychopathic Luddites and would-be genocides among us, no rational individual would ever worry about "overpopulation" again. The present population of the planet—six billion people—could fit, standing room only, into Rhode Island. In Connecticut, they could sit down. In the long run, the object must be to let those who want to, move off the planet into space, to other bodies, first in the Solar System, then among the stars.

A second reason to own guns—and to carry them with you at all times—is the matter of personal self-defense. Violent crime rates in America, which had been on the rise for decades, collapsed in double digits when individuals began to ignore gun laws, to ignore carry laws, and the states were forced to hop for their lives to get out in front again. It's now common knowledge—it was almost from the beginning—that 9/11 would never even have been planned if the Second Amendment rights of those airline passengers had been left unmolested.

Likewise, bloody incidents like the one at Columbine High School are the result, not of too many guns, but of too few. Personal self-defense must not be interfered with in the nation's airports or its schools.

If anybody still wants to argue with you that armed passengers endanger an airplane, there are plenty of self-defense experts who know how to solve minor problems associated with that—including yours truly, in the novels *The Probability Broach* and *The Venus Belt*. Be sure you ask the doubters—and demand an answer, because they'll flop and squirm like a freshly-boated marlin to avoid it—how a .357 Magnum revolver or a .45 automatic could possibly place an airplane and its passengers in greater danger than flying it into the side of a skyscraper—or letting the Air Force shoot it down (yes, that's the kindly, humane, official plan) because they think it's been hijacked.

Even given the most charitable interpretation, victim disarmament, for many of its advocates, is no more than an infantile attempt to deny and evade the responsibilities inherent in self-ownership. Oddly, the relationship involved is asymmetrical. While an armed aggressor can completely overpower an unarmed victim, putting a gun in the hands of a potential victim—even (or especially) a small female potential victim—seems to do considerably more than even up the odds. An armed aggressor will often retreat from an armed defender, just as—according to scientists who study such things— an animal defending its own territory is several times as effective as any would-be invader.

In about 95% of cases studied, it isn't even necessary to fire a shot.

Even if guns did cause crime (which they do—the way that flies cause garbage), even if the violent crime rate were to increase directly or even exponentially with the number of such weapons in private hands, that would not affect in any way my individual right—or yours—to own and carry them. To maintain otherwise is an act of collectivism totally foreign—alien—to the traditional American outlook.

The third reason to defend personal weapons may seem trivial at first, but I assure you it is not. It is exactly the same reason that some individuals may collect coins or stamps, Rembrandts or Picassos, Stradivarii or Stratocasters, Chippendale or Stickley: an intensely private, pure aesthetic, the simple joy of seeing, touching, using, possessing whatever you personally find beautiful, or just appreciate as a significant product of human genius answering dire or everyday necessity.

That joy—the satisfaction of possessing a Collier, a Colt, a Webley, a Smith & Wesson, a Broomhandle Mauser, a Luger, a Glock, or a Schwarzlose (rifles and shotguns are nice, too)—is a prime target, as well, of the bloodless, fleshless, inorgasmic zombies who would be our absolute slaveholders, and it should never, ever be minimized or overlooked.

Just take a glance—it doesn't even have to be a close one—at a typical member of the Obama Administration, the Department of Homeland Security, the Southern Poverty Law Center, or the Center for Science in the Public Interest. What they are inside shows in

114

their strained, pasty faces and nervous gestures. They want our lives to be as miserable as theirs, and they will stop at nothing to have their way.

Those who hunger after power over the lives of other human beings crave it only because they feel they have no power over—and are incapable of experiencing any joy of—their own lives. Deep down inside, in the seething cauldron of bitter dread and self-loathing that serves them as a soul, they desperately hope that controlling others may give them what they can't find within themselves. But history clearly demonstrates that what they suffer is a cancer of the heart and mind that can never be satisfied, and for which there is no cure.

Don't give them an inch. Don't give them an Angstrom unit.

Any compromise with evil is still evil.

Identification and the Security State

Let me get this straight: America is based on the idea that an individual's fundamental rights are his or hers by virtue of having been born—the best evidence of which is that you're standing here, right now. So why, in order to exercise a good many of those rights, are you required to present government-issued credentials?

—L. NEIL SMITH

It never fails to interest me that the first American President to be assassinated was also the first to try to assume the powers of a god.

Abraham Lincoln resculpted history and the law to suit his essentially evil purposes. He intimidated, kidnapped, even deported those who failed to agree with him. He sent army troops to smash the opposition's printing presses and to the polls to make sure he got reelected.

Lincoln oversaw the deaths of 620,000 of his fellow human beings, not to end slavery as was widely (and falsely) advertised after the fact, but because some of those 620,000, those who were paying 80 percent of the taxes, refused to be his slaves, and had the temerity to stand on their rights, instead of meekly bowing to his imperious will.

Before Lincoln, public officials, including the President, could be seen on the streets of Washington City, walking to work, going to lunch, enjoying the evening with their wives, families, and friends. And there was a good reason for that. Before Lincoln, few politicians were in a position to utterly destroy the lives of those they'd been elected to serve. Any who might have been in that position restrained themselves, out of common decency, a positive regard for

116

what America was supposed to be about, or for fear of somebody ruining their lives back.

Then along came Abraham Lincoln, with the evil dreams that he had inherited from Alexander Hamilton and Henry Clay, of buildings roads, canals, and railroads to enrich those who had steamrollered him into the White House, and to manage what was supposed to have been a loose confederation of independent republics as a massive, monolithic super-state.

Along came Allan Pinkerton, whose self-assigned objective boiled down to nothing more than helping the President avoid having to face the individuals he was damaging, and the American security state was born. Today, it takes longer to cycle through White House security than it does to see the Pope, and increasingly, there are millions of cameras everywhere across the country, backed up by face-recognition software.

It is the hallmark of a totalitarian regime that you can hardly go anywhere, or do anything, without carrying your government-approved identification.

"Progressives"—left-wing socialists who used to call themselves "liberals"—can never bring themselves to believe that the Founding Fathers really meant what they said in the Bill of Rights, especially in the Second Amendment, because they're incapable of using words with careful precision themselves, and often say things that they don't mean.

And mean things that they don't say.

Some of them do believe in an armed citizenry—whenever there's a Republican in the White House (they aren't really wrong about that, as far as it goes). And they will defend to your death, their right to say anything they want, no matter how evil, stupid, or crazy it may be.

However, thanks to thousands of hours of "progressive" propaganda, half a dozen decades of broadcast "news" and "entertainment" TV, not many Americans realize that it is a violation of their basic rights to require that they identify themselves in any way in order to buy a gun. Before such laws were passed, especially in the 18th and 19th centuries, violent crime was much rarer than it became in the middle of the 20th, when it began to rise steeply as government at all levels made it increasingly difficult to obtain, own, and carry the means of self-defense.

But as I often do, I have digressed.

We have gotten to a point in America—banks love to blame this on Homeland Security but I don't believe them; they were leaning hard in this direction in the 1970s and blaming it on the government even then—where you need photographic identification to open a checking or savings account. Then you need one to present at the cash register with your credit card. Soon they'll be demanding your fingerprints and a retinal scan just to buy an ice cream cone at the Dairy Queen for cash. Or how about a drop of blood so we can check your DNA and blood sugar at the same time? Can't have the Faux Lady getting mad at us, now.

Because, of course and after all, only criminals use cash. And since there are already ten or fifteen million laws on the books, with more being passed every day in a desperate race with an American public increasingly cynical and suspicious about the very concept of government, and since no one can move a step or take a breath, or blink an eye, or even exist for half an hour without breaking one of those ten or fifteen million laws, we are all criminals—and must be watched.

Totalitarian governments—Mexico, Venezuela, Britain—hate, loathe, and despise cash, and they are taking whatever steps they can, employing their phony War on Drugs as an increasingly shabby and threadbare excuse, to make it illegal. One of the most wonderful things about cash is that it makes identification unnecessary and unjustifiable.

"Hold on, gonna to hafta to see some ID with that half-ounce gold coin."

I don't think so.

Carrying cash also increases the importance of being prepared to defend yourself at any time, anywhere, which—despite the whining and whimpering of giant infants who refuse to acknowledge and accept the responsibilities inherent in self-ownership—is a very good thing.

A.

Very.

Good.

Thing.

"Take a gun with you on all your walks," as Thomas Jefferson put it. I could be wrong, but I don't believe he said a word about photo ID.

So the question arises (or I'll pretend it does), how do we unburden ourselves of all this poking and prying, all this laminated lawlessness on the part of a government that was never authorized to impose these requirements on those who were supposed to be its masters?

At this somewhat revolutionary moment in the nation's history, the authoritarian establishment has some philosophically and therefore politically vulnerable spots. One of them, believe it or not, is the original intrusive and obnoxious identification system, driver licensing.

Originally intended, during the badly-named "Progressive Era," when everything was to be registered and licensed, simply as proof of your proficiency at operating a motor vehicle, it has now become your leash, something you need for practically every transaction with the government as well as what we laughingly used to call the private sector, a means of tracking you right across the country unless you can somehow avoid buying food or gas or sleeping anywhere but your car.

Most drivers' licenses include your photo (notorious for making you look like the uncaught felon that you are) and one or more of your fingerprints. Somewhere they may incorporate your federal prisoner's code—commonly called a "Social Security Number" or more accurately, your taxpayer ID—and there is relentless political pressure to add computerized information like your medical history and status with the IRS.

Did you know, by the way, that it has never been scientifically proven that no two fingerprints are alike? It's just a Progressive Era assumption, backed by questionable statistics, just more phlogiston, phrenology, and globular warmuling. Piltdown Man would be proud—if he had ever existed. It can't be proven, either. You'd have to take the fingerprints of everyone on Earth, six billion individuals, and then crank them through every government computer on the planet for a thousand years, before—hey, isn't that a great idea? Take all the money being spent now on acid rain, ozone depletion, and the menace of video gaming, and devote it to proving what government claims about fingerprints.

And then, if they prove it, forbid them from collecting them.

Similarly, early automobile registration—and the metal plate that went with it—was merely meant to assure all the sloppers at the public trough that you had paid your protection money, as private individuals have had to do for more than a century in America, for anything too large to hide away from the uniformed or bureaucratic racketeers.

License plates now carry your very own personal police tracking numbers and any society organized for the convenience of the police—lately, they've been demanding the power, using OnStar and similar services, to turn your engine off by remote control—is a police state.

A nationwide organization, not just to prevent the imposition of an intrusive universal ID system, but to abolish drivers' licenses altogether, might do more for the freedom movement than practically anything else. If anyone is still concerned with your ability to drive a car, a certificate of proficiency—without anything but your name and account or membership number—could be obtained from your insurance company, the automobile club, even the manufacturer of your vehicle.

The so-called Progressive Era began more than a hundred years ago. Theodore Roosevelt, Woodrow Wilson, and Herbert Hoover are all dead, as dead can be, and the world is in no better shape for their having been here to begin with. Everything these homegrown fascists believed in and shoved, one way or another, down the throats of their fellow Americans, has long since been discredited and is obsolete. All of their numbers, all of their tags, all of their registration and licensing have proven counterproductive. Every social ill that it was claimed they would cure is a thousand times worse today than it was then.

Americans need their liberty, Americans need their privacy, Americans need their personal sovereignty, and Americans need their identities back, not only for their own sakes (although that would certainly be more than reason enough), but if they ever hope to repair the damage done to them by so-called "progressives" of whatever era, from the administration of Theodore Roosevelt, to that of Barack Obama.

It must be illegal for government to track you, using your own cell phone to betray you. It must be illegal for government to eavesdrop on your conversations. It must be illegal for government to open your letter mail, or to spy on your e-mail or other Internet activity.

Given government's past proclivities and abuses, the Fourth Amendment, which presently reads, "The right of the people to be secure in their persons, houses, papers, and effects, against unreasonable searches and seizures, shall not be violated, and no Warrants shall issue, but upon probable cause, supported by Oath or affirmation, and particularly describing the place to be searched, and the persons or things to be seized," must be amended, removing the word "unreasonable" and establishing the harshest possible criminal penalties for judges and other public officials responsible for issuing or serving documents (such as so-called "'John Doe' warrants") that do not meet, in each and every respect and detail, the criteria listed.

Get started with drivers' licenses and automobile registration, then. Move on to the Social Security and gun laws, all of which are unconstitutional. Shame conservatives into joining the fight. Don't be afraid to be made fun of by the left-wing socialist media. In this age, any publicity is good publicity, especially coming from statist idiots whose attacks on you will be seen by others, in effect, as an endorsement.

By a splendid coincidence, I was recently mentioned in a comments section of the Huffington Post as a leading "gun-crazy"; the quote was inaccurate, improperly attributed, but I'm certain, well-intended. And the criticism of me (not of what I didn't say) by ignorant others had absolutely nothing to do with the subject at hand. But my name was mentioned twice, and will stick with those inclined to check out my writings.

May you, too, have such luck.

I Lift My Lamp Beside The Golden Door

"Wake up America," you demand? America doesn't need to "wake up"—by which, of course, you mean pay attention to whatever you think is important. If America weren't already awake, paying attention to what each individual thinks is important, your milk wouldn't have gotten delivered this morning, the grocery shelves would be empty, and you wouldn't have any electricity this afternoon.

—L. NEIL SMITH

I am of two minds when it comes to the hotbutton topic of illegal immigration. Unlike the socialists who call themselves "progressives," I'm more than willing to call it that: illegal immigration. After all, it's immigration, right? And if you don't say "Mother, may I?," jump through the right hoop, and get your forehead rubber-stamped, it's illegal.

Unlike the socialists who call themselves conservatives, however, my sympathy lies entirely with anyone who wants to escape from tyranny and/or build a better life for himself and his family. That's why my ancestors came here—I'm not so sure that they had all the right papers, either—and so did yours, even if they came early, by way of the Bering Strait ice bridge and falsely call themselves "Native Americans." Ultimately, each and every one of us is a refugee from Africa.

The distinction everybody seemed to make twenty years or so ago between political refugees and economic refugees always struck me as patently false and hypocritical. People in the Third World are poor because their authoritarian rulers keep them that way, under

122

political and economic theories that never seem to work for anybody but the nomenklatura.

On the other hand, borders that are open the way ours seem to be—where there's an immigration law on the books, but the federal government refuses to enforce it, and when affected states decide to do it for them, the federal government actively interferes—have very little to do with the basic human right to travel freely over the face of the Earth that I've always been concerned with respecting and enforcing.

I probably don't have to remind the reader of the violent crime now spilling over our southern border. Bodies are piling up by the dozens or being discovered in mass graves. Two friends of mine who both live in El Paso were swapping stories the other day in e-mail about bullets coming across the border and hitting the building they work in.

The reason for this—and the cure—is childishly simple, but those who have the power to do something about it are apparently even simpler and more childish, alternately sitting on their thumbs and sucking them, while innocent individuals on both sides of the border go on dying. The problem is drug prohibition—not drugs, but drug prohibition—the result of an infantile feel-good legislative addiction that, since the late 19th century has caused infinitely more death and destruction than any drugs (or alcohol before them) ever did.

The cure? Everybody but the mouthbreathers among my readers has already figured it out, but I'll go ahead and state what's been obvious for the last hundred years. Repeal drug prohibition and the street price of drugs will drop by 99 percent. The gangs who are fighting each other and the inept and crooked Mexican government will dry up and blow away. Repeal laws against prostitution and unlicensed gambling for good measure, along with any law that prevents ordinary individuals from owning and carrying the weapons of their choice. What's going on now will feel like a bad dream we've just awakened from.

Let me state this flatly so there can be no misunderstanding. My hometown was one of the last, following alcohol Prohibition, to allow the sale of alcohol within the city. It wasn't legal until the 1960s, because all the church ladies (like my idiot grandmother) and the vast number of liquor stores just the other side of the city limits colluded to keep Fort Collins Dry. That's why I know that any politician who fails to apply the measures I've proposed here immediately has something to gain from the way things are now. Yes, that's exactly what I said: something to gain from the way things are now.

Of course, politicians are always eager to compromise—when it comes to your rights and mine. What are rights, after all? Haven't two Presidential administrations in a row told us that the Constitution is just a piece of paper? What is citizenship anyway, but a long obsolete concept, originally thought up by dead, white, European males?

No matter what position you may take on immigration issues yourself (and as you know, now, I am generally for open borders, a border being nothing more than an imaginary line on a map with no genuine counterpart in the real world), one thing is beyond doubt. The current situation is even more complicated than I've acknowledged so far.

There is a genuine conspiracy to flood our southwestern states—Arizona, New Mexico, southern California, southwest Texas—with enough foreign nationals to seize them politically and deliver them, to American socialists, and then to Mexico. This conspiracy is taking place in broad daylight, with the full knowledge and support of the Mexican government, and we are too damned polite to do anything about it.

I use the term "we" loosely.

The whole enchilada (if you'll pardon the expression) is called "la Reconquista"—the reconquest—and it says here it festered first in the academia-decayed minds of far-left Hispanic professors in border-state universities. It's also a lie. For the most part, the land in question never belonged to Mexico. Their plan is that it never will.

Instead, advocates of la Reconquista yearn for their very own socialist paradise they want to call "Aztlan," sort of a Big Rock Azucar Mountain where the same toxic economic system that killed tens of millions of individuals through arctic exile, political execution, and good old fashioned starvation, the system that failed in Russia, virtually destroyed eastern Europe, and is now being rapidly abandoned even by Reddest China, will be given a good old college try all over again.

How do you say "Rah, rah, sis boom bah" in Spanish?

I don't mind people reinventing the wheel from time to time, but when they keep insisting on reinventing it square, it gets a bit annoying. What you're hearing in the background is the establishment Republicans flailing their hands and whimpering like Beaker at Muppet Labs while the Tea parties beat their time. Democrats on the front lines who must worry about re-election carrying Obama on their backs are no less desperate, just a whole lot quieter and resigned to defeat.

But the solution to the Aztlan problem is even easier than the one to drug wars and illegal immigration. The President (whoever she might be) should simply declare that any Mexican state whose voters ratify the American Bill of Rights by a two-thirds supermajority may join the United States. (Just to be fair, we should make the same offer to all the Canadian provinces, as well.) Such a simple declaration will cost nothing, but it'll start brushfires the Mexican government won't put out for a century, and we'll hear nothing about "la Reconquista" ever again.

And therefore our politicos won't have to compromise with it.

In case it occurs to you to wonder if I'm serious, consider the fact, recently revealed, that the current federal regime has placed thousands of acres of park land in Arizona, near the Mexican border, "off limits" to American citizens, apparently because it's being used by heavily-armed Mexican drug gangs who are busily invading the United States.

My readers know that I support the unalienable individual, civil, Constitutional, and human right of every man, woman, and responsible child to obtain, own, and carry, openly or concealed, any weapon—rifle, shotgun, handgun, machinegun, anything—any time, any place, without asking anyone's permission. I also oppose every drug law ever written; they do more damage than drugs themselves ever did.

But as I said, this is not what I meant by "open borders."

It's been argued that the border with Mexico must be closed off because uncontrolled immigration has generated enormous increases in violent crime within the border states. Private land is being trashed, buildings broken into and ransacked, livestock harassed and killed, ranchers and others hurt or murdered. Phoenix is currently cited as having the second highest rate of what might be called "commercial kidnapping" in the world. Yet federal employees only stand at one side and watch, offering victims—and victims-to-be—bad advice, and otherwise doing nothing. In many ways, the situation is strikingly parallel to the failures of King George III's government that the Founding Fathers complained so bitterly about in the Declaration of Independence.

And yet immigration, by itself, is not the problem. A century ago, Italian immigrants inadvertently brought the Black Hand—the Mafia—with them, and Asians brought tongs, and more recently, street gangs.

Once again, the answer is fairly simple.

While Eminent Domain remains in practice (elsewhere, I have called for its abolition) the state of Arizona should seize the land that the federal government is trying to give away and, assisted by sheriffs of the counties involved, begin clearing the gangsters out. The governor should also call upon Arizona's unorganized militia (the one given prominent mention in the Second Amendment) for manpower, relying for leadership on proven combat veterans from the Gulf Wars, Iraq, and Afghanistan.

Although there are still many moral and political points to be resolved before any genuine libertarian can feel satisfied with the result, at the moment, no amount of further debate, no matter how noisy or emotional, is likely to solve the problem. It is vitally important to act immediately—absolutely crucial to the survival of individual liberty and the high civilization it has nurtured, from now on, into the foreseeable future. For every day wasted in dithering, innocent lives are ruined or destroyed, violent criminals gain an even greater foothold here, our own crop of fascist gangsters increases its power over us, and our civilization frays a little more around the edges.

Several outcomes are possible.

The federal government could take the state of Arizona to court, publicizing its many malfeasances even further, regardless of the verdict.

Or the federal government could show up in force to protect "its" property—from the people and the state of Arizona—either driving the drug gangs out as a byproduct, or exposing itself by protecting them.

Or the federal government could leave Arizona alone to solve its own problems, which, in the long run, might be the best solution of all.

If the federal government wanted to help (something that won't happen under the present regime) the best place to begin is repealing every drug law on the books. It is their very illegality—and the risks entailed in producing, transporting, distributing, and selling them—that makes drugs lucrative to those willing to undertake the hazards. In an unfettered market, most drugs would cost only a percent or two of what they do now, depriving the criminal gangs of their profits.

Another point: we hear anti-immigrationists complain constantly about the pressure illegals bring to bear on "social services" in border states. However if there were no "social services" for illegal immigration to put pressure on—that is, if the blatant socialism of public schools, public hospitals, and public everything else were done away with (and that might prove more politically feasible than doing away with illegal immigration)—that set of handy excuses for violating the individual rights of newcomers would dry up and blow away.

But that, of course, in the light of all the idiotic collectivist decisions made every day by America's stupid, corrupt, and irrational politicians, including their failure to stem the tide—or at least offset the negatives—of illegal immigration, would make too much sense.

Instead, open war is likely to break out along the border as Americans there, desperate to defend their homes and livelihood and families, are forced to take matters into their own hands. The federal government will try to stop them, and will exploit the disaster as an excuse to strip them of their weapons (it will fail; most westerners will simply refuse to obey any more gun laws), and even cede large portions of the Southwest "back" to a nation-state that never owned them.

Don't look for big changes if the conventional right takes over from the left. Conservative Republicans always claim to put a high value on individual liberty (and often wonder why libertarians won't throw in with them against the "progressives"). But their party, back during the dictatorial Lincoln regime, gave us our first midnight knock on the door. It gave us a half-baked Hooverian New Deal Franklin Roosevelt only biggie-sized. Recently it's given us Homeland Security, the USA Patriot Act, illegal arrests, false imprisonment, and even torture.

All they'll do about illegal immigration is demand to see your papers.

But if the Tea Parties can stay loose, centerless and leaderless, and resist the attempts of political scavengers and demagogues to organize, credentialize, and co-opt them, we could see a revolution of spontaneous order that will open the door to a better and brighter future.

Keep Your Filthy Hands Off The Internet

Why is it so hard to understand that the reason the first ten Amendments—commonly known as the Bill of Rights—are trampled underfoot by politicos and bureaucrats is that the Founding Fathers neglected to provide a suitably harsh penalty for it?

—L. NEIL SMITH

The subject: "New Bill Gives Obama 'Kill Switch' To Shut Down The Internet."

The story, on PrisonPlanet.com, written by Paul Joseph Watson and published on Wednesday, June 16, 2010, warned that under a new law being pushed by that perennial douchebag Joseph Lieberman, government would have the "absolute power" to seize control of the World Wide Web.

Lieberman has long hated, loathed, and despised—and almost certainly feared—the freedom of unsupervised, uncensored communication among individuals afforded by the Internet. He is far from alone in this. Over the years, he has trudged from one lame excuse to another—"cybersecurity," for example—to justify putting an end to the greatest exercise of freedom human history has ever witnessed.

Naturally, Lieberman's unconstitutional bill has found an avid cheerleader in the fear-mongering demagogue Jay Rockefeller, who has opined that it would be better if we'd never invented the Internet. One can only speculate who he means by "we," since he and his ilk, permanently Crazy-Glued onto the public nipple, almost certainly haven't a clue how the Internet (or a Zippo lighter, for that matter) works.

Not surprisingly, Watson and PrisonPlanet.com report that "the largest Internet-based corporations are seemingly happy with the bill, primarily because it contains language that will give them immunity from civil lawsuits and also reimburse them for any costs incurred if the Internet is shut down for a period of time." Tom Gann, McAfee's vice president for government relations, is quoted as describing the bill as a "very important piece of legislation." I've done my last business with McAfee, or anybody who supports this rape of the First Amendment.

If we did it to Smith & Wesson, we can do it to McAfee.

The National Rifle Association reportedly reached similar accord with those who would become our masters by outlawing criticism of Congress—happily, that particular bill died aborning, although it served very nicely to expose the NRA, once again, as nothing more than the world's oldest, largest victim disarmament (gun control) advocacy—and this sort of crooked wheeler-dealering is beginning to look like a pattern, just one more reason American corporations desperately need to be cut down to size by abolishing the corrupt—and corrupting—institution of limited liability.

Read the article by Watson. He describes what the government wants in chilling detail. Long decades of bitter experience compel us to expect treachery from the Republican Party as well as from the Democrats.

My daughter Rylla, now in her early 20s, was home-schooled. One very important part of her education (she now maintains a 4.0 grade point average in college) was completely unfettered access to the Internet.

When I informed her that I had started writing an article about the importance of resisting threats to Internet freedom, she said, "I have a 'Friends Only' setting on my LiveJournal account, because there are things I only want my friends to see. I no more want government to be able to see what I write than some Internet-prowling sexual predator."

I agree.

Just as there is no place in a nation with a First Amendment in its Constitution for what Lieberman and company are planning for us, nor even for anything remotely like a Federal Communications Commission, there can be no place in such a nation for an "Internet Czar."

Despite the Internet's origin in the late 1960s as a government-sponsored means of communication between the Department of Defense, private industry, and academia, it has been at its best—and generated the greatest economic, social, and technological benefits—since it was "liberated" by the hordes of "geeks" who were originally hired to run it by employers who were not themselves conversant with computers, and couldn't tell when their employees were exchanging official traffic or trading dirty jokes and recipes for marijuana brownies.

Since then, the Internet has often been the only healthy, growing part of the economy, the only thing holding us together as a nation. I believe strongly it is the only reason we have any freedom left. The quintessential exercise of free speech in a culture supposedly built on that concept and dedicated to it, the Internet's development is as historically important to humanity—perhaps even more so—as Gutenberg's invention of the printing press. To paraphrase Carl Jung, the Internet is the collective consciousness of the human race. For those and many other reasons, it must be left unmolested by the government.

The Internet is an interesting thing. You can be communicating with somebody across town today, somebody in another state tonight, and somebody on the other side of the world tomorrow, all with equal ease. If their e-mail address doesn't show it, and you don't know how to read that routing gobbledygook at the top of the message, you can be doing one of those three things and not know which one it is. In terms of "bringing people together" there has never been anything like it.

The Internet serves yet another noble purpose. It invites idiots, crazies, and evil-doers to expose themselves in ways that were never possible before. We learned about the evil machinations of Lieberman and Rockefeller courtesy of the open medium they hate and want to destroy.

And consider the sorry advocates of victim disarmament, for example, commonly—and inaccurately—known as "gun control." They can't even cry out, as they used to, "Outlaw them all!" England and Australia have tried that; they now have the highest violent crime rates on the planet. And—thanks to the Internet—everybody knows it.

Vermont, by contrast (joined now by Alaska and Arizona) is a bloody thorn in the side of victim disarmers everywhere because simply respecting the individual's rights produces results that all the cops and all the laws in the world can't approach. Given the Internet to spread the word, the idea is contagious, and will inevitably spread to even the most backward regions like Illinois, Massachusetts and New York.

It is entirely understandable that backwater satrapies like North Korea or Iran, where the light of individual liberty never shines, routinely scrutinize and censor the Internet, and consign those whose use of it they disapprove of to jail. In true Stalinist style, China has a prison reserved exclusively for the incarceration of "Internet addicts."

Almost alone among the community of nations that share the legacy of Magna Carta, Australia ought to be ashamed of the vile company—that of totalitarian Cuba and Egypt among others—it's keeping online.

And the same to you, New Zealand. Be ashamed.

Teddy Roosevelt is said to have hated the Constitution because it got in the way of his "progressive" ambitions. Woodrow Wilson, another "progressive," exploited the First World War as an excuse to rape the Bill of Rights. Franklin Roosevelt did much the same and more during the Depression and the Second World War, banning the possession of gold and provoking the Japanese into attacking Pearl Harbor. Harry Truman killed a quarter million people with a single signature, and used the army to break strikes. Richard Nixon believed firearms in private hands are "an abomination." Lyndon Johnson used the IRS to persecute critics until they killed themselves, and had people's mail opened by the post office. Jimmy Carter, either of the Bushes, Bill Clinton, and many of the other "great men" in our blood-soaked history, all based their "legacies" on using the Bill of Rights for toilet paper.

Each of them would have hated, loathed, and despised the Internet.

The Clintons certainly do.

Bill and Hillary Clinton were among the first to complain about the degree of unsupervised communication the Internet makes possible and have often suggested that Internet communication be "validated" by government officials and that bloggers be forced to obtain government licenses.

They are far from alone in this view.

Possibly worst of all, from the standpoint of the dedicated enemies of freedom, the Internet is a world that libertarians—having been marginalized for three decades by the establishment media—have made their own, almost without effort. It's an alternative reality (unlike "meat-space" we live in) in which—exactly like intelligence, bravery, or virtue—the human capacity for violence is not additive, and in which it's impossible to initiate force against anybody.

To those, like the Clintons, who believe that there can be too much freedom—or too much information—the Internet represents the direst of threats. The only conceivable reason any politician might have for "regulating" the Internet in any way is to shut criticism off, exactly the same reason that Abraham Lincoln sent his troops to smash the printing presses of newspapers that opposed him and his policies.

New York's Commissioner of Police opines that the Internet is "the new Afghanistan" where Muslims are free to radicalize American youth and turn them into terrorists. The problem, he says, is that you can't do anything about such communication because, until a certain point, nobody has committed a crime. Apparently he wants to arrest people before that point, as they did in Minority Report. I'll point out that we know what kind of fascist bugger this moron is, thanks to the Internet.

Wouldn't it be infinitely better to teach a set of values, rooted in individual liberty, that our kids couldn't be talked out of by anybody?

Of course the real threat to America is this Commissioner, himself—and all other parasites like him who depend on human cowardice and stupidity to write their paychecks—not imaginary youth-radicalizing digital Muslims. Listening to this man—giving him any credence at all—is how the light of civilization starts to go out, all over the world.

Another thing to be wary of is the predatory hunger of politicians and bureaucrats everywhere, from City Hall to the United Nations, to tax the Internet, or the activities it makes possible. Whatever else it is, whatever the reasons given for it, taxation in this context is a step toward control. Daniel Webster pointed out that "The power to tax is the power to destroy," and Chief Justice

John Marshall agreed with him in the historic case of *McCulloch v. Maryland*. Elsewhere, I have set John Maynard Keynes straight by referring to taxation as a "barbarous relic of an ancient past." By contrast, the Internet is the leading element of a future society in which that relic will no longer exist.

Libertarians and conservatives don't generally have much use for the Fourteenth Amendment, one of a handful that were steamrollered through by the victorious Republicans in the absence of effective Democratic opposition, shortly after the War Between the States. There are reasons for this disdain which I'm not planning to go into here and now. I dislike them personally because they are very poorly written.

But consider for a moment, the third paragraph of the Fourteenth, because it offers some tantalizing possibilities to those who defend freedom:

> "No person shall be a Senator or Representative in Congress, or elector of President and Vice President, or hold any office, civil or military, under the United States, or under any State, who, having previously taken an oath, as a member of Congress, or as an officer of the United States, or as a member of any State legislature, or as an executive or judicial officer of any State, to support the Constitution of the United States, shall have engaged in insurrection or rebellion against the same, or given aid or comfort to the enemies thereof. But Congress may by a vote of two-thirds of each House, remove such disability."

What this means, once you hack your way through all the surplusage Mark Twain advised us to eschew, is that anyone guilty of "rebellion" against the Constitution is forbidden ever to hold public office again.

So what constitutes a rebellion? In the words of that great moral philosopher William Jefferson Blythe Clinton, it all depends on what the meaning of the word "is" is. If the First Amendment was written by the Founding Fathers specifically to prevent the government from interfering with the all-important right of free speech, and then some sleazy politician promotes legislation designed to do exactly that, is he or is he not truly involved in an act of rebellion against the Constitution?

And since the Fourteenth Amendment, by the nature of amendments, supersedes, takes precedence over the body of the Constitution, does that not mean that protections traditionally afforded to politicians—under Article I, Section 6 ("…they shall in all Cases… be privileged from Arrest during their Attendance…and in going to and returning from the same; and for any Speech or Debate in either House, they shall not be questioned in any other Place.")—no longer apply?

Imagine a Joseph Lieberman or a Jay Rockefeller stripped for life of the privilege they have long abused of holding public office, employed at meaningless, powerless jobs given to them by corporate America as a charity, writing memoirs nobody will ever read, drifting from talk show to talk show, gradually fading from society like a ghost.

I agree strongly with PrisonPlanet.com's Paul Joseph Watson when he tells us that "The Lieberman bill needs to be met with fierce opposition at every level and from across the political spectrum." He further exhorts us, "Regulation of the Internet would not only represent a massive assault on free speech, it would also create new roadblocks for e-commerce and as a consequence further devastate the economy."

The only hope we have is the Internet.

We must strive to keep it free.

Little Criminals: The Context of Consent

*You say we have a "disagreement" over my intellectual
property rights and I should submit to arbitration over
what's already mine? Then by all means let's have a
"disagreement" over something you own, too. What kind
of car did you say you drive?*

—L. NEIL SMITH

Have you ever noticed—in movies, books, or real life—that when
a mugger attacks someone, he never says "Give me your money!," but usually says "Give me the money!" or even "Give me
my money!" instead?

There seems to be a basic human drive to justify one's actions, no
matter how heinous they might actually be. Sometimes it's a matter
of self-deception—"I'm doing this for your own good!"—sometimes
it's a matter of propaganda: "We had to destroy the village to save
it." It's the basis on which millions of Jews, Gypsies, homosexuals,
and others were stripped of their perceived humanity in the 1940s
and massacred.

I was probably only eight years old when I realized that socialism is nothing more than a fancied-up excuse for stealing other
people's property and killing them if they resist, that collectivism is
just a shabby attempt to make theft and murder appear respectable.
Later on, I came to understand that this is true of all "philosophies"
of government.

We all live in a kleptocracy.

Lately, we have witnessed the rise of a movement—a thuggish
crusade wrapped in the tattered robes of academic "respectability"

against "Intellectual Property Rights"—dedicated to stripping creative individuals of whatever they create, depriving the rightful owner of the lawful benefits of his work, to expropriate it for some imagined "greater good," and to attack the creators viciously and defame them if they should be so gauche as to object to being stolen from.

Their principal "argument" seems to be, now that almost everything is digitized and can be duplicated, manipulated, and transported by means of electronics, that this somehow removes the moral obligation of civilized beings to respect the rights of others and honor their propriety. It's fundamentally the same argument that victim disarmament advocates make when they claim—ignoring the principle involved—that the authors of the Second Amendment couldn't possibly anticipate machineguns.

Even more, it's like a rapist saying afterward, "Hey, if you were a virgin, at least that's taken care of now. And if you weren't, then you haven't really lost anything, have you? True, I have benefitted from your sexuality, but you still have it, don't you? And if you didn't want to get raped, you had no business going out in public and spraying pheromones all over. In fact, I think I'm the real victim, here."

I am currently thinking these thoughts, and many more besides, because, when they thought I wasn't looking, a small handful of literary muggers and rapists have taken something that I am fairly famous for having written—my "Covenant of Unanimous Consent"—inflicted alterations on it which they falsely claim makes it a different document, and then fraudulently passed it off as their own work.

Which means any signatures it gathered were obtained fraudulently, too. They would want me to mention who they are and give you their URL.

I've seem plagiarism before. In ninth grade, I won a short story contest because the guy who "beat" me had typed up something by Robert Scheckley or Richard Matheson and passed it off as his own. I'm not the one who turned him in, although I had immediately recognized the story. The idiot had to get on the PA system and confess to his crime. Whether it ruined his life forever or was the making of him, I have no way of knowing. I had no sympathy for him because what he did is a crime, in the legal sense but more importantly, in the moral sense, as well.

Back to the present.

In time, several individuals warned me about what had happened, and I contacted the plagiarists directly, myself. Imagine my surprise when, instead of apologizing humbly and abjectly, as they ought to have done, and sought to make restitution, they became obnoxious and aggressive, so that, in the end, I was considered the villain of the piece, and called names, simply for having defended my own work from theft.

You will be interested to learn—and falling-down amused, if you know me or my work at all well—that I am, officially, a "statist asshole." In part, this is because I politely informed them I was sharing our correspondence with my attorney, to whom I had started blind-copying everything. My attorney is also among my very closest friends, and I had decided to blind-copy him to keep his Inbox clear of the heady liquid excrement (ever see the uncut final sequence of The Magic Christian?) I was having to wade through to protect my rights.

Never forget that I am a statist asshole.

Please note: I had never said that I was planning to sue this gang of little criminals, only that I was blind-copying my correspondence with them to my attorney. It was they who jumped to the conclusion that I wanted to sue them. Even when I told them that I wasn't planning to sue them, and instead mentioned private adjudication—a process, I assume, that can legitimately involve attorneys—they childishly went on calling me a statist, not because it was true, but because it was such a swell smelly ball of excrement to smear on the wall.

This is not unlike the way, whenever they sensed dimly that they were losing the argument at hand, my grandmother Mabel and my wife's grandmother Bertha (no, I am not kidding), both of whom were Roosevelt Democrats with minds so narrow they could look through a keyhole with both eyes, would resort to calling anyone who disagreed with them a communist.

Thus I am a statist asshole.

I have a small bet with myself that if I had informed these opponents of common, civilized behavior that I consider what they have done amounts to an act of initiated force against me—with all of the consequences that entails—intervention on their behalf by the State, most likely in the form of badged and uniformed policemen who could prevent me from dealing with them directly, myself, would suddenly, miraculously appear a whole lot more attractive and morally acceptable.

But, statist asshole that I am, I have digressed.

At some point, I realized that the topic of intellectual property rights (about which I have never before been particularly interested) would have to be dealt with in *Down With Power*, the book you're reading at this very moment, and that if I were to write an article about this little flapette for my editorial journal *The Libertarian Enterprise*, it might be suitable for the book. I conveyed that idea to the plagiarists as politely as I could, and put off any further argument with them until the article could be written and published.

The very next thing I knew, I was being defamed, by the leader of these scavengers and parasites, to all sixteen of the listeners to his Internet radio show, and all over the Internet. But, of course, had I decided to sue the guy for libel, slander, and defamation, in addition to his plagiarism, that would have made me a statist asshole all over again.

A double statist asshole.

Ever hear a mugger or rapist complain bitterly when it turns out his victim is armed and can defend him- or herself? I have. He sounds exactly like a left wing anti-gun politician. He also sounds exactly like the second-handers who stole my work and offered it as their own.

Like many another pack of thieves, the Hole-In-The-Head Gang (to borrow a phrase) had an ideology with which to alibi themselves. The first tenet is that there is a distinction between physical property and what some—especially its creators—claim to be "intellectual property."

They informed me, loftily, that just because I think of an idea, that doesn't mean it belongs to me. That if I don't want something I created stolen, then I shouldn't communicate it to the world. Fine—and if everybody followed this "advice," these creeps wouldn't have any opposition to their thievery, and no stories or books would ever be published, no songs would ever be written, no music would ever be composed.

What a swell world that would be.

True, I had backed off pressing the Covenant as it became more and more obvious to me the movement had deteriorated so badly that the Zero Aggression Principle was now considered controversial, and even oppressive.

Believe it or not, one of these scavengers defended his crime by asserting that the Covenant of Unanimous Consent did not appear on one of the more prominent pages of my website. That's exactly like ordering me to turn in my Yves Saint Laurent suit (believe it or not, I own one, and a nice Calvin Klein, too) because I don't wear it very often.

"You are a dinosaur and your assertion [presumably of my personal property rights] is invalid," another of them informed me grandly. He'd want me to mention his name. "Innovation is impossible under your worldview."

As an individualist, I'm not generally interested in Utilitarian arguments. However, it is worth noting that the past 300 years have seen the greatest progress in human history, and it's exactly the same era in which copyright has been respected and stringently enforced. In this connection it's worth asking, since there is no actual difference between intellectual property and physical property, when some self-appointed committee of sticky-fingered little rodents will "discover" that fact, and decide that you don't really need your wallet, your car, your house, or especially your guns. It's been done everywhere else, during the last couple of centuries, all over the world. Why not here?

Only we'll call it libertarianism.

As I say, I had pretty much ignored the issue of intellectual property rights, even though arguments about it had been raging all over my blog at BigHeadPress.com, and in the virtual pages of my opinion journal, *The Libertarian Enterprise*. For the most part, I had been too busy creating more intellectual property, notably my vampire novel, *Sweeter Than Wine*, and the policy guide, *Where We Stand*. Now I was going to have to think about it and say something coherent.

Damn.

My first observation is that, in a moral context, there is no discernable difference between physical property and intellectual property. As I first learned at the age of thirteen from the pages of Jack Finney's 1959 novel *Assault on a Queen*, virtually everything we have, we have purchased at the price of little bits of our lives which we dedicate to fulfilling some employer's interests rather than our own.

We trade the seconds, minutes, hours, days, weeks, months, and eventually the years of our lives for our homes, cars, and everything else.

Traditionally in civilized property theory, "mingling your labor with the land," the concepts of "sweat equity," and of "selling little bits of your life" in order to acquire whatever you need or want, abolishes any meaningful difference between physical and intellectual property. The farmer begins with a tree-covered lot that he must clear and plow and plant, and the writer with a damnedly blank page or screen.

Property is property and theft is theft. Or as my wife Cathy, who can be refreshingly straightforward, puts it, unless you can go out in a field somewhere and pee me a bicycle without reflecting on it, all property is intellectual property. Somebody had to think of it. Somebody had to build it. And somebody had to use his mind to earn the money "or other valuable consideration" that was exchanged for the bicycle.

When I first went to college as a freshly-fledged "admirer of Ayn Rand," I was informed—by leftists deeply involved in what was billed as the "Civil Rights Movement"—that there are human rights and then there are property rights; only the former existed in reality and are legitimate. Some of them asserted mockingly that property couldn't have rights, others that defending property rights is somehow reprehensible and evil. Doomed never to be popular at school, I disagreed. It had been my experience that those who disparage property rights most vociferously usually do it because they want your property themselves.

Almost to a man (if that's not giving these poor creatures too much credit; I have noticed that none of these would-be looters seem to be female, perhaps because women are the ultimate creators and the fiercest guardians of that which evolution has put in their charge) these illiterati seem to be very poorly educated where history in general—and the history of the libertarian movement in particular—is concerned. One of them actually quotes one of the original ideological expropriationists for the common good, collectivist anarchist Pierre-Joseph Proudhon, in his messages: "Property is theft."

That's like a Jew leaning on Adolf Eichmann for support.

They seem a little unendowed in the imagination department, too. I have spent my entire adult life writing novels about how the mechanics of civilization can be reengineered to exclude the very concept of government.

I hereby sentence them to read *The Probability Broach, Pallas,* and especially *Forge of the Elders.* Just because it was the state that protected intellectual property rights in the past doesn't mean intellectual property rights don't have to be protected. Just because it's difficult to imagine how, that doesn't relieve us of the moral burden.

Judges, Juries, and Justice

Politicians, bureaucrats, judges, and cops all see the Constitution in about the same light in which your great-grandmother saw the Sears-Roebuck catalog: a fine useful thing to have around—although its principal application may be somewhat different than its authors intended.

—L. NEIL SMITH

Most Americans today understand that something is very wrong at the heart of their civilization. It would be fair to guess that most of them don't know what it is, how to fix it, or whether it can be fixed.

They know that whenever it's most important for their rights to be recognized, respected, and enforced by government, those rights nearly always turn out to be rather less than what they grew up thinking they were.

They understand that, even if they could afford to bring the matter to court, in almost every dispute they have with government or large corporations, they're bound to lose. They've come to understand that it's a lawyer's job—as he sees it—to tell them what they can't do, rather than help them with what they want to do. Mostly, they understand that "justice" belongs to whoever can pay the most for it.

There are reasons why this is so. Consider judges for a moment and the hideous conflict of interests they find themselves in. The great libertarian educator Robert LeFevre observed generally that if you want to know what side judges are really on—or, in criminal matters, why they seem to think of themselves, more and more, as a part of the prosecution team—just look at who signs their salary checks.

Sad but true, in the final analysis, political party means very little, and ideology means absolutely nothing. Government pretty much belongs to whoever has the most money. "Public choice" scholar James Buchanan won himself a Nobel Prize (back when that actually meant something) pointing out that officials will almost always pursue and protect their own interests in preference to those of the public they have sworn to serve. In any conflict between the source of a judge's income and practically anybody or anything else, who do you expect to win?

As an old saying has it, "He who pays the piper calls the tune."

It is vitally important that a source entirely separate from government be discovered or created to pay judges and resolve the conflict of interests, preferably involving the people of each judge's jurisdiction who will be subject to his decisions. A small town near where I live holds a village fair every year, just to underwrite their volunteer fire department. There are old fashioned bake-sales, three-legged races, raffles, and tugs-of-war employing worn-out firehoses. Enormous fun is usually had by all. It would change the working of the justice system fundamentally—and for the better—if judges had to rely on good will and direct public support of this kind for their livelihood.

In addition to being pulled from the government teat, all judges should be required by law to inform juries of their 1000-year-old right—and duty—to rule on the law, as well as on the facts of the case. Similarly judges must no longer be permitted to muzzle defendants or their attorneys who appeal to their rights under the Constitution.

All prospective judges must be tested harshly on their knowledge of and allegiance to the Constitution—exactly as it was conceived and written by the Founding Fathers—and to each article of the Bill of Rights. Once they are elected or appointed, should they violate their oath of office, they must be removed from the bench and prosecuted for perjury.

Finally, just as attorneys on both sides have a right to examine prospective jury members and reject those who, for one reason or another, they find unsuitable, so they should have a right to reject judges.

Lawyers, too, are involved in a fundamental conflict of interests that very few of them like to think about, let alone discuss openly.

Most of the nation's legislators are lawyers, who pass laws which then become the province of lawyers to interpret and argue over in court on behalf of clients affected by them. Most presiding judges are lawyers, as well. Lawyers must be forbidden to hold legislative office at any level of government to avoid this obvious—and highly profitable—conflict.

Furthermore, as "officers of the court," lawyers are public servants, absolutely obliged to uphold and defend the Constitution. They should not be permitted to pass the bar and practice law unless they sign off separately on each and every article of the Bill of Rights exactly, once again, as it was conceived and written by the Founding Fathers. As it is at present, most firearms enthusiasts know the case law in their area of expertise better than either lawyers or judges.

They should also be required to consent to "loser pays all" legislation.

By the way, how is it that defense attorneys, who used to be the heroes on TV—remember Perry Mason?—are now the badguys, or at least the badguys' accomplices, and "lawyering up" is an admission of guilt? I'd heard that the trial lawyers have a better lobby than this would indicate. They certainly do when it comes to preventing tort reform. On the other hand, look at the peace movement today, silent and invisible now that the war-mongering president is a socialist Democrat.

All of this probably became inevitable from that moment in March of 1989 (ironically, the same year that the Berlin Wall fell and the Soviets collapsed), when the extremely long-running television show COPS first began its despicable work of desensitizing Americans to police violence, brutal intimidation, and other unconstitutional and questionable "law enforcement" activities that have no place in a free society.

But, as often happens, I have digressed.

It is impossible to know with any certainty what's going on in the mind of another human being, or to know what happened at a given time and place when we weren't there ourselves to see it happen. Even then, the testimony of eyewitnesses is notoriously unreliable and usually contradictory.

Throughout history, whenever knowing the truth seemed necessary, various cultures have hit upon many different methods in an attempt to take the uncertainty out of the equation. In some, a red hot iron was applied to the tongue of a suspect or witness on the theory that a liar will have a dry mouth and be burned worse than someone telling the truth. In other cultures, being able to whistle was indicative of innocence. Other examples of "trial by ordeal" made less sense, such as pouring molten lead in a suspect's hand to see how long it took to heal. If it took too long he was guilty. If it healed quickly, he was innocent. And if it healed too quickly, he was probably guilty of witchcraft.

Something like a thousand years ago, European society in general, and the British Isles in particular, began to rely on juries, composed of "ordinary members of the community" (juries and the phenomenon of "jury nullification," which we'll get around to momentarily, actually go back as far as ancient Greece), to determine, as best it can humanly—and humanely—be done, the truth in matters criminal and civil.

Early on, juries proved useful to the ruling class, putting the king or the lord or the squire at a remove from the dirty process of deciding innocence or guilt, while establishing him as wise and just for leaving such matters to the community and abiding by the jury's verdict.

Now and again, however, a jury would arrive at a conclusion the boss didn't care for. Surprisingly often, these juries would stubbornly stand by their verdict "in spite of dungeon, fire, and sword." Any aristocrat who imprisoned, tortured, or killed jury members stood to lose a great deal of credibility with the people he ruled.

Inevitably, juries that stood their ground in this manner came to believe (and there were well-established historical precedents) that they could judge the law itself as well as the individual accused of breaking it, deciding for themselves if a law was unconstitutional, unjust, or just plain stupid, and demonstrating this judgment by refusing to convict those who were obviously guilty of having broken the law. A jury cannot be required to explain why they reached their verdict, all that was supposed to have happened already, in the courtroom.

In short, the jury today acts as the eraser on the legislature's pencil.

In a civilization that turned out to be rather more democratic than the Founding Fathers intended or desired (in their minds, democracy meant "mob rule" and the ascendency of those "men of the mob" we call demagogues, and they provided many guards, such as the Electoral College, the indirect election of U.S. Senators, against it), the English jury system remains one of our few unanimous consent institutions.

Many people believe that alcohol Prohibition in the 1920s and 1930s ended because the political allies of Franklin Delano Roosevelt repealed it. In fact, Prohibition actually came to an end because juries refused to convict people accused of violating it, one reason Al Capone had to be convicted of income tax evasion rather than any of the many other crimes, victimless and otherwise, of which he was guilty. Repeal of Prohibition only made the failure of an idiotic law official.

For the same thousand years that there have been juries, those who stood to have their authority questioned have been looking desperately for ways to get around to power of the jury. Certainly no individual who is fully aware of the thousand-year-old power and duty of the jury to rule on the nature of the law as well as "the facts of the case"—and advertises it in any way—will be allowed to sit in the jury box.

Hilariously, no ruler can get rid of jury nullification without getting rid of the jury itself. It's built right into the concept. In some jurisdictions, judges will attempt to threaten juries just before they retire to decide on their verdict, to which the obvious answer, sotto voce, is, "Yeah, right." In some, jurors are required to sign a document surrendering, in effect, a precious right won for them by their ancestors the hard way, in the face of torture and imprisonment. The answer to that demand has to be, "Take your document and shove it!"

Probably the commonest way prosecutors try to steer the jury (and judges let them) is by interrogations that take things far beyond what is necessary to exclude friends or relatives of the parties in a case, or who harbor some irrational prejudice for or against them. Often using psychologists or sociologists as consultants, prosecutors look for jurors who are stupid, not particularly well-educated, or inclined to believe in the authorities no matter what those authorities say or do.

Vast, complicated, elaborate mathematical and statistical systems of selection have been cooked up to create such pre-decided juries, something the defense has very little in the way of power or resources to counter. Exact methods vary from jurisdiction to jurisdiction, but the process is generally referred to as "voir dire" which journalist Vin Suprynowicz reminds us, effectively, is medieval French for "jury tampering."

Juries must be chosen completely randomly from among all of the citizens in any given jurisdiction, with no selection being done until they are actually in the courtroom, and only then to determine their relationships (if any) to the parties, and whether they are inclined to pre-judge others for their color, religion, accent, or nation of origin. Any individual who, for any reason, doesn't want to serve on a jury must be released immediately and without prejudice, lest the Thirteenth Amendment's ban on "involuntary servitude of any kind" be violated.

The key to a healthy practice of jury nullification has always been advertising and education. Obviously, the more people who know and understand their age-old rights and duties as jurors, the fewer that prosecutors and judges can ferret out and bend to their autocratic will.

Add a better public understanding of the Constitution and the Bill of Rights, and, following a period in which juries level a mountainous pyramid of unnecessary, stupid, unjust, and unconstitutional laws, the "justice" system will be left with prosecuting parking violations, rare bank robberies, and employing many fewer judges, prosecutors, defense attorneys, recorders, bailiffs, jailers, and, ultimately, policemen. Taxes will be reduced and law schools shut down by the dozen.

Everybody wins—except those who don't deserve to.

And Sow Salt on the Ruins

*Better the "Me" generation than the "Duh" generation.
It is not the purpose of education to produce good citizens,
but to help children become successful human beings.
The former is properly identified as "indoctrination"
and, when undertaken at the taxpayers' expense, should
be illegal.*

— L. NEIL SMITH

When I was a little kid, about ten thousand years ago, I made a terrible vow never to forget what it was like, having one's life— one's body, one's belongings, one's clothing, one's bedtime, and everything else—controlled by another human being. That, more than anything else, is almost certainly what made me the libertarian I am today.

The rights of children have always been a matter of deep concern to me. In the 1970s, I prepared a Children's Rights plank for the Libertarian Party's national platform committee that was entirely consistent with established libertarian principle, but considered by many a chicken-hearted would-be politician to be too controversial, too radical, and too embarrassing for them to have to discuss in public.

When he was on trial for his life in Israel for crimes against humanity, Nazi official Adolf Eichmann, known as "the architect of the Holocaust," testified that Hitler's nightmare reign of terror occurred because "Germans lack civil courage." Here is as good an example of that deficiency, which always begins with small things, as I have ever seen. The first chance they got, the crawling, craven cowards carved the Children's Rights plank out of the platform with a dull-edged knife, leaving a bleeding, gaping wound where the LP's integrity had been.

What that plank said (and it was party founder David F. Nolan who helped me push it through on the convention floor) was that children have all the rights—especially as laid out in the remainder of the platform—that are possessed by anybody else. The fact that they might have problems, now and again, exercising their rights wisely, in no way separates them from adults, who often have exactly the same problems.

Every argument used today to deny children self-determination was once used in the past to deny exactly the same thing to blacks—and women.

There are even those, outside the freedom movement and within, who, for reasons of their own, routinely accuse children's rights advocates of being closet pedophiles. One cretin who said this about me—he was angry because I criticized Republicans—turned out to be an Arkansas hillbilly who drove a manure truck for a living (I swear I am not making this up) and also lived off his girlfriend's disability checks. Somebody told me recently that the fellow is now in jail.

One of the kindest, gentlest, smartest, and most principled women in the Libertarian Party was smeared in exactly this manner in 2008 by a rival for the party's Presidential nomination, who now expects to win the nomination himself in 2012. What he really most needs to be nominated for is a vacant position in rural Arkansas, driving a manure truck.

But once again, I have digressed.

Of course the petty tyrants of the public education establishment wholeheartedly (or whole-organedly of some kind) agree with the LINOs and faux libertarians who excised the Children's Rights plank. It was bad enough when these worthless bureaucratic drones and wasters began searching the persons and private property of those individuals so unwisely placed under their oppressive thumbs. It became vastly worse when this illegitimate power was extended to search students' cars.

Unfortunately, the students' rights situation is pretty bleak at the moment, and was long before 9/11 and Homeland Security. Probably because kids can't vote, judge after stupid, evil, and insane judge has ruled that students have no Fourth and Fifth Amendment rights, that their lockers can be rifled through without any kind of excuse, that their cars are not their own, and, of course, that the idea of Second Amendment rights for kids (my particular hobbyhorse, and the reason, I suspect, New York agents and publishers don't want to touch me with the proverbial ten-foot cattle prod) is completely beyond the pale.

Never forget that liberals, especially, are afraid of their own children.

Now, according to something I saw recently on TV, the Kiddie Kommissars have started seizing their captives' cell phones, so they can read and "log" (and place in the kids' "permanent record") text messages that might reveal whether said kids are smoking (gasp!) or seeking some other pitiable way, physical or otherwise, of evading, if even for a precious moment, these ever-present dealers of intellectual and spiritual death. To this observer it looks like what they really want to know is whether the kids are making fun of them and mocking their authority. Of course the ACLU is flailing its usual limp wrist at them, exclaiming in its screeching falsetto, "Oh, don't do that, please?"

Lawyers for the school district guilty of this savage invasion of individual rights claim it's perfectly legal. That may very well be. So does the Supreme Court. But the law is an ass, as Shakespeare warned us, and the Supreme Court once approved enthusiastically of slavery, declaring it a crime not to return runaway slaves to their masters.

Lawyers and judges to the contrary, this school policy is just plain wrong, not only morally, not only pedagogically, but legally, as well. It's extremely important to remember, in this connection, that the Bill of Rights isn't really about you or me or about any other individual. Its name is misleading because it doesn't concern any of us at all. The Bill of Rights is not a list of things we're allowed to do, it's a list of things that government is absolutely forbidden to do. As such, there's no age limit on whose rights it protects.

The same petty tyrants prowl the World Wide Web like the virtual child molesters that they are, calling children to task and punishing them at school for things they have said and done online, on their own time, that have nothing to do with the school system and are entirely outside its proper jurisdiction. Authoritarian excesses like this are obviously intended to condition yet another generation of Americans—who were once a proud, brave, resourceful folk who regarded "a little rebellion now and then" as a good thing—simply to resign themselves and uncomplainingly give in to the sadistic practices of the police state being erected around them, for the most part as their parents cheer.

From time to time, news stories inform us that politicians and bureaucrats positively ache to tattoo our children as if they were already the concentration camp inmates the government plans for them to be someday. Or they want to inject radio transponders under their skin, begging the question how long will it be before such a device can deliver a healthy shock if they won't do whatever is required of them?

Self-evidently idiotic and blatantly unconstitutional school policies—such as "zero tolerance," not only for weapons but for thoughts about weapons—are the basic cause of atrocities like the Columbine High School massacre, which happened not because there were too many guns there that day, but too few. If the bucketheads who run the nation's schools actually cared about the lives, health, and safety of America's school children—rather than striving to give the public, political appearance that they care—schools would instruct the kids in the safe and effective use of firearms for self-defense.

That's right. I said exactly what you thought I said. Schools should teach children the safe and effective use of firearms for self-defense. Or they should be abolished, leaving parents and the free-market system to take over the basic functions that they have abdicated.

There is absolutely nothing wrong with America's public education system that can be fixed by tinkering with America's public education system. It has nothing to do with education. Having begun as a carbon copy of state indoctrination machinery in 19th century Prussia, the public school establishment has long been a major contributor to the systematic Nazification of this country. It served George W. Bush and his predecessors. It serves the interests of the state so well that, beyond cosmetics, Barack Obama isn't going to change anything about it.

At present rates, America's schools will continue serving as incubators for fascism long after both politicians are gone—until, as I have written on many another occasion, Americans finally shut down all the government's mind-control mills (which increasingly have begun to resemble maximum security prisons) raze the buildings so that not a single stone remains standing on another, and sow salt on the ruins.

I used to describe American child-rearing practices as the "Darwin Deadfall" method. The basic idea is that children must be shielded as completely as possible from the sights, sounds, tastes, and smells of real life. Television must be censored until there is nothing to watch but infantile pap. Movies and popular music must have warning labels if they say or show the same things ordinary people say and see every day. When kids are finally old enough to send to college, the full weight of reality—drugs, sex, alcohol—falls on their innocent and unsuspecting heads. Those who don't survive the process become the next generation's walking wounded. Those who do—or at least give the appearance they do—are fit to pass the torch of civilization to.

All that has changed in recent years. Thanks to Bill Clinton, for example, I had to explain what oral sex is to my daughter when she was six years old. For better or worse—not necessarily the worse— the Internet opened up to all of us a wider view of the real world—not merely sexually, but with regard to the vastly greater obscenity that is politics, as well—than many a full-grown adult had ever seen before.

New York's Commissioner of Police reportedly claims that the Internet is "the new Afghanistan" where Muslims are perfectly free to radicalize American youth and turn them into terrorists. The problem, the man complains, is that you can't actually do anything about such communication because, until a certain point, nobody has committed a crime. Apparently he'd like to arrest young people before they commit a crime, as was the common practice in the movie "Minority Report."

Wouldn't it be better to teach—and behave consistently with, ourselves—a set of values our kids couldn't be talked out of by anybody?

It is impossible—again for better or worse—to teach children personal responsibility if you deny them every chance to exercise it. Those today who lobby for regulating the Internet—or shutting it down altogether—simply want to return to the Darwin Deadfall method.

Aside from asserting the supremacy of the Bill of Rights, and adding a stringent—no, let's make that Draconian—penalty clause to it, among this country's highest priorities must be to establish, clearly, once and for all, that those individuals we call children, especially those over the age of sixteen, who are being maintained, largely against their wills, in a contrived and unnecessary state of childhood, have exactly the same rights as anyone else, whatever their age.

I am far from the first thinker to observe that adolescence, as we have experienced it in Western Civilization, is a completely synthetic phenomenon, a purely social artifact that has been created by a number of different factors for a number of different reasons. Mommies and daddies don't like to see their little kids grow up and away from them. Labor unions don't want competition. School administrators and teachers worry, as Mel Brooks would put it, about their phony baloney jobs.

My understanding of history and human nature leads me to believe that many of the difficulties associated with being young or living around young people could be solved simply by reducing the age of majority to what it has been over the greater part of the last thousand years. If a sixteen-year-old could drink alcohol, smoke tobacco, own and carry the means of self-defense, (yes, and marry, too—how old were Romeo and Juliet, after all?), and especially vote, the stresses caused by being kept in infancy for an extra decade would evaporate.

There are those who will assert that the majority of public school teachers are dedicated contributors to civilization. That may very well be true. But in the same way that schools attract pederasts and sexual predators, they also attract petty dictators who badly need to be weeded out of the system if we wish to have a free society in the future.

Like murder, crimes against the Constitution have no statute of limitations (and never can, owing to the matter of conflicting interests involved). Those in the school system who smugly believe it's smart or cute to strip away children's rights for the sake of administrative convenience (or plain old sadistic pleasure) will someday face those former children in a jury box, possibly in a small town in Pennsylvania that will lend its name to the Nuremberg II tribunals.

The Medium and the Message

*The function of government is to provide you with
service; the function of the media is to supply the Vaseline.*

—L. NEIL SMITH

Somebody once described the libertarian movement as "30,000
people trying to make a living selling newsletters to each other."
We have been a movement, from the inception, of folks with
something to say, even when getting it said—and spread around—
proved arduous and expensive.

I can still smell the mimeograph fluid.

I once observed that, if Americans ever learned how they'd
been lied to all these years, from Lincoln's War Between the States,
through Roosevelt's attack on Pearl Harbor, Johnson's trumped-up
Gulf of Tonkin "incident," George H.W. Bush's Ruby Ridge, Bill
Clinton's Waco and Oklahoma City, George W. Bush's September 11, to the Bush-Obama so-called "War on Terrorism," there
wouldn't be a television station left standing above its own ashes
anywhere on the North American continent.

Apparently a great many more people than I have managed
to learn the truth, because, second only to the moribund newspaper industry, television has begun dying a well-deserved lingering
death, as more and more viewers turn to talk radio, and especially
to the Internet.

Springsteen said it: "Five hundred channels and nothing on."

When I started working in the freedom movement in the early
1960s, the situation with the mainstream media (which was all
we had) seemed pretty hopeless. These were the stuffed suits, the

hairsprayed heads, the gentlemen of the evening as I was later to call them, who appeared physiologically incapable of telling the truth about anything. For 20 years I never heard a true word about gun ownership from **ABC**, **CBS**, or **NBC**.

Instead of anything resembling honest investigation, they stuck a finger into the wind (or somewhere else) to determine what side they'd take on the current issues as predetermined by what conservatives call The Liberal Template. And despite the fact that I vehemently opposed Johnson's disastrous trip across the Big Muddy, to this day I recall my utter disgust at their craven, unprincipled turnaround regarding Vietnam.

If you were gonna change sides, you had to have a real reason. I did.

Mostly, instead of performing their proper function as envisioned by Thomas Jefferson, acting as a perpetual adversary to the government (even he had his doubts, saying that the only thing in the newspaper you can believe is the advertisements), they seemed to be playing some game completely internal to their industry, one that meant nothing to anybody but themselves, over what issue or event was hot and what was not, who had the power to make the choice, and which politician they would build up to near godhood one day, only to tear him down the next.

Apparently many other individuals felt the way I did; together, almost without knowing it—and starting with the unlikely foundation of a cybercommunication system built by government for the military industrial academic complex—we "grew" the Internet as we know it today.

In the beginning of the Internet era, the mainstream media, those congenital purveyors of one-way disinformation consisting almost entirely of government lies and threats, attempted to trivialize and marginalize the new interactive communication system by making fun of it and especially of those who used it, questioning its motives, its accuracy, and its reliability, despite their own deeply unenviable, decades-long track record of shameless and unrelenting propaganda generation.

Now, as the cold, dark waters of obsolescence and rejection rise about them, and they feel themselves going down for the third time, they want the government to tax the Internet, to subsidize the very institutions it should be rewarded for rendering obsolete, like taxing automobile manufacturers to subsidize the manufacturers of buggy whips.

Others want the Internet "regulated"—for which read monitored and censored—and those who use it forced to beg for some sort of credentials like "respectable" journalists (for which read government indoctrinated and vetted for abject compliance) as if respectability were more important than the truth the mainstream media refuse to tell. This is Hillary Clinton's bonnet-bee and it should never be forgotten.

Others have different ideas.

Before he wrote his blockbuster novel *The Da Vinci Code*, Dan Brown authored a thriller he called *Digital Fortress*, which spotlights as strange a moral inversion as I've ever seen in American literature.

In the book, from the viewpoint of some of the protagonists, the worst possible disaster that could ever befall Western Civilization is about to happen unless Our Heroes can stop it. Our Heroes work for a gigantic computer center run by the National Security Agency that supposedly monitors every single electronic message sent by anybody anywhere.

The oncoming catastrophe they must prevent is the public release of encryption software—like PGP, one gathers, only massively more powerful—which will give any individual absolute privacy in his communications.

The guy who wrote the software (he's Asian, but I think he's meant to be Phil Zimmerman), a villain of the worst kind, must be stopped at all costs before the government loses its ability to spy on us. Our Heroes, again, are snoops who believe your e-mail is their property. There are a lot of twists and turns, but in the end, I couldn't figure out whose side the author is on, or who the heroes and villains really were. This is what comes of getting too much technical advice from those whose jobs are illegal under Article I, Section 8 of the Constitution.

The fact that privacy might be viewed by anyone in government as a world-ending calamity pretty much sums up what's wrong with America today. I take it as a good sign that, in the end—but that would be telling.

Back to what we laughingly call "reality."

Naturally, not all is hunky-dory with the new medium. Wikipedia, for example, seems to have forgotten what it's all about, apparently attempting to ingratiate itself with the dark side—possibly because it thinks they'll win and kill the rest of the Internet—acquiring a bad case of political correctness that's going to destroy it in the end.

Thomas Paine talked about "the summer soldier and the sunshine patriot."

And we all know about Benedict Arnold.

According to the badguys, of course, all these proposed controls are "for the children," a shiny excuse rapidly losing its charm, especially after I found myself attempting to explain to my daughter what oral sex is, not because of anything she'd seen online, but because of that great protector of children, Bill Clinton. Or they'll claim it's to protect the security of our precious Homeland from vile "Islamofascist cyberterrorists," who apparently possess some dark, mysterious hypnotic power—sort of like snake charmers, I guess—to use Internet chatrooms and blogs to transmogrify squeaky-clean Productive Class kiddies into cursing, screaming, bomb-throwing neoMuslims.

Lately, a more subtle, but equally deadly threat to freedom of expression has arisen with various individuals and groups asserting that anything you happen to think of, write down, attach your name to, and send out into the world, from articles and columns to whole books, is up for grabs. There is no such thing as intellectual property rights. You have no right to claim what you've created as your own, and exclusively derive income from it, while anybody else may copy it, make any alterations they wish, remove your name, and replace it with their own. Or simply present it as if you approved of what they're doing.

Of course they claim that what they're advocating is a new kind of freedom, that copyrights and patents have become oppressive mechanisms of the state. One of them told me he doesn't want to live in a world he feels is shackled by intellectual property rights. I'd rather not live in a world shackled by gravity, but both are features of natural law. I do not regard a lock on my door as a limit to anybody's freedom.

But when you argue with them, the real shape of what they want eventually emerges. Like the socialists they are, most of them appear to envy and hate the creators of intellectual property, and relish a future they imagine in which it's impossible to earn a living by writing.

There can be, of course, no moral distinction between physical and intellectual property, and just because advancing technology makes something easier to steal, that doesn't make stealing it any less immoral. Opponents of intellectual property rights are nothing more than thieves, and, no matter what they may claim, neither are they libertarians.

But I have digressed.

Where the Internet is concerned, the simple truth, which those on both sides of the issue know perfectly well—just as both sides know perfectly well that the other side knows it—is that the new media, especially the Internet, are all that are currently propping up a deeply wounded and deliberately sabotaged economy, and preventing America from being taken over completely by the forces of domestic totalitarianism.

Lately, those who hunger to command those forces, to begin with at the Transportation Safety Administration, and now by order of the Department of Homeland Security's Jackboot Janet Napolitano (or is it Dolores Umbridge, I have trouble seeing any difference) have responded by forbidding their orcish minions to employ company computers to log onto "controversial"—meaning freedom-oriented—websites. Porn sites—remember what I said about propping up a deeply wounded economy?—are conspicuously absent from the forbidden list. The next logical step, of course, will be monitoring their Internet activity at home, exactly the same way the public schools do with their helpless prisoners.

When the other side sticks its fingers in its ears and starts chanting to itself about how it isn't listening, you can tell you're winning. If Obama were a liberal, in the old-fashioned meaning of the word, instead of what he really is, he would order these agencies to reopen their eyes and ears, to see and hear the individuals they're supposed to be serving, but whose lives they relish controlling and destroying.

Since its inception, the Internet has consistently frustrated the worst enemies of individual liberty—the Clintons, Bushes, Cheneys, Rumsfelds, Chernoffs, Obamas, Pelosis, Reids, Holders, Napolitanos, and Emanuels—and when it hasn't prevented their machinations, it has exposed them to public view so they can eventually be repealed, nullified, or otherwise disposed of. Any attack on the completely open and egalitarian character of the new media, is an attack on everything that has ever made America "the best idea that anyone ever had for a country."

There is nothing that anybody who initiates or supports such an attack can do afterward—Joseph Lieberman, the least principled individual in American politics today, comes to mind, as does Jay Rockefeller, the world's foremost electronic Luddite—to remove the ugly stain it places on his resume. He might as well pack up his bag of tricks right now, and get ready to emigrate to Venezuela, Cuba, or North Korea, where his snotty disdain for individual liberty can be appreciated.

Critics whine constantly that the Internet is as full of falsehood as it is of truth, as full of hatred as it is of real communication. In these ways, of course, it is no different from "real" life, where we are obliged each day to sort out lies and ugliness from everything else. Are these people infants, that they feel unequal to such a grown-up task? Do they assume that everybody else is as infantile as they are?

And what of their "cure": gatekeepers, credentialization, and an inevitable return to the bland, polished lies of past generations, to what amounted to mass religious faith in kindly, reassuring con-men and establishment propagandists like Edward R. Murrow, John Cameron Swayze, Douglas Edwards, Chet Huntley, David Brinkley, and Walter Cronkite?

That era is over. One way or another, it is never, ever coming back.

And that's the way it is.

The Money of Your Choice

*Money, first and foremost, is a medium of communication,
conveying the information we call "price." Government
control of the money supply is censorship, a violation of
the First Amendment. Inflation, ninety-nine times out
of a hundred, is a government lie.*

—L. NEIL SMITH

It should be abundantly clear by now that government-issued "fiat" money (so called because of the Biblical use of a Latin term that means "let there be")—paper currency, plastic or junk metal coins, and what might be called "magic wand credit" with nothing of actual, intrinsic, tangible value to support it—has been an unmitigated disaster for everyone, everywhere, except for the corrupt politicians who foisted it on the rest of us and certain of their privileged pet mercantilists.

A mercantilist, you may—or may not—recall, is one of those businessmen whom Adam Smith complained about in his famous 1776 book *Wealth of Nations*. Basically, a mercantilist enlists the government—or powerful individuals within it—as an ally to help him against his competition in the marketplace. By contrast, a private capitalist competes honestly, by producing the highest quality goods and services he can, at the lowest possible prices. Although they are, in point of fact, complete polar opposites, the two, mercantilism and private capitalism, are often confused—all too often willfully—by politicians, media, and educators who hate, loathe, and despise individual freedom and the free-market system which is its economic expression.

For the most part, disappointingly to freedom lovers, America is, and always has been, mercantilistic, rather than capitalistic. For that you can thank master mercantilist Alexander Hamilton and his friends.

Many of this nation's current difficulties have deep roots in this bitter but almost invisible conflict between two distinct political and economic systems. For example, "fractional reserve banking" is a corrupt and fraudulent mercantilist practice in which the government allows—in fact it encourages, or even compels—banks to lend out many times the amount of money that they actually possess. The effect is the same as writing a bad check, or better yet, as counterfeiting, but without the costs associated with actually acquiring press, paper, and ink and printing the stuff. A common type of trouble arises when, for one reason or another, borrowers can't pay their loans back, and the banks get stuck with many times the debt that they themselves can pay.

On the other hand (although this may seem to fly in the face of what libertarians and conservatives have been saying for decades), any attempt, well-meaning or otherwise, to create a gold "standard"—imposed or administered by government or by anybody else—must be resisted just as vigorously as we resist the present system, if we are interested in preserving freedom of individual choice, and building a genuinely unfettered and secure market for money and for everything else.

Instead, individuals and organizations must be left alone to generate tokens consisting of, or representing, real wealth, in any substance, form, or denomination that those they do business with find acceptable. Establishment politicians and their "intellectual palace guard" on campus and in the media (especially academic economists), detest this idea, often denouncing gold as a "barbarous relic of the past" precisely because it cannot be created politically, out of thin air.

Over the ordinary course of events, money consisting of—or based on—something of real value cannot be inflated by government counterfeiters, one of whose objectives is to fund programs that seek to buy votes from millions of fools who, thanks to public schooling and the mass media, have little or no understanding of economics or history.

Regardless of what you may have been told, money did not put an end to the barter system, it enhanced it. All free-market transactions are barter. Money is just another commodity—admittedly, a superior commodity—to be traded for food, clothing, shelter, transportation, or various necessities of self-defense, including medical attention. As long as the commodity being used as money has real value, in and of itself, everybody wins, something most left-wing economists assert is impossible.

There is room in a free society for things like privately issued paper certificates (for gold, silver, or what have you) which are nothing more, for all intents and purposes, than glorified IOUs. Does the person or institution offering these certificates in exchange for goods and services promise to redeem them with real wealth? And does he actually hold the wherewithal to back that promise? These questions must be left to the individual, not the government, to answer and decide whether to accept the certificates as money or not. Handing over such a certificate is the same as signing a contract, and the terms must be agreed upon by buyer and seller, and ultimately enforced—by adjudication, if necessary—by the individual accepting the IOU.

In all honesty, given the checkered history of money, the author's own personal experiences with it, and a free society offering private currency that weighs heavily in the pocket and makes jingling noises, I'm uncertain whether I would ever accept paper money again, from anybody.

But I have digressed.

Gold, silver, platinum, nickel, or copper coins, manufactured by private parties, represent the best kind of start toward a reformed economy. Laws against this kind of private issue must be repealed, nullified, or otherwise disposed of. Thuggish raids against coin companies must be forbidden, and those who conduct them strenuously prosecuted. Likewise, levying sales taxes on transactions involving precious metals—that is, on the metals themselves—must cease immediately.

If there is any role for government in this connection (something that calls for rigorous debate) it lies in assuring that such coins are what they advertise themselves to be. If a coin is marked "Silver, one ounce, .999 fine" it must really be an ounce of 99.9% pure silver, or it is as fraudulent as fractional reserve banking and magic-wand credit.

And let me be clear: I am speaking, here, about enforcement of already-existing laws against fraud, not creating some new regulatory agency.

Privately-issued coins could be disks (which practical history appears to prefer), octagons, hexagons, pentagons, squares, or even triangles. They could be cubical or spherical. Ultimately, it is transactions in the marketplace that will determine what works best. If, for some reason, a shoemaker, for example, decides that he prefers spherical or triangular coins to any other kind circulating, then in a free market, he might accept fewer spherical or triangular coins per shoe, and that is his right as an individual, a collector, and a businessman.

One thing is certain: free-market money must be denominated in weights—ounces, grams, etc.—rather than use meaningless and deliberately misleading words like "dollar," "franc," or "peso." At one time in history, the British "pound," which is currently worth less than a buck and a half, meant an actual pound of silver, at today's prices, about $225.00. (In the decades immediately following the American Revolution, a dollar was worth about five shillings, or a quarter of an English pound.) Silver hasn't mysteriously grown more valuable over the centuries, British currency has become less and less trustworthy thanks to government counterfeiting that commenced, if I recall correctly, during the reign and at the insistence of Henry VIII.

He wanted the extra money so he could fight more wars.

The huge difference in value—from $225 in ancient times to $1.50 today—reveals the amount of real wealth sneakily stolen from the British people over the centuries, about 99.33 percent of the value of the pound, through inflation by greedy politicians and royalty.

Similarly, twenty dollars would have bought an ounce of gold in the late 19th century, whereas a hundred years later, it's over twelve hundred. Again, gold hasn't changed, the dollar has, by about 98 percent.

Mind you, there is absolutely nothing magical about gold, or any other single substance, only that it has been acceptable as money by billions of individuals for thousands of years. Free-market activity could also be based on stores of various commodities not ordinarily thought of as money: petroleum, grain, various ores, precious gems, even computer chips and so forth, all of them fluctuating constantly and minutely against one another to produce an economy that's stable overall.

When this author was visiting London back in the 1970s (before the European Union and its own phony fiat currency were imposed on tens of millions of unwilling individuals), I noticed that all the banks hung chalkboards up in their windows every morning, divided into grids that showed the relative value of various national currencies: how much the franc was worth in pesos or the peso in drachmas. The same thing would work with various monetary commodities, except that computers would now make calculating and displaying such information a great deal easier.

This could prove important in the long run. In the 16th century, the economy of Spain was more or less destroyed when conquistadores brought home tons of gold they'd looted from the New World. It's said that Pizarro took every ounce of gold the Incas possessed. The value of gold, relative to other things, plummeted because the more there is of anything, the less any of it is worth. Economists refer to this phenomenon as the "Law of Marginal Utility." Spanish fortunes based solely on gold tended to suffer as gold became more abundant and therefore cheaper. Spain ceased to be a world power and became, instead, the first "sick man of Europe." In many ways, it has never recovered.

The Law of Marginal Utility is not a law of economics or any kind of physical phenomenon. The physical qualities of a commodity do not change simply because there is more or less of it. Marginal Utility is actually a law of psychology. If Individual A possesses a thousand gold ounces, and Individual B has only a hundred, Individual A will be less concerned about spending ten of his gold ounces, because he will have many more left at the end of such a transaction than would Individual B.

If the Spanish had based their economic life on a broader variety of commodities, it might have prevented the economic disaster that followed the discovery of gold in the New World. The future of money today may lie in the stars, or, more accurately, in the Asteroid Belt, where roughly one-third of the millions of "flying mountains" circling the Sun between Mars and Jupiter are composed of metals. Mostly it's iron and nickel. But other metals—gold, to name one— are present in lesser amounts. It has been said that a single metallic asteroid a mile in diameter contains more gold than has ever been mined on Earth, most of it lying within relatively easy reach of the asteroid's surface.

Owing to the Law of Marginal Utility, importing so much gold would halve the perceived value of the gold we already possess. Given a future that offers relatively easy and inexpensive means of importing precious metals from space, probably within this century—current proposals for "space elevators" present just such an opportunity—the entire future global economy could be affected in exactly the same way that Spain's was 500 years ago, if America (and humanity) relies on gold—and gold alone—as a monetary standard. On the other hand, allowing the market to decide, and constantly re-decide from day to day, what is money, and what is not, would readily prevent such a catastrophe.

The lesson in all of this is that for money to work in a society, and not damage it, it needs to be based on something of real value. The market must be open, and flexible enough that it can adjust to changes like the one that damaged Spain. Unless government and its hangers-on cause civilization to collapse altogether in the next few years (a real danger, I believe), most of the technological pieces are nearly in place—cheap space travel, access to the Asteroid Belt—and metallic inflation is bound to arrive sooner than many might expect.

But in a free market, if gold (or any other single commodity) declines in value (for whatever reason), people can switch instantly to using other commodities, and civilization will keep rolling right along.

Which is more than anyone can guarantee right now.

Read My Lips: No New Laws

"No man's life, liberty, or property is safe when the legislature's in session."

—JUDGE GIDEON J. TUCKER, 1866

Every day we seem to be confronted with yet another legislative bonnet-bee buzzing around in politicians' heads that threatens in one way or another to deprive us of our lives, our property, and our rights.

It never seems to stop.

For each of us who demands nothing more from the civilization that we live in—and to which we contribute our efforts—than absolute ownership and control of our own lives (and, as Ayn Rand frequently noted, all of the products of our lives) there has been nothing but increasingly bad news for as long as anybody who is now living can remember.

Since the turn of the 20th century, collectivism—referred to by every conceivable euphemism: communism, progressivism, socialism, fascism, liberalism, environmentalism—has taken more and more and more away from us. Its appetite is insatiable. It wants everything we earn, everything we own, everything we ever hope to own. It wants our homes, our land, and our children. It wants our cars and especially our weapons. It wants our very lives and it strives for the means to observe and manipulate them at every minute, every step, and every breath.

Any ally we ever hoped that we might rely on, every organization that we turned to—or created ourselves—to put a stop to this never-ending horror, has wound up betraying us sooner or later.

The Republican Party, the Democratic Party, the Libertarian Party, the American Civil Liberties Union, the National Rifle Association, labor unions, even the Boy Scouts of America all seem to be run by idiots, lunatics, crooks, and outright traitors. Most of these desk-bound chair-warmers are simply weak-willed sponges, chosen for their abject compliance to whatever may be considered politically correct at the moment.

There isn't a university in this country worth the sewage it generates.

Those who understand me best are aware that I'm not anything even remotely resembling a conservative. Basically, I think of myself as a radical individualist in search of biological immortality and on his way to the stars, possibly by way of Ceres or Mars. But before any of that happens, I want America back the way I remember it. No, I'm not being blindly nostalgic. It was never perfect, not by a long shot. But it was one hell of a lot better when I was a little kid than it is now.

As I write this, for example, the Federal Trade Commission—of which there is no mention among allowable government practices in the Constitution—is said to be attempting to seize control of the Internet.

Various special interest groups—for which read advocates of state terrorism—are attempting to put pressure on the Federal Communications Commission (which also has no legitimate place in any nation dedicated to freedom of speech) to trash the First Amendment completely by muzzling various conservative radio talk show hosts like Rush Limbaugh, Sean Hannity, Glenn Beck, and presumably G. Gordon Liddy, as well as the Fox News Network. I have no doubt my own *The Libertarian Enterprise* is way down at the bottom of somebody's list somewhere.

And two United States Senators, who took a solemn oath to uphold and defend the Constitution, are scheming with others of their unsavory, criminal ilk to legally define any dissent at all against government policies as treason—and treat dissenters, whether they happen to be anti-war protestors or Tea Party demonstrators, as terrorists.

And that's just today.

I want an America with no more grand utopian plans (A) to save an environment that doesn't need saving, (B) to prevent global warming, acid rain, ozone depletion, deforestation, or desertification that aren't happening, or (C) to force individuals to participate in an illegally collectivized medical system that is a hollow farce and little more than a justification for government snoopery, robbery, and tyranny.

I want an America where the few, remaining pitiful, starving, underpaid bureaucrats that are left—eking out their final days before their positions are abolished forever, along with their pensions— have nothing whatever to say about what I eat, what I drink, what I drive, what I keep in my gun cabinet, who I love, how I do it, and what, in the immortal words of the great George Carlin, I shoot, snort, smoke, or rub into my belly. Maybe it seemed like a good idea at the time, giving these subcreatures the power to interfere in all of those things. Now we know it was a mistake and we must correct it.

With prejudice.

I want an America where there are no more hidden schemes— or at least no money to encourage them—like rounding up the population and forcing everybody to live in gigantic hundred-story tenements (this is no paranoid fantasy: the United Nations calls it Agenda 21) while the socialist aristocracy, the nomenklatura, ride to hounds in an emptied countryside and shoot peasants. I want an America where the eternally smoldering ruins of the United Nations building in New York City stand as a monument to freedom and a warning to collectivists of every stripe, everywhere, no matter what rock they choose to hide under.

It is time to forge a mechanism for restoring individual liberty to America and for utterly destroying every last remaining trace of collectivism—both tasks are vital—a mechanism that can never be compromised, broken, or betrayed. I have a pretty good idea what that mechanism ought to look like, and that's what this article is all about.

Nearly everyone acknowledges that America has somehow lost its way, and is in some kind of deep and serious trouble. Individuals will disagree on details, but they understand that something is very, very wrong.

In 1972, when I was 26 years old and had been a libertarian for a full decade already, I was extremely fortunate to be invited to a week-long seminar in Wichita, Kansas, very generously hosted by the local 7-Up bottlers and the Love Box Company. It was conducted by one of modern libertarianism's early thinkers, journalist, editorialist, and almost surely the freedom movement's greatest educator, Robert LeFevre.

If you're a Heinlein fan, you know him as Professor Bernardo de la Paz.

He wanted everyone to call him "Bob."

Bob told us a great many things during those almost magical 40 hours, and I remember a surprising amount of what he said verbatim, even to this day, almost four decades later. (At my age, I have discovered, time flies whether you're having fun or not.) One of the things he said is that there were on the books at that point in time, an estimated 15,000,000 federal laws—and no way to tell how many state, county, and municipal laws there were, in addition to that.

Fifteen million.

"How many laws are enough?" he asked his students. "How many laws are too many? Can there be too many?" That was way back in 1972. And even then, it was clear that there were already too many laws "on the books."

"I'll remind you," Bob added, "that 'ignorance of the law is no excuse.'"

Over the years, a number of individuals have argued with me about that figure. Nobody has ever offered me a credible counter-estimate. I have seen the endless rows of law books myself, in libraries and lawyers' offices. If the true number of laws was only a third of that estimate, or even a tenth, clearly we would still have far too many laws.

Now, in the early 21st century, it's almost impossible to do anything without running afoul of some ordinance, statute, or decree. In places like "the People's Republic of California," a person can hardly take a breath or blink an eye without some kind of government permit. A burden like that slows commerce or stops it altogether (in many cases, that's the specific intention of business-hating left-wing legislators). It prevents progress in vital areas like energy and medicine. You can lose your savings, your property, your children, even your life, for breaking some petty prohibition you never knew existed.

Some of those millions of laws represent legislation "properly" introduced, shuffled through committees, and voted for on the floor of the House of Representatives or the Senate. But a great many more of them—possibly as many as 99 percent—consist of various rules and regulations voted on by nobody, but simply promulgated and shoved down our throats by various agencies full of appointees and bureaucrats, often in direct contradiction to what the legislators originally intended.

And of course, a number of those laws consist of nothing more than judicial reinterpretations that many complain actually constitute the passage of new legislation by judges. Even worse, as America continues to slide down the slimy slope into fascist dictatorship, there is an increasing tendency of "law enforcement" agents to make up the law as they go along, out in the field. With so much legislation already on the books, and its precise meaning perfectly unclear even to those who wrote it, the law becomes whatever minions of the police state say it is.

The vast majority of the existing body of law, and of new laws passed every year is, of course, thoroughly unconstitutional. Article I, Section 8, of the Constitution lists those functions of government—and they are very few—that are legally permissible. Anything the government does that does not appear on that list (probably 95 percent of its current activities) is a clear and open violation of the law. Moreover, the individuals who perform those functions for government—all the politicians, bureaucrats, and cops of various kinds—are criminals.

When I was a kid,—in case you've ever wondered how we got into this mess—I often listened to the local and national news media, newspaper and radio editorialists, whimpering about the "do-nothing Congress" (or state legislature or county commission or city council) condemning them for failing to crank out enough new legislation in a given session to satisfy the same statist crackpots—they were usually left-wing socialists in those days—who were doing the editorializing.

These were the Eisenhower years, I confess, and even as a fairly naive youngster, I had an intuitive sense that "No man's life, liberty, or property are safe when the legislature's in session," and that a "do-nothing Congress" is a good thing. Also, it occurred to me that, after almost two centuries, the Powers That Be ought to have passed more than enough laws by now. At that point, you understand, I'd spent my entire life—exactly like any other little kid—being told what to do and what not to do. It seemed to me there was enough of that crap already going around to last us at least another hundred years.

The more I've thought about that idea over the years, and after long study and consideration, the clearer it has become to me, almost every day, that a significant first step—indeed, an absolutely indispensable first step—toward understanding the mess we're in and fixing it, toward restoring our traditional liberties in this country, as well as preventing any future threats to it (and this should be the principal goal of any organization that claims to advocate freedom) ought to be a Constitutional amendment, absolutely forbidding the passage of any new legislation, at any level of government, for a century.

Let's call it "The Moratorium."

What I am proposing here, at minimum, is a new amendment to the Constitution, that would provide, from the date of passage forward, for a full century, that no new legislation could be passed at the federal, state, county, municipal, or any other level of government—especially including rulings by any part of the court system that, in effect, would constitute new law—or treaties of any kind. Nor would any new regulation or promulgation be permitted by any agency of government.

To be clear, this Moratorium would strictly forbid all lawmaking of any kind, at any level of government, for at least the next ten decades.

The one and only exception, of course, would be bills of repeal, getting rid of old laws that already exist, initiated referenda, lawsuits, criminal complaints, rulings that declare existing laws to be null and void, and the official disbandment, dissolution, or abolition of various arms, wings, legs, or other appendages of the government.

Or perhaps I should have said, amputation.

Because nothing political occurs in a vacuum, and the opponents of this concept would be inclined to see the handwriting on the wall and attempt to make the most of whatever time they believed they had left, the amendment would automatically repeal any and all legislation rammed through in the final year (or two, or five, or ten) before its ratification.

Or perhaps since my articles about it first appeared in public "print."

Naturally, there would be Draconian penalties for any violation of this new "highest law of the land." For a long while now, I've been interested in seeing the ancient federal prison on Alcatraz Island in San Francisco Bay fully rejuvenated and dedicated exclusively to the incarceration of government lawbreakers. I'm more than confident that tourists on excursion cruises would pay a reasonable amount for small packages of meat, maybe with expired sell-by dates, with which to keep the bay's famous sharks interested in hanging around the prison island.

You probably think I'm kidding.

I am not.

In the meantime, having nothing better to do with themselves (nothing that would show above their news desks, that is), the broadcast media would have no choice but to begin measuring the accomplishments of the nation's legislatures, not by the number of laws they pass, but by the number of laws they repeal. A "do-nothing Congress" (or legislature or county commission or city council) would be one that failed to repeal enough laws to suit the media and the public.

My goal—and yours, too, if you understand and agree with my proposal—is to make the Moratorium a hot issue in every national election from now on, until it finally becomes the last law of the land.

During a century completely without any new laws of any kind, Americans will be free to reconsider—and possibly to get rid of—millions of old laws and regulations. Like the so-called USA Patriot Act, that Congress voted for without even reading. Like the more than 22,000 items of anti-gun legislation, each of them a violation of the highest law of the land, the Bill of Rights. Like the equally unconstitutional Federal Reserve Act. Like the Sixteenth—income tax—Amendment which some historians believe was never legally ratified anyway.

I am not claiming that this single legislative measure can solve all of America's many problems—although when Great Britain did something somewhat similar in the early 19th century (the Reform Acts and Repeal of the Corn Laws), it ushered in a lengthy period of unprecedented peace, prosperity, and progress. But it's a good beginning.

And when the resulting American century of unprecedented peace, freedom, progress, and prosperity finally draws to a close, unlike the British, who, within only a couple of generations, buried themselves all over again under a new avalanche of idiotic legislation and regulation, Americans will make their Moratorium permanent. Perhaps ultimately there will remain only one law "on the books," the Zero Aggression Principle, forbidding the initiation of physical force by anyone—especially government—against anyone else, for any reason whatever.

We might then begin to count ourselves as civilized again.

Enquiring Minds and the Oil War

*The most dangerous and successful conspiracies take place
in public, in plain sight, under the clear, bright light of
day—usually with TV cameras focused on them.*

—L. NEIL SMITH

Now and again, I receive e-mail asking me about libertarianism and libertarian views. Sometimes these questions seem so important that I feel a need to answer them in public, so others who wonder about the same things, but are too shy to ask, can get an answer, too. My policy has always been that the only stupid questions are the ones that go unasked.

A few days ago, a friend of mine asked me the following question: "I would like to know your opinion about the current U.S. military operations in Afghanistan...I understand that libertarians tend to oppose foreign military intervention, but Osama bin Laden is believed to be hiding in Afghanistan, and the Taliban would not turn him over....What do you think should be done about Osama bin Laden?"

Here is my answer:

As I have written on many occasions, if the government story on the atrocities of September 11, 2001, is to be believed (which requires a severe stretch and a great deal of charity), it reveals certain departures from logic, common sense, and sanity that we ought to be deeply concerned about—although it may already be too late for that.

The first is that, although the Pentagon and World Trade Center were allegedly attacked by a group of men of whom the overwhelming majority carried Saudi Arabian passports, the United

States government responded by invading Iraq and Afghanistan, employing a series of rationalizations that seemed to change—just as they did in daily briefings at Mount Carmel during the Branch Davidian siege—every day.

It's a little like—no, it's exactly like—my punching you in the mouth and, in retaliation, you slug the guy who's standing beside me.

Think about Saddam Hussein's "weapons of mass destruction" that never quite managed to materialize. The argument—which I was deeply dismayed to see and hear on one of my favorite television shows—that nearly every intelligence agency in the world reported that the WMDs were there, and that the Bush Administration, "in good faith" believed and acted on these reports, is pure horsehockey. The record clearly shows that those agencies reported what they were ordered to report, often over the strenuous objections of those who worked for them.

Sounds a lot like global warm—pardon me, "climate change."

Now the latest two-party line is that the elusive WMDs, large and conspicuous enough to poke both your eyes out in views from satellites so technologically advanced and powerful they can see the pack and tell you what brand of cigarette you smoke, were secretly smuggled off, somehow, to Syria, a pathetically transparent excuse to invade and destroy that country, too, should Presidential whim ever demand it.

A similar array of justifications has been offered for the invasion of Afghanistan, among them, as my questioner indicates, that the arch villain Osama bin Laden has been hiding out there—at the same time that he was being observed by the usual reliable eyewitnesses, hanging with Elvis and Amelia Earhart in Pakistan, Chechnya, and the French Riviera.

It's important to remember in this context that United States policy created both Saddam Hussein and Osama bin Laden and installed them in place. Similarly, the folks we now refer to in contempt as "insurgents," back when they were fighting Soviet invaders, were the "Mujahedeen." It was said, admiringly, that these mountain people, from whom the resistance was drawn, were uniformly warm, gracious, and friendly—unless you messed with their dogs, their rifles, or their women.

To these noble freedom fighters, we gave a great deal of money and sophisticated weapons—mostly to shoot down Russian helicopters. Now we're the ones fighting them, and we're buying helicopters from the Russians.

If I were Osama, and the United States government were actually looking for me, I'd be clean-shaven by now, crewcutted, wearing jeans and a ZZ Top T-shirt, and living in a nice little house in Lincoln, Nebraska. But the government isn't looking for Osama, it needs him out there, somewhere, a Cheshire cat, evil eyes and fangs glowing in the darkness.

So here's a question: how do we know that Osama was the master fiend behind the fall of the twin towers? It struck me as more than suspicious that he was named as the badguy within just a few hours after the attack, by a police culture that still can't tell us who killed JonBenet Ramsey. It reminded me of the way the authorities ran a counterfeit Montag down and killed him on national television in Fahrenheit 451. Lee Harvey Oswald was identified the same way, out of thin air, immediately after the Kennedy assassination, and that story has more perverse twists and logical disconnects than *Naked Lunch*.

The fact is, Osama bin Laden has nothing at all to do with what the government is really up to in the Middle East. He only serves as a focal point to prevent Americans from asking questions that are more dangerous and important. The establishment desperately needed somebody like him—if only for the Five Minute Hate—and the guy had every reason to accept the role that was assigned him because it reinvented him as a hero of legendary proportions to something like a billion and a half Muslims who (not entirely for no reason) see the United States as an oppressor and cheered the images of its collapsing towers on television.

He didn't have to die to get his 27 or 72 virgins, or whatever. He's the equivalent of a rock star, the Mick Jagger of international terrorism.

Scream about it as conservatives may—they can't make a reasoned argument against it—there is sufficient evidence to open inquiries as to whether the Bush regime destroyed the towers, hired someone to do it, or knew that it was going to happen and did nothing to prevent it. I know what buildings look like when they're destroyed from the inside.

And so do you.

Likewise, artificial controversies about what general, with which strategy and tactics, and against whom they ought to be applied, are irrelevant and distracting. It's exactly like what I've observed about the War Between the States: scholars and hobbyists concentrate on the smallest details of this battle or that battle, but fail to ask the really important questions about why the war was fought, and on whose behalf.

Clue: Grenville Dodge, in the parlor, with a money clip.

The reasons why this government has done what it's done—and has failed to do what it ought to do—are no great secret. It's all about oil. It doesn't matter that the majority of the 9/11 hijackers carried Saudi passports. This government and the corporations that own it don't dare antagonize Saudi Arabia, no matter what crimes they may commit, because the Saudis are the world's largest producers and exporters of oil, and we get a significant portion of our oil from them.

Iraq, on the other hand, sits atop what has been called the world's second largest pool of oil, which was controlled by a dictator who was increasingly hostile toward the west despite the fact (or possibly because of it) that we installed him as dictator in the first place.

Incidentally, the next time some war-mongering wise-ass tries to tell you that one reason we're in the Middle East is to enhance the civil rights and social equality of women, remind them that we very enthusiastically destroyed the most secular country over there, where women could dress as they liked, have good jobs, be literate, and vote.

Purely by coincidence (of course) Afghanistan lies on the route of a central Asian pipeline western companies and their pet governments dreamed of building decades before the current unpleasantness. The decentralized, independent regime in that country—those who beat the Russians twice, the British, even Alexander the Great, wouldn't have been able to prevent tribesmen from damaging such a pipeline, to extract protection money or simply obtain oil for themselves. It had to be replaced with a government that was Big Oil's wholly-owned subsidiary.

Forget all the white papers and scholarly tomes issued by august institutions of political and economic thought. Forget the White House briefings and Presidential press conferences. Forget everything the military claims. America's effort in the Middle East is summed up on the nastiest bumper sticker I ever saw: "Kick Their Ass And Take The Gas."

There were other beneficiaries, of course, other birds that could be killed with one stone. Foremost among them is the Israeli police state. Some investigators even believe the towers were brought down by Mossad. In any case September 11, 2001, provided the perfect excuse for anything.

Which is why, whenever you hear about the only rational, ethical, effective action people of a free country can take against crimes like 9/11, you hear conservatives and neocons scream hysterically against it.

The action?

You must understand that terrorists, although they may ultimately derive their financial resources or other assets from a government or governments, are theoretically stateless themselves—they're rather like international corporations, in their way—because they reject the idea of a state, they don't wish to be controlled by a state, they have had their state taken away from them or destroyed, they have been denied a chance to create a state of their own, or they were created to provide some government somewhere with what's called "credible deniability."

When individuals not affiliated with a national government commit violent acts, they are—and ought to be dealt with as—criminals, nothing more and certainly nothing less. Rather than indiscriminately destroy entire nations full of innocent people in retaliation for the criminal behavior of a few, guilty individuals should be pursued and either killed, or captured, tried, and on conviction, appropriately punished.

As reluctant as I am to rely on government for anything, I believe that, for now, a very small team of experts in investigation, covert operations, and combat should be assembled under the aegis of the U.S. Marshal's office (established by George Washington himself, in 1789), to pursue individual criminals of this type when their violent acts involve more than one state (as 9/11 did) or the suspects have fled the United States. Given a good housecleaning which includes the abolition of the Department of Homeland Security, the jailing of Janet Napolitano, and a thoroughgoing investigation of the activities and objectives of supporters of state terrorism like the

Southern Poverty Law Center, they could also act as consultants to local peace-keeping authorities.

An organization like this could even form the core around which a Department of Bill of Rights Enforcement could be constructed. I have more detailed ideas on this proposal that might be discussed at length elsewhere.

At the same time, a reward should be offered for the apprehension of such criminals that is actually effective. If those around Osama won't betray him for a million dollars, then make it ten million or a hundred million or a billion. Or forget dollars and make the offer in pure gold. It is said that everybody has his price. I seriously doubt whether this excludes even the most devout and pious of religious adherents.

Rationalization—like love—will always find a way.

Compared to what the United States and its diminishing number of allies have squandered in declining dollars, in irreplaceable human lives, and in precious individual liberty, a system like this is so easy and inexpensive that it defies adequate description. Yet, if you describe what happened on 9/11 as a criminal act, and suggest that it should have been dealt with as a police problem rather than an act of war, or suggest that we should offer bounties that are adequate to get at the guilty parties, conservatives will scream and tear their faces off.

In reply, I can only ask, if a rational system like this had been in place on 9/11, if we had managed to avoid this Ninth or Tenth Crusade or whatever it is, how many lives, Iraqi, Afghani, American, British, others—how many hundreds of thousands—might have been saved?

And which of them might have discovered a star drive or a cure for cancer?

Toward a Police Reform Movement

The police are like parents. They're not interested in justice, they just want quiet.

—L. NEIL SMITH

The Problem

When you see three police cars pulled over at the side of a city street to deal with a single miscreant bicycle rider, you realize that there are too many cops. When all the heroes on television carry badges and a government franchise, you know we're in real trouble as a culture.

Every day we hear of some act of brutality—people beaten and kicked when they're unconscious, or "Tased" until they die—carried out by federal, state, or local "law enforcement" (which is a terrible misnomer, since most of the laws enforced today are unconstitutional, and therefore unlawful in and of themselves) against individuals or groups whose only crime was exercising their unalienable individual, civil, Constitutional, and human rights. "Policemen" at every level of government have become, more than any mere military organization, the "standing army" that was hated and feared by America's Founding Fathers.

There are reasons for this, foremost among them a shocking failure on the part of those same Founding Fathers to provide for any kind of proper enforcement of the first ten amendments to the Constitution, commonly known as the Bill of Rights. The warning signs were already plain, many years before this century's "Reichstag Fire"—the attack on the World Trade Center on September 11,

2001—which gave the government all the excuse it needed to turn the entire country into a prison.

Today's freedom movement (Libertarians, Constitutionalists, "Tea Partiers," and a growing number of "progressives") is attempting to identify the causes of America's ills. As long as they are being addressed, there's no harm in ameliorating symptoms, as well. You may get a CAT-scan to see why you suffer migraines, but you also take an aspirin.

Accordingly, we suggest the following steps—many of which libertarians have thought about for decades—to begin dealing with the signs by which we understand that we're all living in a police state. Any one of these measures (or even all of them together), may be pursued by concerned individuals and organizations who find them interesting and worthwhile—without regard to their political ideology—as conventional legislation, constitutional or charter amendments, initiated referenda, or as a part of settlements in lawsuits.

Short-term, what's important is to create as much discussion of these matters as possible, so the authorities among us will understand that, if they don't change their ways, their ways will be changed for them.

Some Answers

First, there being no provision whatever in the Constitution for a national police force of any kind—and in compliance with the 9th and 10th Amendments, as well as with Article I, Section 8—all federal "law enforcement" and investigative agencies must be abolished and their present and former employees subjected to legal scrutiny of their current and past activities for possible criminal behavior and crimes against the Constitution. As "interim" measures, these agencies and their employees will be forbidden to use or carry weapons of any kind (except off duty as ordinary individual citizens), and will be permitted to operate at all only under close supervision by local police.

All military-style weapons, military vehicles, and military aircraft presently in use by any of these agencies—or by local police—will be surrendered for distribution to those who paid for them.

Independent civilian review boards, perhaps one in each of America's 3088 counties—will be established to ensure that federal conduct remains fully consistent with the Bill of Rights. No pleas of secrecy or "national security" will be permitted to impede access to government documents (including routine police reports) or their investigations in general. Willful misunderstanding, for political or any other purposes, of any article of the Bill of Rights on the part of any elected or appointed official will be considered prima facie evidence of an intention to commit a crime or crimes against the Constitution.

Local Police

All police officers at state, county, and local levels will be required to wear traditional police uniforms on duty and be forbidden to act in a professional capacity when off duty, or wearing civilian clothing. All uniforms must bear individual name patches and badge numbers easily legible from a distance of fifty yards, and it will be unlawful to cover or obscure them in any way. It will also be unlawful for police officers to conceal their facial features with any sort of helmet or mask, or to wear camouflaged or military-style helmets or battledress.

All vehicles employed by local police must be clearly marked and readily identifiable, with highly-visible registration numbers. With the exception of emergency medical and rescue services, agencies at every level of government will be forbidden the use of helicopters, fixed-wing aircraft, or unmanned drones which, in recent years, have more and more become instruments of state terrorism and statist oppression.

It is long past time to demilitarize the police and reintegrate them as individuals into the society they're supposed to protect. To reestablish a proper relationship between them and the people they're supposed to serve, police officers may not possess, carry, or use any weapon prohibited to civilians within their jurisdiction, nor carry a weapon of any kind off duty, concealed or otherwise, until all laws forbidding civilians to do so in exactly the same manner have been repealed.

In general, so they will be dependent once again on the good will of armed civilians, police officers must be limited to the traditional six-shot revolver and four-shot slide or pump shotgun. They must be forbidden to use or carry rifles, Tasers, stunguns, or fully automatic weapons of any kind. Likewise, bullet-resistant clothing and equipment—which appear to have engendered an increasingly contemptuous disregard for the lives, property, and rights of civilians—will be forbidden.

Handcuffs or other restraints will not be used gratuitously on anyone arrested for nonviolent crimes—especially for the purpose of a humiliating public display. Arresting officials will be held fully and individually responsible under civil and criminal law for any loss of repute suffered by arrestees treated this way who are later proven innocent.

In "siege" situations (which may not be initiated merely because an individual expresses a wish to be left alone, locks himself in his house, or is known to possess weapons) authorities will be prohibited from interrupting telephone service or other utilities, or restricting free access by the media to the subjects of their operations. No incendiary devices, purposely built or otherwise, may be employed by police.

To avoid conflict of interest and prevent over-zealous enforcement of statutes and ordinances, all fines and other traffic revenues will be divided equally between the American Civil Liberties Union and Amnesty International, provided, of course, that these groups adopt a view of the Bill of Rights which is consistent from article to article.

All illegal activity on the part of individual police officers or groups of officers should be treated as felonies and punished accordingly.

A Newer Covenant

Individual members of the military and police must be required to prove themselves at regular intervals by publicly taking an oath to uphold, defend, and enforce—without reservation—each and every separate article of the Bill of Rights, as written and intended by the Founders.

Any individual member of the military or police who refuses to obey an order which he or she considers unconstitutional or unlawful, in good faith, will receive executive clemency and, should the order prove to have been unconstitutional or unlawful, an appropriate reward, promotion, and reinstatement, if necessary, to full pay and benefits.

Privacy and Civil Liberties

Like many other such events in history, the attacks of September 11, 2001, have been exploited as an excuse to destroy every value that once made America a unique civilization. If the Bush Administration was correct in saying that "they hate us for our freedom," then the terrorists have won, because the government has destroyed that freedom.

Americans will have their privacy again, whether government and government-chartered corporations want them to or not. In general, owing to a long-established pattern of abuse by police agencies and individual officers, all eavesdropping, wiretapping, Internet surveillance, infrared photography, and other invasions of individual privacy—or any procedure, including taxation, that requires disclosure of private financial information—will be absolutely forbidden.

It was a grave mistake to extend such powers and privileges to government and its surrogates in the first place and now they must be revoked. For the foreseeable future, in order to restore the balance, the Fourth Amendment must be read as if the word "unreasonable" did not appear in it, since it is essentially meaningless. Given the unmistakable injunction of the Second Amendment, possession or use of any device for the detection of personal weapons—by government at any level or by corporations—will be illegal and severely punishable.

It is inappropriate for sovereign individuals to be labeled, sorted, and tracked as if they were livestock. Naturally, there is no provision for these activities to be found in the Constitution. Fingerprint records and other identification systems presently maintained by government or its surrogate corporations must be destroyed. Voiceprinting, retinal photography, and the "preventive" collection of DNA samples must be forbidden. Electronic tracking systems must be banned, and government forbidden to use Global Positioning Systems, especially in telephones, to track or find individuals.

A Personal Message

To individual members of the police and military, we say the time for denial is over. If these proposed measures anger you, remember that Bill Clinton did it to you. Janet Reno did it to you. Louis Freeh did it to you. Larry Potts did it to you. Lon Horiuchi did it to you.

George W. Bush, Richard Cheney and their minions did it to you. And now, Barack Obama, Janet Napolitano, and Eric Holder are doing it to you.

You have let them do it.

Thanks to them, you are despised by the very populace that you're supposed to be protecting. You are feared—and if you enjoy that, there's something deeply wrong with you—and you have forgotten that frightened people are dangerous. Until you are willing to prove the contrary to those you have sworn to serve, you are no different from the politicians listed above. You're exactly the same as those who:

Firebombed a whole neighborhood out of existence when a group of residents was accused of nothing more serious than disturbing the peace;

Assassinated a harmless old man merely to steal his valuable real estate;

Shot a little boy and his dog to death and then blew his mother's head off with a scoped high-powered rifle as she held her baby in her arms;

Confined, terrorized, gassed, and machine-gunned dozens of innocent men, women—and 22 little children—in the church that was their home;

Tortured, intimidated, and tried to dispose of political prisoners—not foreigners overseas, but your fellow Americans—by denying them necessary and lawfully prescribed medication and proper medical assistance;

Threatened and confiscated evidence from independent investigators when they questioned the cover-up of an airliner crash that killed hundreds;

Viciously stomped kittens to death underfoot trying to frighten the innocent victims of a narcotics raid carried out at the wrong address;

Kidnapped, illegally imprisoned, and even tortured individuals never proven in any court of law to represent any kind of threat to anybody;

Committed hundreds of thousands of similar brutal, illegal, and unconstitutional travesties that have inexorably transformed the once free and noble American civilization into a dark, horror-filled dictatorship.

Time to Stand Down

The Cold War is over. The immensely destructive "War on Drugs," which has done vastly more damage to American society than drugs themselves ever threatened to, was meant from the beginning to replace it, and to destroy the very Constitution you have sworn to uphold and defend. When the "War on Drugs" failed to produce the desired results, it was replaced with the equally fraudulent and destructive "War on Terror."

Don't allow a gang of socialist trash, elected by the mass media and a noisy minority, to exploit you as a tool to force illegal, immoral, alien ideas on an unwilling populace. They have stolen your honor. Your one duty, your only goal must be to regain it by enforcing the highest law of the land, the first ten amendments to the Constitution, commonly known as the Bill of Rights. Indeed, that's the only possible justification for what you do, and for the existence of government itself.

Don't let deskbound, overpaid SINOs—"Superiors In Name Only"—tell you what the Bill of Rights means. It wasn't written to be obscure. It wasn't written for them to interpret away. Remember your oath. Don't let corrupt judges and lawyers—who only stand to benefit from eliminating the Bill of Rights—tell you what it means, either. Do what most Americans haven't tried to do for over half a century.

Think for yourself.

Ask yourself this question: if you were one of America's Founders and you'd just surprised the world (and yourself) by winning a war of secession against the most powerful, heavy-handed government on the planet, and the last thing you wanted for yourself, for your children, or for your grandchildren was to fall beneath the heels of its jackboots ever again, what would you want the Bill of Rights to mean?

And if the first act, under martial law, of that powerful, heavy-handed government had been to try to take your guns away at Lexington and Concord (yes, that's what those battles were all about), would you have written a Second Amendment to guarantee government's exclusive "right" to own and carry weapons? Would you have written a Second Amendment that was subject to whatever the whims of government claimed was a reasonable regulation? Or would you have written it strictly to forbid government from having anything to do with your guns, ever again?

Anything whatever.

We say once again, it's time to end the "War on Drugs." Think back: isn't it true that every dime ever spent on it has only made the problem worse, not better? Many decent individuals have come to believe that, from the outset, it was never meant as anything but a war against the people of the United States of America and their freedom. It's time to end it forever, and to abolish the DEA, the FBI, the BATFE, and every other federal agency not specifically mentioned in the Constitution, and which is, for that reason alone, a criminal enterprise.

Likewise, it's time to end the "War on Terror" and abolish those agencies—each and every one illegal—charged with waging it. All laws, regulations, decrees, and promulgations passed in connection with it must be repealed, nullified, or otherwise disposed of, immediately.

All hiring for these illegal agencies must also cease immediately, and those individual officers who manage to survive legal scrutiny of their past activities should be encouraged to find employment in the private economy, or be transferred to the US Marshals Service, given a new assignment—Bill of Rights enforcement—and be turned loose on crooked politicians, bureaucrats, and judges, rather than the American people.

It should have been obvious long ago that the worldview of the typical "law enforcement officer" has become so contaminated and corrupt over the years, so pathologically contemptuous of everyone around him, that, for the sake of public safety, every one of them will have to be removed and replaced by newly-trained personnel with a proper respect for the rights of the individuals they serve. One possible exception may be made in the case of "Oathkeepers" who are trying to stem the tide of brutal authoritarianism in the police and military.

In the long run, provided that care is taken to avoid the election of unapologetic fascists like Maricopa County, Arizona's Joe Arpaio, municipal police forces and their multiple layers of bureaucratic protection must be outlawed and abolished, in favor of local sheriffs who are directly accessible by and accountable to the people. Also, stringent limits must be set on the ratio of officers to the civilian population.

Above and beyond everything, the Founders' hideous, destructive omission must be corrected and the Bill of Rights equipped with a "penalty clause" for politicians, bureaucrats, or policemen who violate its precepts. The point must be made that no portion of the Constitution allows it to be set aside in the case of an "emergency." The Posse Comitatus Act of 1876 must be reinstated in full, and the most Draconian punishments imaginable established for its slightest violation.

Creating and enacting such a penalty clause must become the highest priority for Libertarians, Constitutionalists, "Tea Partiers," and any others who are interested in restoring freedom to this once great country.

Property

Over two centuries, American democracy has acquired something analogous to an immune system to protect it from the merest threat of wisdom, intelligence, honor, decency, individuality, or courage. Anyone entering the system who exhibits any of those undesirable attributes will sooner or later find himself broken and cast aside— if he is fortunate—or assimilated.

—L. NEIL SMITH

This nation, the United States of America—and the near miracle of human progress that it represents—owes its power, prestige, and prosperity solely to the sanctity that it traditionally afforded to individual property rights. In the 18th and 19th centuries, the worst thing that a human being could be accused of being was a horse thief, and the customary punishment, at least out in the West, was death by hanging.

Second only to that, the most detested criminal was a claim jumper, somebody who stole somebody else's prospecting site— make note: a mere potentiality, an as-yet unrealized, and therefore entirely abstract entity—and claimed it as their own. Most often, this resulted in a firefight, with justice administered by Messrs. Colt and Winchester.

Or Remington and Smith & Wesson.

In the 18th and 19th centuries, especially out in the West, crimes against persons or property were so vanishingly rare that today we can still remember the names of the individual criminals. Whatever connection there may be (if any) between that fact and those set forth in the paragraphs above will be left for the intelligent reader to determine.

There are customary ways that human beings mark their temporarily unused or unoccupied property so that nobody will claim that they've abandoned it. They write their name in a textbook or affix it to their computer. They sew nametags in their underwear. They pile stones up in a traditional way to stake their claim to land. And they make certain that the copyright mark or assertion is printed in all of their own writings.

For the most part, people have respected these customs, either because they were worried about all that hardware coming into play, or, much more frequently, because they wanted their own rights to be respected. Today, however, and for at least the last century, the principal threat to persons and property has not been the individual, "freelance" marauder, but the very entity that attempts to justify its existence by claiming that it protects persons and property, the government.

However, thanks to processes like "eminent domain," a medieval travesty that should have been abolished, right along with *droit de seigneur*, when we gave George Hanover the boot, "civil forfeiture," re-engineered specifically to deny legal representation—and the presumption of innocence—to the politically incorrect, "tax liens," an age-old means of stealing real property when there's no more money left for the government to steal, and, in general, the boosting of whatever politicians want, for reasons of "public health" or "national security"—or because some bought-and-paid-for judge has ruled what you own to be a "public nuisance," the near-miracle is nothing but a memory.

As America slides into another Great Depression, and from there into a new Dark Ages the world may never recover from, there's no need to wonder why, no reason to look for answers elsewhere, no point in listening to bucketheads proclaiming that it happened because we angered some nasty-tempered neolithic deity or another. What kept the United States afloat for their first century (note my use of the plural), what made them work better than any other civilization in the world, or in history, was the amazing phenomenon of absolute property rights.

If you can't be sure of what is yours, then you can't be sure of anything, a fact I'm absolutely certain that socialists have relied on to spread their deadly poison—their mental malware—around this battered planet since at least the time of Plato. If nobody else is sure of what is his—and what is yours—then everything is up for grabs.

These observations apply to so-called intellectual property as well as they do to ordinary, physical property. All property, in fact, is intellectual property, since no kind of property can exist without being preceded by the thought that first allowed it to be claimed or created.

Intellectual property rights are under an intense attack at the moment, both socially and politically, because the concept seems more difficult to defend than that of physical property rights. And indeed it is—once you accept the lie that there's any moral difference between the two. In any case, the ultimate objective of its attackers is simply to discredit the concept of any kind of private property at all.

And then cash in.

In the view of libertarian author and lecturer Robert LeFevre, there are only two kinds of entity in the universe: people and property. Only property may be owned; no one may own another human being.

There are, according to LeFevre, three distinct kinds of property: (A) lawfully and ethically held property, (B) improperly held (stolen) property, and (C) unclaimed or abandoned property. Even libertarians argue among themselves—more or less constantly—about what is required for property to fall unmistakably into category A, one reason libertarians have enjoyed little success, so far, either socially or politically.

I was first inspired—when I was about thirteen years old, in eighth grade—to think seriously about the nature of property, and an individual's purpose in life, not by any philosophical treatise (I wouldn't be reading *The Fountainhead* or *Atlas Shrugged* for another couple of years) but by an unusually interesting action-adventure novel (and caper story) that, to me, at least, bordered on science fiction.

Jack Finney's 1959 novel *Assault on a Queen*, later made into a Frank Sinatra movie, concerned raising a scuttled World War I German submarine and using it to stop the RMS *Queen Mary* in midcourse, in order to rob her and her passengers at torpedo-point like a western stagecoach.

For as long as I can recall, I've been fascinated by submarines. That's what brought this science-fiction-reading kid to buy a mundane novel. The story was pretty exciting, and there was just enough sex to satisfy a thirteen-year-old's curiosity. But there was something else, too.

Setting aside the rationalizing that attempted to justify stealing from frightened first-class passengers and the purser's safe (in this, Finney almost perfectly anticipated Harry Harrison's *The Stainless Steel Rat*), that "something else" was the way that the viewpoint character found himself getting talked into becoming a part of the operation.

You have a finite life expectancy, he was told, you only have so many years to live, so many months, so many days, so many hours. And in order to stay alive, to keep yourself fed and clothed and housed, you sell relatively large chunks of your remaining life expectancy to somebody else who pays you to do what he wants you to do with your time, instead of what you'd rather do yourself if you were free to choose.

By the time you've saved enough money to become independent—provided that you ever do—you're too old to do half or more of what you wanted to do. You've sold that part of your life, and now it's gone. And with those words, or something very much like them, Our Hero joins the merry crew of submarine bandits and the story really gets started.

I suppose I might have read or heard this idea—that you have to sell portions of your life in order to stay alive—in a thousand other places, but I didn't. I read it in an adventure novel and it stuck. At the time, supported as I was by my father who was selling enormous portions of his life to the Northeast Air Command, it seemed pretty bleak and cynical, but it stayed with me because it was—as it remains to this today—perfectly true. Today, people talk about being credit card slaves, or the indentured servants to corporations, but this was a purer, cleaner, simpler notion and it led straight to another.

If you sell portions of your life—a very scarce commodity, as it turns out—to obtain whatever you need or want, then what you have purchased at such an irreplaceable price is necessarily a part of you, an extension of your being, of your self. Anybody who tries to steal it from you, whether it's a burglar, a mugger, the IRS, or (if you're a writer) a plagiarist, is kidnapping the part of you that's represented by what they're trying to abscond with. If they succeed, if they manage to separate it from you, they have killed that part of you.

When I finally read Rand, and she informed me that I'm the sole proprietor of my own life and all the products of my life, the lady didn't "convert" me to anything. I already knew all of that. Part of it was my reading, of course. A large part of it was the way I'd been brought up, by parents who were both Westerners, had led something of a pioneer life themselves in isolated Walden, Colorado, and Tuba City, Arizona, had survived the Great Depression and the Second World War, and knew that life is hard enough without some criminal jerk making it worse.

Since then, times have changed, not always for the better.

We live in bizarre age when, just as a single example, athletic "competitions" for children self-righteously refuse to keep score—apparently because losing is so unpleasant, or winning (one would infer) is fascistic. No attempt whatever is made on school playgrounds to determine, in the case of a conflict, who threw the first punch—that is, who initiated force—(and teachers will peer at you as if you're speaking a foreign language if you try to explain to them how that policy is both morally and pragmatically wrong), and the worst crime that an adult can commit, especially in places like Chicago, Denver, New York, San Francisco, and Washington, D.C., is premeditated self-defense.

But these are hardly new developments, nor did they occur without antecedents. I recall being shocked at about age eight (this would have been around 1954, when I was in third grade), when I learned that other children were not given the authority by their parents to kick kids out of their yards who started fights, stole things, or made themselves unwelcome in other ways. Some of my friends were explicitly forbidden to do so, because it was "rude," unchristian, or because whatever young people said or did or thought or felt was unimportant. As I've observed, most parents don't want justice, they just want quiet.

If you are not permitted—or prepared to seize—propriety over your own environment, you will never achieve propriety over your own existence. There are those, of course, who understand this perfectly well and wish to take full advantage of it. Any attack on the right to property is—before any other consideration—an attack on personal sovereignty.

The United States of America are in big trouble now, politically and economically, and the greatest part of that trouble has arisen because people no longer have property rights, and the nation has become a kleptocracy—that is, its government is no longer based on principles of liberty, or even on the will of the people, but on theft.

Most—if not all—governments in the world, and throughout the course of history, have been kleptocracies, although, thanks to the indoctrination camps we call public schools, people tend to learn that fact too late in life for it to do them any good. Most—if not all—governments are kleptocracies. Ours was supposed to have been different.

We can change that, all at once, with a Constitutional amendment or a revolution, to restore the absolute right to own property, or incrementally, in step by step. A good place to start might be to abolish the power of government to take anybody's property for any reason.

Nobody should ever be deprived of their home because of taxes. In the first place, a government that can't get along on what people are willing to give it voluntarily doesn't deserve to exist. And if it's possible for government to seize somebody's property simply because they failed to pay it, then what good is it? A government like that exposes itself as nothing but a criminal protection racket: "Pay us and we'll 'protect' you (right out of everything you own)—from ourselves!"

Put a stop to government theft and we'll have taken not just an incremental step, but an enormous stride in restoring civilization and with it, peace, freedom, progress, and prosperity for our entire species.

An Act of Sanity

Always attack in perpendicular fashion, from an unconventional and unexpected (but relevant!) direction. The enemy will be unprepared; you can strike him with your full strength while he finds nothing to attack effectively.

—L. NEIL SMITH

Immediately upon passage of this measure, every act, bill, decree, directive, edict, executive or administrative order, initiative, law, mandate, ordinance, proclamation, regulation, resolution, or statute, promulgated or enacted by any agency or any other part of the United States government between January 19, 2008, and January 21, 2013, or the end of the Barack Obama Administration, shall be null and void.

The Coathanger Lobby

Just what "life" is being defended here? I seriously doubt
whether 99.99% of the anti-abortionists who wave their
gory photo-placards around at demonstrations could tell
a human fetus from that of a rabbit or a rat.

—L. NEIL SMITH

S omewhere south of Denver, along I-25 toward Colorado Springs
or Pueblo or Trinidad, there is a five-foot white homemade sign
with big stenciled black letters that proclaims, "Abortion Stops
A Beating Heart."

The immediate, reflexive thought that such a display provokes
is, "So does a mousetrap." I seriously doubt whether the individuals
who put that sign up are vegans or members of PETA. The con-
flation—and there can be no doubt that it's deliberate—of life in
general with human life in particular is only one of several dishonest
tactics used by those, fixated in their foolishness, who refuse to take
that final step into full adulthood and give up trying to control the
lives of others.

When I was struggling to survive high school, back in the 1960s,
there didn't appear to be as much public controversy about abortion as there seems to be now. The important point back then was
that, no matter what the law demanded of her, a woman determined
to have an abortion would get one, one way or another. Tens of
thousands of young women were dying every year because the only
abortions they could get—or give themselves—were extremely dangerous. In a modern age of antibiotics, they were dying of ancient
and unspeakable infections. They were also dying of hemorrhage.

They were dying in droves, and if they survived then there were plenty of self-righteous assholes around, quiveringly eager to make their lives as miserable as possible afterward.

When *Roe v. Wade* came along, as usual the Supreme Court got it all wrong. The issue of privacy may be tangentially involved (and I disagree with Robert Bork that the Bill of Rights doesn't guarantee it), but what's actually at stake here is the absolute right of the individual to direct her own life—a right that every court in the land would greatly prefer never to acknowledge. However, if a woman isn't free to choose whether or not to bear a child, then the rest of her "freedoms" mean absolutely nothing; she's just a breeding slave to the state, to the church, to her husband, or to her father. And the United States of America is no different from the Middle Eastern religious satrapies that warmongering neo-conservatives are so fond of denouncing.

Americans seem more or less equally divided over the issue of abortion. It doesn't appear that many minds get changed, one way or another, from year to year. The libertarian movement, too, seems to be divided about abortion, although the division may not be quite so equal.

Libertarians who oppose abortion do so, more or less commendably, because they believe it is a violation of the rights of an individual human being, namely, the unborn child in question. Basically, they view abortion as an act of murder which must be prevented at all costs. If they're consistent (and many of them are) they won't even countenance the termination of a pregnancy brought about by incest or rape. After all, the bad behavior of its father isn't the fetus's fault.

Libertarians who support a woman's right to abortion do so for a number of reasons. First and foremost, they see an unwanted pregnancy as a form of slavery, a violation of a woman's inalienable rights to self-determination and personal sovereignty, and an assault on the absolute self-ownership which is the foundation of all other human rights.

At the risk of repeating ourselves, let's look at it from another angle: if a woman's neighbors or the government can force her to carry a baby for nine months—in effect, expropriating her as an incubator to satisfy certain moral or political stances she doesn't necessarily share with them—then what other rights does she retain that mean anything?

I've often argued that it doesn't do children any good—and it may even do them lasting harm—to discover that their father was forced, more or less at gunpoint, to provide them with financial support. Far better to let the bastard go his own way. But how much worse must it be to learn that your mother didn't want you, but was forced—again by the guns that lie behind any law—to carry you to term?

There is also a view that a fetus is neither legally nor morally a person, because it fails to meet certain criteria that define a human being, and therefore has no rights. I happen to agree with that: a fetus lacks a critical quality called "sapience"—the ability, among other things, not just to think, but to think about thinking—which is the very definition of humanity and the wellspring of every human right.

However, even if the unborn child were considered a person with rights, they wouldn't include a right to live at the involuntary expense of someone unwilling to nurture and sustain it. Its presence constitutes trespass and the woman has a proprietary right to evict it.

In my experience, the post-abortion guilt and depression that only anti-abortion groups ever talk about is a myth. I have known many women who had abortions because it wasn't the right time in their lives to have a baby. These women, free to go on with their lives and to achieve their ambitions, often chose to have a family afterward, when the time was right. It is up to the woman—and the woman alone—to determine when the time to have a baby is wrong and when it's right.

I do disagree, however, with the commonly-asserted view that men have nothing to say about this issue. It's a cowardly position we used to call a "cop-out." There are certainly plenty of men on the other side; in fact it sometimes seems like all the other side consists of is patriarchal males and a handful of intimidated token females. Real men should feel a knightly obligation to defend the sovereignty and freedom of the women in their lives, and perhaps even of all women in general.

I agree with feminists that, if it were men who got pregnant, abortion would be a sacrament. Ayn Rand said, in defense of abortion, that sacrificing an actuality, a fully grown up woman with her future shining brightly ahead of her, for the sake of a mere potential—an unborn, nonsapient, not-quite-human parasitic organism—is an obscenity.

There is also a First Amendment question. That amendment provides, in essence, that as civilized participants in society, we will refrain from making public policy based on our religious beliefs. If the laws forbidding abortion don't fall into that category, I don't know what does.

I'm extremely skeptical of anyone who claims their opposition to abortion doesn't spring from religious motivation. People on the other side of the issue maintain that abortion is murder, the wrongful death of a human being. But if they're not moved by religion, I wonder what their definition of "human" can possibly be. Can a fetus write a sonnet, formulate a mathematical theorem, play chess, or tell a dirty joke? Can a fetus use tools, start a fire, or say, "Please don't abort me!"?

Clearly, there is some other definition of humanity at work here, and almost certainly, it is a religious one. We're certainly entitled to think so until it's proven otherwise. I myself have never believed in souls or in any other variety of supernatural entity. Nor will I be compelled—by the law or by anything else—to behave as if I did believe.

Those who are honest enough to support their moral position with the claim that children are "gifts from God" are usually the same people who view children as a punishment for sin. (Later on, they tend to see them as cannon fodder.) I have heard many arguments such as, "You were having sex, therefore you deserve to get pregnant," and "If you're not ready to have a baby, maybe you shouldn't be having sex."

I wonder how consistently they follow this advice, themselves. The human and historic truth is that for every deliberate act of attempted procreation, people have recreational sex a hundred or a thousand times with no intention or expectation of starting a baby. That young people should be subject to a different standard—"Here, carry this egg around for a few days before you contemplate having sex."—when older adults are not, represents a ludicrous and unacceptable double standard.

I also oppose all sex "education" in the public school system—in fact I oppose the system itself—because it is not the proper business of the government, through its propaganda mills, to tell young people how to conduct their lives, especially where intimate personal matters are concerned. Moreover, so-called "abstinence-only" sex education is especially farcical, if for no other reason than that it flies in the face of almost four billion years of evolution. A biological imperative impels all organisms higher on the ladder than an amoeba. It is utterly idiotic to expect to be able to thwart this imperative.

It's a cheap dodge to assert (as so many political candidates, including those who called themselves libertarians, have) that abortion is an issue properly left to the state, rather than to the federal government. Interference with an individual's life, liberty, and property is wrong no matter what level of government is guilty of it, and suffering the intrusions of fifty small dictatorships is no better than suffering the intrusions of a single big one. Any political candidate who replies that abortion is a state-level matter is simply afraid to stand up bravely, face the issue squarely, and answer it honestly.

As I have said, rights derive from that particular quality of the mind called "sapience." Only human beings appear to have it. Rights (exactly like purpose) are wholly and exclusively a human concept. While it may help some people feel good to assert that animals—or fetuses—have rights, that doesn't make it so, and I have never heard anyone make a coherent argument for it that went beyond the mere assertion.

Some years ago, on one of my websites, I conducted an admittedly unscientific poll on abortion in which I asked my readers (who range all over the political spectrum) whether—if it would lay the issue to rest once and for all, and allow humanity to get on with other matters—they would be willing to accept an agreement under which abortion would remain legal, but not one cent of tax money would ever be used to provide it. The measure was approved by 85% of those who responded.

The leaders at each end of the argument wouldn't agree, but the whole idea was to strip them out of the process. It should be obvious that the left wants abortion to be paid for by the government because it's part of an overall irrational desire of theirs to mix Marxism and medicine.

The right has its own problems. If they got their way, if abortion were outlawed, the logistical details and difficulties would be overwhelming. Among other things, it would require all pregnancies be reported, registered, and monitored. In the end, every second of a pregnant woman's life would be observed and controlled by the very kind of regime they complain bitterly about with regard to socialized medicine. The resulting police state would make the present mess seem appealing.

And yet, conservatives do support Obamacare—for pregnant women.

For more about this, see "Abortion: An Excerpt From *Hope*" by Aaron Zelman and L. Neil Smith in THE LIBERTARIAN EN-TERPRISE, Number 485, September 21, 2008 at:

http://www.ncc-1776.org/tle2008/tle485-20080921-02.html

If abortion is a sin, those who oppose it must respect the First Amendment and leave those they regard as sinners alone to face whatever punishment they deserve in the afterlife they believe in so fervently.

Anything else reeks of hypocrisy.

The Algore Uncertainty Principle

It is an unfortunate—and possibly fatal—sign of our times that, to paraphrase Robert A. Heinlein, one man's science is another man's belly-laugh.

—L. NEIL SMITH

Although it's one of my favorite movies of all time, there is a certain attitude written into *Twister*—a 1996 Helen Hunt and Bill Paxton film about tornado-chasers that was the first to be sold as a DVD and the last to be sold as an HD-DVD—that never fails to annoy me.

If you don't know the story, it pits a sort of lovably rag-tag gang of eccentric academic researchers with battered vehicles and equipment against the elemental forces that kill many Americans every year in the heartland, and destroy what they have labored so hard to build. I live at the western edge of "Tornado Alley" and my eyes are often on the sky looking out for "greenage" practically every summer afternoon.

The characters in *Twister* also have to confront a rival team of atmospheric scientists equipped with brand-new shiny cars and gear, slick company outfits and bright orange windbreakers. Their leader was a colleague of the two principal characters, but finally left them to go to work for private enterprise. Our hero calls him a "corporate suck-butt."

Now hang on just a minute, I always want to say to Bill Paxton. Your "evil adversary" works for a collection of people who have no power of any kind to force their customers to buy whatever it is they have to sell. They can only produce the highest quality goods and services that they can, and then sell them at the lowest possible price.

You, on the other hand, as cute and adorable as you and your cohorts may seem in their beat-up jeans, worn hoodies, and faded T-shirts, tossing catchy dialogue back and forth that was written for you by Joss Whedon, and playing Eric Clapton music videos in your funky-looking equipment-crammed truck—you don't have to produce anything.

You have armed thugs who go out into the world for you and threaten and terrorize Productive Class individuals into paying for your hobby whether they—the Productive Class—are interested in what you do or can afford it or not. Should any among them prove unwilling to cough up, they will be arrested, their homes and other property will be stolen out from under them, and they may be beaten up, kidnapped, and even killed—so that you can be all winsome and cool.

So who's really sucking, here, and exactly what butt? "Yes," said Huey Long. "We will have Fascism in America—only we will call it antiFascism."

Now there are certain things that every five-year-old knows—what torture is, for example, and what it is not, or that it's very bad to plagiarize the work of others (an issue that arises in the story when the "bad" private enterprise guy appears to have stolen both the noble socialist guy's invention and the credit for having invented it)—that most people tend to evade or blank out as they grow up.

One of those things is that it's morally wrong—and not very nice—to steal money and other stuff from one human being or group of human beings with the excuse that you're giving it to some other individual or group, however worthy the recipient's cause may seem to be.

For that reason alone, government funding of the sciences is unacceptable.

Just as I live at the edge of Tornado Alley, thanks to what my wife does for a living, I have lived at the edge of the academic environment for something like 30 years now. Believe me, there is no "suck-butt" like some university scientific johnnie applying for a grant.

Government subsidy, however—and perhaps even more importantly, the ever-present threat to withhold it in the interest of "political correctness"—has corrupted the practice of science in this country almost beyond recognition. Possibly beyond redemption. All by itself, "global warming"—not really a scientific theory, just a highly lucrative shell-game and article of environmentalist faith among the hopelessly stupid—has made us the scientific laughing-stock of the planet.

The gods alone know what the future will make of us.

The fact that the fatuous former United States Vice President Albert Gore could actually be given a Nobel Prize (not to mention an Academy Award) for furthering the global warming hoax would be almost terminally repulsive and depressing—if it weren't also morbidly funny.

In my 1983 novel *The Nagasaki Vector*, I predicted the collapse of the Soviet Union. One way I knew the culture was doomed was that, for purposes of "security," its scientists weren't free to communicate with one another in their own country, but had to attend international conferences just in order to learn what their own colleagues were up to. The effect of political correctness on science is every bit as harmful.

It's not just global warming, and not just climate science. Over the past several decades, we've been warned, in the most hysterical of terms, about the dire threats represented by horrors like acid rain, ozone depletion, deforestation, desertification, the reduction of biodiversity, and overpopulation. If we're sane, we file these pronouncements away with other "menaces" that confront us, like smoking in bed (very big when I was in first grade), video arcades, and platform shoes. If we're not sane, we obligingly start to "run in circles, scream and shout" the way the con-men and the media want us to do. Along come the politicians to "fix" everything, and invariably we end up with less freedom, and more government control over our lives.

Yet, despite claims that practically everything we eat, drink, or breathe is toxic, we continue to live longer than our predecessors. Of course that's a dire threat, too, to demented individuals who, like the Discovery Channel gunman, hate their own species because they hate themselves.

It never fails to astonish me how many people don't understand what science is. Listening only to evolution-deniers, one would get the impression that it's some kind of cult or religion comparable with what they themselves believe, and that one accepts science on the same basis—the desire to believe it—that they have accepted what they believe.

Science is none of those things. At the same time, it is a very simple thing. Science is nothing more—or less—than a way of looking at reality that has produced vastly better results than any other way that people throughout history have tried. And it works for everyone, every day. You don't have to be an official, certified scientist.

Here's how it works: observe some aspect of the world around you. Find or think up an explanation for why that aspect is the way it is. Test your explanation. Form a new, improved explanation based on your test.

My rooster makes a lot of noise every morning. The sun comes up every morning. My explanation is that my rooster makes the sun come up. I test the explanation by gagging my rooster somehow, and then watching what the sun does. When the sun comes up anyway, I abandon my explanation and try to think of another that coincides better with reality.

Those simple steps, repeated a million times over a thousand years have taken us from the oxcart to the spaceship. They have shown us the true shape of reality from the whirling of unimaginably tiny subatomic particles to the great lacy fans formed by millions of galaxies, each of which is made up of billions of stars. They have lengthened human life expectancy from a little over 20 years to nearly 80 years. They have fed and clothed and housed the people of Western Civilization better than human beings have ever been fed or clothed or housed in history.

The opposite of science, shamanism, in any of the thousands of forms it assumes, always boils down to believing what you believe, not because it's consistent with reality, but because you want to believe it. Although it's been around for thousands of years, and may in fact predate our species, shamanism has failed to produce an inch or an ounce of progress, nor has it enabled people to live a microsecond longer, or—without the generosity of individuals who happen to be in better touch with reality—fed, housed, or clothed a single human being.

Science is often seen by government as a political weapon. The National Aeronautics and Space Administration has absolutely no interest in seeing large numbers of taxpayers move away into space on a permanent basis, and for years, they have done whatever they could to prevent vital research in certain areas such as the effect of fractional gravity on human physiology. Similarly, the American Cancer Society, which might as well be a government agency, is infamous for controlling funds to prevent cancer research that they don't approve of.

And which might actually cure cancer, putting them out of a job.

In a more general sense, the substitution of statistics for actual science has had a negative effect on progress. Statistics teach us nothing new; they can be "cooked" to prove or disprove anything you like. For years, "social scientists" lied about the effect of private gun ownership on crime rates, causing countless individuals to lose their lives by being unequipped for self-defense. A so-called scholar, Michael Bellesiles, was caught falsifying data about gun ownership and was banished from academia, although he's currently trying to make a comeback.

On the other hand, Dr. Peter Duisenberg, among others, has been severely and unjustly punished, ostracized by establishment science for publicly pointing out certain questionable research practices and attitudes about Auto Immune Deficiency Syndrome, Legionnaires', and several other diseases.

While it's undoubtedly true that corporate funding is generally results-oriented (which is supposed to be a good thing in engineering, but a bad thing in science), government funding of science is no less results-driven, and almost inevitably involves the misallocation of money for purely political reasons. What institution, for example, is going to pay for research that proves there's no global warming or that AIDS is caused by lifestyle choices rather than a pathogen? We've seen this clearly with stem cell research. We are left to wonder, if all this corruption is going on in plain sight, what's going on in areas of science too esoteric for the public to be interested in or understand?

In the same way Abraham Lincoln didn't really end slavery, as his admirers claim, but only nationalized it through military conscription and the income tax, frauds like Piltdown Man, the *New York Sun* Moon hoax, and the Cardiff Giant were not eliminated through government involvement in science, they were just taken over by the government—an excellent example is secondhand smoke—to be used for its own purposes.

Often it works the other way. The brilliant promise of thermal depolymerization, which could solve most of our energy problems while dealing effectively with landfill pollution and used tires, has been brutally suppressed. I remember misleading headlines in *Science News* claiming that nobody could replicate Pons and Fleischmann's "cold fusion"—mostly large "prestigious" universities that changed the experimental design—when the body of the article listed many more that had stuck with the design and proven that catalytic fusion is real.

There is another danger to real science here: the transparent fraud that is "climate change" is now being used by unscrupulous religionists to cast doubt on the reality of evolution by natural selection. This particular slippery slope leads directly downward into a new Dark Age. Thanks in large measure to Albert Gore and humbugsters like him—and what their behavior has to teach us—we can no longer be confident with the results produced by what is represented today as "science." Did smoking or chewing tobacco ever cause cancer? Who can say? Will using cellular telephones give us brain tumors? We might as well consult someone who looks for the truth in chicken entrails.

Science is too important to be left in the hands of government. In 19th century England, before the development of the greedy, voracious, income-taxing state, it was possible for "amateur" scientists, "living on the interest" to make all of the important discoveries in fields ranging from bacteriology and chemistry to astronomy and what became astrophysics.

What the United States of America need most, if they wish to undo the damage done to them by political correctness, and regain their previous position as the world's leaders in scientific endeavor and the exploration of the universe, is a Constitutional amendment mandating formal separation of science—especially medicine—and state.

Separation of science and state.

If At First You Don't Secede

You cannot force me to agree with you. You can force me
to act as though I agreed with you—but then you'll have
to watch your back. All the time.

—L. NEIL SMITH

I heard an idiot on the radio this morning proclaiming grandly that the sovereign remedy for all the nation's problems is to impose a heavy tariff on all imported products, so that people are economically compelled to buy only those things that are produced in America, by Americans.

A log-jam immediately began to pile up in my mind, consisting of all of the many things that are not only wrong, but wrong-headed about this silly-assed notion, the first being, by what right does this guy think he can steal from me or tell me with whom I will be allowed to do business?

Right behind it, came the realization that it has all been tried before, time and time again, and has, virtually without fail, almost invariably generated nothing but disasters of historically heroic proportions.

I confess that I have only included the weasel-words "virtually" and "almost" so you'll think I'm more reasonable than I really am. The fact is, this is one of the worst ideas ever generated by a power-hungry human brain, nakedly greedy for the fruits of somebody else's labor.

But, as usual, I digress.

A tariff, in case you're feeling shy about asking, is a special tax levied on merchandise or materials imported from other countries.

Back in the 1960s, for example, American automobile companies and the automobile workers' unions were unwilling to compete with the cheaper, higher-quality products being shipped here, mostly by Japan. Instead of trying to make better, cheaper products themselves, they leaned on their bought-and-paid-for politicians, who obligingly added about four thousand dollars (in 1960s money) to the price of the average Japanese import.

Sounds like a good deal all around, doesn't it? The car companies get to stay in business. The workers get to keep their jobs. The government gets a lot of extra moolah. The only ones who get screwed are the Productive Class who have a crappy choice between driving a pile of Detroit road-garbage or paying four grand extra for a decent car.

Four grand they might have spent on a better home (that was a lot of money in those days), a better bathroom, modern appliances, their children's dental bills, their college educations, or several hundred pairs of shoes. Four grand savagely ripped out of their pockets by corrupt politicians, lazy and obsolescent manufacturers, and union drones whose products—if they came out of the factory on a hangover Monday or a Friday being celebrated early—consumers were wise to avoid.

There are many historians and economists who will claim that one of those disasters was World War II that, if not directly caused by the Smoot-Hawley Tariff Act of 1930, which raised the import taxes on over 20,000 items to record levels (and without a doubt lengthened the Depression by at least five years), was certainly made unavoidable by it. I cannot attest to this myself because it is not within my area of expertise. I do know for sure that the American conflict erroneously known as the "Civil War" was the direct and inevitable result of tariffs.

Prior to 1860, although Southerners amounted to only a minor fraction of the American population, they were paying 80% of the national government's bills, through the taxes extorted from them because they concentrated on producing crops, rather than finished goods they needed that were cheaper to obtain from Europe which was also willing to pay more for Southern cotton and sugar than the North was.

Already restive about this inequity, Southerners became incensed—and rightfully so—when the newly-elected Lincoln government made moves to double or quadruple the tariffs, which would have reduced every member of the Productive Class below the Mason-Dixon line to peonage.

It is by no means any accident of history that the first shot of the resulting unpleasantness—a war of secession, exactly like the American Revolution, fought for almost identical reasons (a civil war is one in which two sides struggle for control of the same government, something that does not describe the War Between the States at all)—was fired symbolically at a federal customs collecting establishment known as Fort Sumter, located in the harbor mouth of Charleston, South Carolina.

The War Between the States happened because the politicians and mercantilist lords of the industrial North didn't give a damn—any more than they appear to do today—that they were making life impossible for those who labored to pay the bills. They had the brass gall to criticize the "peculiar institution" of black chattel slavery, while often keeping slaves themselves, and seeking to make slaves out of everybody—black and white alike—who lived in the agricultural South.

Which brings us to today...

A teacher of mine once told me that there are more than fifteen million federal laws. You can get arrested, fined, even imprisoned for exercising many—if not most—of the rights once guaranteed to Americans by their Constitution. While the average federal employee receives twice the salary that his private sector equivalent does, and politicians fly across the country and around the world in luxurious jets or ride with their mistresses or trophy wives to their mansions in limousines, taxes, and the burden of regulation, deprive the Productive Class of at least seven eighths of what we work so hard to earn.

That's right, I said seven eighths. Taxes consume half of what we earn. Taxes double the price of everything we buy. And regulations double the price all over again. We all live on one-eighth of what we earn. A once-free people have been reduced to the status of medieval serfs.

Tax slaves.

Repeating all of the mistakes made by antebellum Washington, the most recent couple of regimes have seemed intent on making it too expensive once again—and too humiliating—to remain an American citizen.

They have increased taxes and regulations to the breaking point and made it virtually impossible for ordinary individuals to do business.

They have created and unleashed on Americans one brutal, intrusive, dangerously armed, unconstitutional bureaucracy after another. You can be arrested, fined, and jailed for filling in a mud puddle on your own property. Or shooting a thief driving off in your car.

They have forced massive alterations to the nation's architecture for the sake of handicapped individuals, which would have paid for medical research into growing new limbs and curing degenerative diseases. They even tell you what kind of toilet you can have in your home.

They have imposed a "healthcare" system on us—against our clearly-expressed will—which is actually a gigantic tax hike and an endless supply of excuses to peer into every intimate crevice of our lives. And for the sake of your health you can be jailed for not complying.

They have repeatedly accused anyone who disagrees with them about virtually anything at all, anyone who reads the wrong books written by the wrong authors, anyone who upholds and defends the Bill of Rights, anyone who practices a religion that embarrasses them or of which they disapprove, anyone who owns firearms, anyone who votes for politically incorrect candidates—or anyone who happens to be one of those politically incorrect candidates themselves—of being potential terrorists.

In so doing, they have provided local and state police officers with a license to kill—at the sight of an unapproved bumper sticker.

Refusing, for the lowest, dirtiest, most political of reasons—they burn to give non-citizens the power to vote for them—to control the nation's borders from armies of kidnappers and murderers, they have attempted to prevent states like Arizona from protecting themselves.

Maybe our glorious leaders are simply jealous of Russia's Putin because they don't have Chechens of their own to slaughter and oppress. Maybe they're anxious to show the United Nations gangsters they look up to how eager they are to impose Agenda 21—the 21st-century equivalent of the Highland Clearances—on an unwilling populace.

Whatever their reasons—it may be that they crave an excuse to use troops, tanks, and perhaps even neutron bombs to control an unruly population—they are making it more and more likely that large areas of the United States of America where people value what the Founding Fathers carved out for us, will decide to go their own, independent way.

When the country was born, and a central government was formed by the original thirteen colonies, it was assumed that any of those colonies—independent republics—was free to make that choice. On more than one occasion, the threat of secession—by New England, for example—was sufficient to correct the policies of that central government. The possibility of secession became one of the "checks and balances."

However, when the Southern states attempted to exercise their legal right to withdraw their sanction from the central government, Abraham Lincoln's Administration knew it could never survive the loss of revenue it needed to convert the country into a firmly knit-together fascist state. It illegally crushed the South in a war that took 620,000 lives, injured many more, and destroyed billions of dollars of accumulated assets that it took more than a century to rebuild. Today, "Honest Abe" would be arrested, tried, convicted and hanged for war crimes.

As a science fiction writer, I've made many accurate predictions about future events. I predicted the laptop computer (although it looked more like an iPad) and the Internet (I called it the Telecom system). I predicted the collapse of the Soviet Union, a world trend against Marxism. I predicted that the United States would run against that trend, embrace Marxism, and start a long, agonizing slide into ruin.

At this point, I believe that the right of states to secede from the federal union is about to be tested again. Many state legislatures have passed resolutions underlining the Tenth Amendment which ignores the coercive "resolution" forced on them by Lincoln's war and reserves the unenumerated powers to the states. Others have asserted a right to ignore federal gun laws. Arizona is being pressed to the limit, and the governor of Texas has openly discussed the possible necessity of secession.

It will start with federal thugs and bureaucrats being thrown in jail by local peace officers when they attempt to interfere with people's rights by enforcing unconstitutional laws. Where it will end—given a national government absolutely bereft of anything even remotely resembling moral scruples—nobody can predict, although I don't believe this government or these politicians would hesitate to reduce a rebellious city to glowing radioactive slag as an example to others.

On the other hand, there is some evidence that there are still individuals within the U.S. military—possibly a majority—who take their oath seriously, would resist unlawful orders, and would never permit the civilian government to commit such a murderous atrocity.

One thing is absolutely certain: even with all of the attendant inconveniences and perils of independent nationhood, a free Texas, or Arizona, or Montana would be better off than they are now, sucked dry by the gaping and insatiable maw of government run amok, crushed under the thumb of the left-wing socialist Obama Administration—or than they were, crushed under the thumb of the right-wing socialist Bush Administration.

Shall we let Texas go? If we do, given decent constitutional guarantees of life, liberty, and property, how many of us would move there? I've told correspondents I would head for the border myself so quickly I would leave bright blue streaks of Cherenkov radiation in my wake. A Texas republic that genuinely and enthusiastically enforced individual rights—particularly rights of property and the freedom to do business—would quickly become the wealthiest nation in the world.

On the other hand, should the United States of America secede from New York, Massachusetts, Illinois, and the People's Republic of California?

That might be an even better idea.

How Many Stupid Years?

Manned spaceflight versus robotics? Let's see...on your wedding night, would you be satisfied to send in a remote, and receive telemetered progress reports?

—L. NEIL SMITH

For a long time, thanks principally to the great teacher Robert LeFevre, I have been saying that the overarching tragedy of the human species is that all of our best attributes—courage, integrity, and more than any other characteristic, intelligence—are not additive in quality. Two people aren't braver than one person, nor are two people more principled than one under pressure, nor are two people any smarter.

On the other hand, all of our worst attributes—primarily brute force—are additive. Two people are inarguably stronger than one person.

Another attribute human beings possess is a regrettable propensity to react to sufficiently shocking events by allowing themselves to be stampeded like buffalo, straight over the nearest cliff. You may even call it "Chugwater Politics," that being a little town in Wyoming, named by Indians for the noise a herd of buffalo makes when they hit the ground after being stampeded over a cliff. We properly call that attribute stupidity; it is perhaps the most additive of all human attributes.

Four decades ago, as a result of the voluntary cooperation of tens of thousands of human beings attempting to add their intelligence together (admittedly and deplorably at the involuntary expense of the American taxpayer), three men clambered into something like a large conical dumpster and allowed themselves to be blasted into space toward the single large natural satellite of humanity's native planet. Once there, two of them descended from orbit, walked around, planted a flag, took some samples, then climbed back into lunar orbit and came home.

If you doubt that it happened that way—or that it happened at all—you might as well stop reading right here, and go look at the funny papers or something. Unquestionably, there have been a lot of ugly conspiracies in the history of the world, but this wasn't one of them.

A great deal has been said, in the many years that have passed since that event, and five similar landings that followed, about that mission and its meaning. Four pretty stupid decades, forty-one stupid years, in the view of those of us who had hoped that landing on the Moon might somehow change the outlook, and, thereby, the destiny, of humanity.

In some ways, it was the noblest thing that human beings ever accomplished. In other ways it was the silliest and most futile. We all supposed that it was a first step—for all of humanity, not just for USDA Grade A-stamped supermen—to the stars. To our disappointment, that part turned out to be a very nasty, very painful lie. What NASA's Apollo XI mission has come to represent instead, historically and psychologically, is a not-so-cheap publicity stunt, commemorating not the great purposefulness and the power of the unfettered human mind, but the purposelessness—and the power—of the modern managerial state.

Others have said it far better than me. Victor Koman's monumental novel *Kings of the High Frontier* identified and forced us all to confront a grim reality that many of us were loath to acknowledge: any rational analysis of the government's "space program" reveals that its principal assignment is to prevent ordinary human beings of the non-government-approved variety from ever leaving the Earth. I don't recall that Koman ever offered a coherent reason for this policy, beyond a reluctance we know all too well, on the part of those who believe they own us, to let go of our lives. As Freeman K. Dyson put it, once we get out there among the asteroids, the IRS will never find us.

And they know it.

But there's another reason, one I don't remember if I've written about publicly before (I've mentioned it in private correspondence), but which I think represents a much more compelling motivation for those who believe they own us to keep all of humanity penned up on this mudball than the mere enjoyment of power. Unless something very difficult to change changes nonetheless, we'll all be penned up here forever, and our children, and their children, until the sun burns out.

Remember Robert A. Heinlein's saga of the Lunar revolution, *The Moon Is a Harsh Mistress*, one of the cornerstones of the libertarian movement? Remember how it ends? If I'm right, it's also one of the cornerstones of the government's effort to keep us all trapped here on Earth.

The other cornerstone, as it were, is the epoch-making studies of scientists Luis and Walter Alvarez, who discovered that the dinosaurs were probably wiped out by a giant rock falling on this planet from space.

The Alvarezes showed us what falling rocks can do.

Heinlein showed us how to make them fall.

You and I read works of literature like Heinlein's to inspire us in our struggle for individual liberty. But there are dweebs who work for the government who read books like *The Moon Is a Harsh Mistress* to feed the paranoia of a new parasitic class. Remember those geeky kids you run into at science fiction conventions, usually unkempt, pimply-faced, and overweight, wearing makeshift uniforms and armbands or badges that say "Security"? Well, eventually, some of those kids grow up to populate the NSA, NASA, and the Department of Homeland Security.

Sieg heil.

They are the Security Class; they will be the death of the human race, or at least of its dreams, which amounts to pretty much the same thing.

Yes, I know that there are purely civilian efforts to get mankind into space. I find their delicate, fledgling spacecraft, so different from the crude, lumbering hardware the government uses, incomparably beautiful, and just seeing them on the ground or in the air gives me hope.

Yet at some point, I suspect, they will hit a limit, beyond which government won't let them pass. Unless we manage to change things, you and I will never be allowed into space because we might launch a rock from the Moon (or simply nudge a handy meteoroid) and do to Chicago or Beijing what nineteen murderous fanatics did to the World Trade Center. And now that 9/11 has actually happened, the Security Class has all the "proof" any lunatic requires to believe that you and I can never, ever be trusted. Earth is forever to become one enormous, high-walled, inescapable sanitarium, run by its sickest, most pathetic patients.

And we will never get to the Moon again. We will never get to Mars. We will never get to Pallas or Ceres or 5023 Eris or to the stars.

Unless.

It may strike you at first as odd, but the place to begin to set things right, I think, is at the nation's airports, where the Security Class was born. I'm going to say again—until one of the culprits twitches or burps or screams in protest (I accept that none of them will ever apologize or admit that I was right)—that I tried as hard as I could to warn members of the 1977 Libertarian Party national platform committee of the danger to liberty that the then-new airport security measures represented. I predicted that they would grow more Draconian, and that they would inevitably spread out to destroy the freedom of an entire nation. I was sneered at and shouted down by the same LP morons who now approve the insane, immoral wars in Iraq and Afghanistan.

A popular war is all the proof anyone needs that intelligence isn't additive.

There's another reason to begin with the airports. They are the Security Class's greatest weakness, its soft underbelly. The simple, horrible truth is that, had these idiots not been in place, violating the unalienable individual, civil, Constitutional, and human right of every man, woman, and responsible child to obtain, own, and carry, openly or concealed, any weapon—rifle, shotgun, handgun, machinegun, anything—any time, any place, without asking any-one's permission, the atrocities of September 11, 2001, would never have happened.

A single individual on each airplane, armed with a .22 caliber revolver, could have stopped those criminals with their pathetic box-knives cold. Even if the hijackers had had their own guns, under a relaxed security regime, they would not have been willing to face an aircraft full of armed passengers. Criminals don't want a fair fight, they want things easy. Knowing that American aircraft passengers were commonly armed would have kept them from even planning such a crime.

For once, I have not digressed. Demonstrating that ordinary people can keep the peace, perfectly well, all by themselves, is absolutely crucial to getting them (meaning us) into space to stay. We will never convince the Security Class that ordinary people can take care of themselves and each other without their "help." Or that, without their "help," ordinary people won't hijack airplanes and drop Moon rocks on Earth's cities simply for the hell of it. To the typical member of the Security Class, civilians are nothing more than criminals who haven't been arrested yet; what's called for there is some very deep and lengthy psychotherapy. But if we can convince a sufficient number of other people, then what the Security Class believes is no longer relevant.

Everyone who ardently hopes that he or she—or maybe just our species in general—has some kind of future Out There beyond Earth's increasingly stuffy atmosphere needs to begin right now to exert every bit of political pressure possible to accomplish three tightly-braided objectives.

First, all 25,000-odd gun laws in this country must be repealed, nullified, or otherwise disposed of. Second only to this country's psychotic foreign policy, they are what make America vulnerable to terrorism.

Second, as a subset of the first objective, universal reciprocal "Vermont Carry" must be the rule all across this country. That means no government could require you to get a carry permit. It is what the Constitution mandates, and with the exposure of victim disarmament as a proven killer, it is what experience guided by intelligence must demand.

Third, as a subset of the second objective, both the government and the nation's airlines must be prevented from keeping passengers from carrying personal weapons with them in flight. Contrary to the opinion of many, airlines are corporations, and as such, they are simply an extension of the government. Despite the recent maunderings of the Supreme Court, corporations have no rights. On the other hand, they do have the same positive obligation that the rest of government has, to uphold and enforce the Bill of Rights, including the Second Amendment.

Likewise, if millions of individuals are active in space, free to pursue their own selfish interests, they stand a vastly better chance of preventing, stopping, or intercepting an interplanetary 9/11 than any government body. Exactly as it happened on Earth, where violent crime soared at the same time one administration after another spent billions on police personnel and technology in a futile attempt to deal with it, but fell precipitously when civilians started carrying guns, an armed citizenry will beat the Space Patrol to the punch every time.

Ending victim disarmament is only the first step. The abysmal political events that have followed September 11 are a clear signal that it's time to dismantle the security state totally and forever. It's the whole argument about freedom versus security in a nutshell. Every time some idiot suggests that you give up another part of your liberty for the sake of "safety," remind him that the most famous advocates of that philosophy ended up being tried and hanged at Nuremburg.

All of this will be difficult at first. It will be embarrassing and quite possibly dangerous as the government grows bolder and more violent every day. But September 11 is a demonstration, a remarkably vivid one, of the "clear and present danger" that victim disarmament poses. And the alternative is giving up, allowing this poor battered planet of ours to become a dark, dreary futureless prison from this day until the end of time. Personally, the prospect of never getting to see the rings of Saturn from one of its inner moons is too sad to contemplate.

And unacceptable.

We're supposed to be satisfied—entertained and mollified—by spectacular photographs from unmanned flights to places like Jupiter, or by robotic missions to sift the sands of Mars. And yet it isn't the composition of soil on some random planetoid that I give a damn about, but a chance to stand on the surface of that planetoid ourselves, our feet spread wide, our hands on our hips, surveying humanity's new domain.

I want that future for my child.

Hell, I still want it for myself.

What was it you always wanted to see...Out There?

Cigareets and Whiskey

Mrs. Grundy is dead. Tell me what you think, not what you think other people think. If you voted in terms of what you're ready for, instead of what you've convinced yourself others are ready for, we'd have had Constitutional government, a Libertarian society, and eradicated socialism half a century ago.

—L. NEIL SMITH

My paternal grandmother Mabel Fern Boot Kidd Smith (as she often called herself) may have been one of the last living members of the Prohibition-era Women's Christian Temperance Union. She voted the Prohibition ticket whenever she could, which, amazingly, a person can still do here in Colorado. She wore a corset (not the fun kind) and jersey dresses (not the sexy Pointer Sisters kind) and dressed and undressed in her bedroom closet whether anybody else was in the house or not. Best of all, she referred to intimate relations with her husband as "bedroom duties." She must have been loads of fun in the sack.

My grandmother was Mrs. Grundy in the flesh.

Somehow, Mabel managed to color my dad's attitude toward alcohol (a single drink could make him throw up, although he didn't care if other people drank) and my own, in turn. It took a long time and a lot of growing up to teach us both better. While it's absolutely true that certain individuals drink too much, and that others probably shouldn't drink at all, it's equally true that such a decision rests with nobody but the individual involved. Alcohol is a benign pleasure for most people, one that's sometimes all that makes living tolerable. And more lives have been destroyed by Prohibitionism than by beer, wine, or whiskey.

When "our boys" were busy out of town, putting Kaiser Bill in his place, their do-gooding womenfolk—including the self-sainted Mabel—gulled by religious snake oil salesmen, put the wheels under the campaign to steal the beer right out from under their menfolk's noses with the 1919 Volstead Act. What a splendid reward to come home to, after making the world safe for democracy: no booze, and "bedroom duties."

And if you believe that turf wars, drive-by shootings, deadly overdoses and poisonings on bad product, violent and power-hungry federal thugs trampling down the Bill of Rights, and a general misuse of fully automatic weapons on all sides, are exclusive features of the War on Drugs, then you need a little serious self-educating. (Robert Stack was a gun-guy and fine gentleman, and I have nothing against Kevin Costner; however, you wouldn't have wanted to know the real Elliot Ness.) Each of those items, along with many another charming and gory custom, were gifts to American society bestowed by alcohol prohibition.

Alcohol consumption, of course, is far from the only activity demonized by the mental midgets and ethically stunted prigs who are sick and driven to control the lives of others because they have no lives of their own in what we used to jokingly call the land of the free. Every time nobody is looking, they add something new to the list.

The mirror that the issue of smoking holds up to our vaunted civilization presents a disturbing, shameful, and revolting image composed of bald-faced lies, ill-disguised bigotry, rank hypocrisy, and naked oppression. It fully confirms my mother's observation—which she first shared with me when my age was still in single digits—that the lower that an individual sinks in some moral sense, the more he needs to keep somebody lower than he is, so he can look down on them.

Let's begin by dismissing the question of smoking and health as the red herring it is. In light of the recent, massive, worldwide pseudoscientific hoax called Global Warming, it might even become appropriate to reexamine whatever "science" may have originally been employed in the determination that tobacco smoking causes cancer and other respiratory diseases. I was young at the time, but personally, I don't remember ever seeing any studies quoted, do you? And now that we know how science really works in today's world, why should we believe them?

I do know that Prohibitionists are liars when it comes to things like "secondhand smoke," because I watched that lie being carefully constructed, right before my eyes. During the first Bush regime, the Environmental Protection Agency was ordered to "study" the presumed health hazards of secondhand smoke. When that agency reported (uncharacteristically for an outfit like the EPA, which is why I believe them) that there exist no such hazards, an infuriated Bush Administration ordered them to go back and find some. Failing, they presented their results in the form of a bar graph—only they pulled an old Madison Avenue mind-trick—displaying only the tops of the bars, to exaggerate differences where, in fact, there were almost none.

And this is the kind of "scientific integrity" that eventually brought us to a point where another snake oil salesman, Albert Gore, can win an Academy Award and a Nobel Prize, among other things by claiming with a straight face that cigarette smoking causes global warming. If I were a Nobel laureate—especially after they gave one to Barack Obama—I'd bundle the damn thing up and send it back to Scandinavia.

Postage-due.

If it's real science that we're looking for here, why isn't the apparent therapeutic value of tobacco ever mentioned by any of these "researchers" with regard to Alzheimer's Disease and Parkinson's? Why don't any of these medical "authorities" ever remind us that tobacco smoke was commonly used by physicians at the turn of the 20th century to treat asthma in young children—and that it appears to have worked?

I haven't smoked a cigarette since 1993, when I had two mild heart attacks and needed to stop. Before then, I smoked two packs a day for thirty years, having started back when I was a freshman in college. I thoroughly enjoyed smoking, and was genuinely sorry I had to quit. In my time, beginning in 1964, I happily consumed Camels, Luckies, Pall Malls (both filtered and unfiltered), Winstons, Salems, English Ovals, Half & Half (pipe tobacco in cigarette drag), Parliaments, Kools, Marlboros, Gaulois, and Gitanes. I may be the last individual alive ever to have smoked Sweet Caporals. The final decade, it was mostly Marlboros, but I was smoking Nate

Shermans—in an attempt to cut down (because they're extremely good but were prohibitively expensive, even way back then)—when I experienced the first of two myocardial infarctions.

When I first came to Colorado State University in 1964, a pack of Winstons cost a mere 35 cents (a gallon of gas was about the same) and there was a little store near campus that sold Mexican cigarettes (no, not that kind of Mexican cigarettes), in pinstriped brown paper for 20 cents. Thanks to the form of government larceny we call inflation, the prices, for cigarettes, gas, and everything else, rose over time. Having quit, I hadn't paid much attention to prices for a while, so you can imagine my surprise and horror when I was in a liquor store recently and discovered that the price of a pack of smokes is up to $4.76!

Almost all of that increase is taxation, usually justified by a phony concern for people's health or for the healthcare system. And yet, even if smoking does cause cancer or emphysema, it's purely a matter of individual choice, and nobody else's business. Don't let them hand you any of that crap about smokers being a burden on taxpayers who are forced to pay for their medical care. This is the same line of guff we hear about motorcycle helmets. It isn't the smoker's fault (unless he voted for collectivists) that this crybaby culture has foolishly adopted socialized medicine—long before Obama or even the Woman with One Eyebrow—along with all the liabilities that entails.

There are three types of individuals where the political issue of smoking is concerned: smokers, non-smokers, and anti-smokers. As I have said, I was a smoker myself for thirty years—at least two packs a day—until I was compelled to give it up for health reasons. I had two heart attacks, and nicotine, it turns out, causes corpuscles to clump together, greatly increasing the likelihood of another heart attack.

I never claimed that smoking was a good or healthy thing to do, but I enjoyed it, as I had every right to do, and I still rather like the smell of people smoking. I remember very well the first cigarette I ever smoked, in 1964, and I remember the last, nearly twenty years ago.

Now, perforce, I have become a non-smoker. I can't say that I feel particularly better, but I do get a lot more done (cigarettes are, hands down, the most effective procrastination devices ever invented) and the dust in my house miraculously changed almost overnight from this brown, tacky substance (nasty on the shoulders of your clothing in the closet) to something gray and fluffy. Nor can I say I miss smoking—I certainly don't miss paying for it—but it would never occur to me to begrudge anyone else whatever pleasure they derive from it.

Anti-smokers are something else altogether. The political battle in my hometown—over whether restaurant owners ought to be allowed to exercise their unalienable individual, civil, Constitutional, and human right to run their business as they decide—convinced me that it isn't smoking itself that anti-smokers are violently against, it's the enjoyment that others find in it. If an anti-smoker saw a smoker 100 yards away through a 10-inch plate glass window, taking a puff, leaning her head back and closing her eyes to enjoy it, then exhaling the smoke from her mouth and nostrils, the anti-smoker would collapse in a tizzy of anger and frustration. French inhaling would leave him comatose.

As H.L. Mencken observed, what we're dealing with here is a broken personality, somebody who wakes up in the middle of the night, sweaty and trembling in terror at the idea that somewhere, someone might be happy.

Now we hear that the Obama Administration, thanks largely to a round-heeled Democratic Congress greedily spreading its legs to the proposition, like the sanctimonious, hypocritical, power-hungry, dogwhistles they truly are, will call upon the federal Food and Drug Administration to regulate tobacco products as if they were narcotics, when in fact the FDA shouldn't be regulating narcotics, and shouldn't really exist at all, under the United States Constitution as it was written.

So much for the Democrats' fabled sympathy toward the working poor who do most of the smoking, drinking—and cigarette-tax paying—in this culture. Here's hoping that all you union guys will remember this day. Otherwise, another day will come, sooner than you believe, when you will have to go to a dreary government store, stand in a long gray line, and when you finally reach the window, surrender your money, your signature, and your Social Security Number (you will already have surrendered your face to the camera on the wall behind the counter) to some slovenly, unshaven bureaucrat smelling of sour, unwashed clothing, in exchange for a ten-pack of horrible-tasting generic cigarettes manufactured under the close supervision of the federal government.

As time goes on, they'll want your fingerprints, and your DNA and retinal scans, too. And as the filtered part of your cigarette grows longer, the tobacco part will shrink. Ever see what they smoke in Russia?

It says here 21 percent of the American public smokes cigarettes. (I'd bet almost anything the real number is higher; I've seen the same pollster lie about guns and the Vietnam war.) There being 300,000,000 Americans, that means at least 63,000,000 of them smoke, a number comparable to that of gun owners, and half again the number of blacks or Hispanics, two minorities politicians tend to pay close attention to.

The same pollsters assert that smokers are "too diffuse" a group to be useful to any party or individual candidate; besides, most smokers say they want to quit. (That much is true; I spent most of my 30 smoking years saying I wanted to quit, and occasionally trying, but it took the poleaxe of a heart attack to make me do it for once and always.)

Another reason it's hard to organize smokers is that government, the media, and the schools have been making them feel guilty about their habit for more than three generations, and now that Gang of Three—schools, media, and government—holds most of them by the gonads. Guilt is a solitary affliction and keeps people apart from one another.

Nevertheless, any pro-freedom candidate or party worthy of the name must include, high in its priorities, the abolition of all taxes on alcohol and tobacco. Tens of millions drink and smoke. Some of them are pretty tired of being extorted for it. The votes generated by that one promise could change the course of history. What's more, under the Fourteenth Amendment, which offers equal protection for everyone under the law, such taxes are clearly discriminatory, and therefore illegal already.

Alcohol and tobacco have paid more than their fair share, if there is such a thing. It's long past time to remove exorbitant, punitive, religiously motivated taxes on them, along with the oppressive and unconstitutional requirement that any stage of their cultivation, manufacture, distribution, or sale be licensed and supervised by the single most corrupt and murderous bureaucracy within the federal government.

What smokers need is a smokers' union—I'd join up in a minute, as a "smoker emeritus"—to identify their common interests, provide certain benefits, and put a finger on the disgusting politicians who prey on them. It might begin as a smokers' caucus of the Libertarian Party—but beware of opposition from LINOs: Libertarians In Name Only.

However that turns out, if you smoke—if you ever smoked—you must promise yourself, right now, that as long as you live, you will never vote for another Democrat or "country club" Republican again. These are the lowlives who helped to ram the Patriot Act through. Twice. These are the lowlives who expanded the War on Drugs until it became a War on Everything. These are the lowlives who, at the local level, find excuses every day to steal your property, your pets, and even your children. And these are the lowlives who casually decide for restaurant owners whether to allow smoking in their establishments or not.

These are the lowlives who did this to you—the FDA regulation, the $4.76 a pack, the no smoking even in restaurants that would prefer to allow it, the huddling in the broiling sun or freezing rain outside your office building trying to get a nicotine break—and they are the lowlives who must be forced to pay. Vote for any candidate or party that will treat you with respect. I'd be very interested to see where Congressman Ron Paul, a physician and libertarian, stands on all this.

In the end, there can be only one resolution: abolish the Food and Drug Administration and the Bureau of Alcohol, Tobacco, Firearms, and Explosives, as well. Neither is sanctioned by Article I, Section 8 of the Constitution, which makes them nothing but gangs of outlaws, bent on stealing our money and destroying the last tattered vestiges of our freedom. Both have murdered more individuals than they claim to have saved.

Now if you're gonna write to tell me smoking's bad, or that people who do it—especially near kids and pets—should be castrated with a rusty chainsaw and baked in clay over a slow fire, you can just save it.

Better yet, stuff it.

Having never been permitted to hear half of all the facts about tobacco, you are operating out of an ignorance thoughtfully provided by the schools, the media, and the government. Check out those connections it has historically with Alzheimer's, Parkinson's, and asthma.

Whatever the truth may be, my life is none of the government's business.

And neither is yours.

What this demonstrates to me, all over again, is that we need a new Constitutional amendment mandating a formal separation of science—especially medicine—and state if we're ever to get at something resembling the truth about smoking or any of a dozen other medical issues.

A third-party presidential candidate isn't going to win. Get used to it. His best value to the cause of freedom lies in the fact that he and his party can afford to tell certain otherwise "unspeakable" truths, among them the fact that tobacco smokers are being treated today the way black people were treated 75 years ago. It is nothing short of barbaric to force them to huddle out in the rain, snow, or in the blistering heat. In many cities, they're not even allowed to do that anymore! It's even worse to tell the owner of a restaurant what he has to do with his own property with regard to smoking or anything else.

Raising the political consciousness of smokers could awaken a sleeping giant and place a freedom-oriented party in at least second place, displacing one of the traditional parties. On the other hand, if self-styled freedom advocates continue to display the same bigotry and intolerance toward smokers that people in other parties do, they don't even deserve the place—a very distant third—they occupy today.

Start with the kids. They already know, thanks to Clinton, Bush, and Obama—plus crippling taxes politicos are so fond of extracting from those who actually do something for a living, plus regulations that bind the Productive Class hand and foot—that they have no real future to look forward to, nothing but endless grubbing on an assembly line or in some blind corporate cubicle, plus the prospect of endless war.

And yet some of you idiots out there would make it worse by begrudging these poor, futureless waifs, these orphans of history, a crummy beer or a smoke? Maybe you ought to spend the same time and energy that you're wasting now—trying to keep young people from drinking and smoking—on making this a free and decent country again.

Try giving America's children a future worth looking forward to, so they won't feel a need to escape it, before you start nagging them again.

Political Taxonomy

Believe what you like about "wasting your vote,"
nothing will ever alter a fundamental assumption on
the part of Democrats, Republicans—and the vast,
despotic bureaucracy they've created together—that even
the slightest manifestation of individuality (let alone
of individualism) is a threat that must be dealt with
immediately and harshly.

—L. NEIL SMITH

Left, Right, Center.

Okay, class, let's review what life has taught us so far.

To begin with, forget the old, conventional right-left political spectrum that has failed so pathetically to describe or predict actual behavior in the political universe. I know, it's what we were taught in high school and college. It's what they still blather about on television.

But it's television, get it? It's TV.

And when the old, conventional right-left model doesn't work (at what point, for example, on the conventional right-left political spectrum can you find the position or people who won't tax you?), when it runs into some activity or object that it can't explain, then its practitioners and apologists—I've heard them admit this openly to a classroom full of students—simply throw out the inconvenient data. So if you're a Randite, say, or a Henry Georgist, or any one of a small handful of other "unconventional" political persuasions, your views and your votes won't count, not in the Bizarro world of PoliSci 101.

Thanks, Justin Raimondo, for a concept that explains so much.

For the sake of this conversation, you can even forget about the lovely diamond-shape of the Nolan-Fritz diagram ("The World's Smallest Political Quiz") that libertarians have been circulating for decades, and which is a quantum leap away from what got pounded into each of us in civics and political science classes. At the root, all politics breaks down into a choice between some variety of collectivism, and individualism.

Between those who believe that, at need, you or I can be killed, and cooked, and eaten for the greater good of something that they've defined as bigger or more important than we are—and those who do not.

Individualism is a pretty straightforward proposition, as concepts go, although it's a choice that hasn't been particularly popular over the last ten thousand years or so among those who run things and those who want things—but don't want to have to think them up, or work for them.

Individualism is the choice that's closest to the truth, the most consistent with physics and biology. Not to reiterate the greatest advocates of the idea unduly, individualism argues that the individual is the only real component of any given group—that, in a physical and moral sense, there is no such thing as a group, but only an aggregation of individuals—and that no individual is under any obligation that he doesn't explicitly accept to recognize the existence of any group or to inconvenience himself in any way for its sake.

It's up to them, of course, members of the group, to make the individual's participation worth his while, which is the great bargain upon which all civilization rests. Break that bargain, cheat the individual—and I mean any individual—out of what he is due, and whatever else is left that falsely calls itself civilization deserves nothing except contempt, ignominy, and destruction. That's the reason civilization today is in a state of collapse. Ayn Rand was right, and Thomas Hobbes had it exactly the wrong way around. "Leviathan"—the so-called Sovereign—desperately needs the individual for its survival.

There are, indeed, some things that I would willingly give my life to defend, but I reserve the absolute right to choose them for myself, I refuse steadfastly to let those things be chosen for me, and I refuse to recognize anything as bigger or more important than I am, myself.

I am not a national resource.

And neither are you.

Those who don't feel secure enough to stand on their own two feet, physically or mentally or morally (or who have dedicated their lives professionally to exploiting the sad unfortunates who suffer from that shortcoming)—and, as a consequence, are inclined to identify more with the group than with the individual—naturally hate and fear individualism. They have done everything within their power, by all evidence over the entire span of those ten thousand years, to destroy it.

That they have failed abjectly to do so, and feel compelled to keep up a constant and clamorous cultural litany against it—in myth and legend, poetry, literature, and drama, not to mention virtually every form of music—is a strong indication of its powerful natural validity.

Robert A. Heinlein warned us that slavery—the use of one human being by another as property—is a vile, pernicious, and persistent predilection, a filthy habit that always, sooner or later, finds a way to worm its way back into any civilization in an endless number of guises.

One of those guises is socialism, a criminal scam masquerading cynically as a legitimate ideology that—at best—promises to enslave each and every one of us to one another, but which, in point of historical fact, merely enslaves us all to an aristocracy—the nomenklatura—as arrogant and privileged as any royal bloodline ever was, but which lacks the faintest redeeming shred of noblesse oblige.

If you need an example, take a hard look at the ranks of bizarre cartoon characters, each of them more evil, dimwitted, or insane than the others, who have comprised both the Barack Obama and Bill Clinton Administrations.

I believe it was Ludwig von Mises who noted the central fallacy of socialism: that customs and relationships that exist naturally between members of a family can be extended to others—say, to a community, to a region, to a nation, or to an entire planet—and function as well as they do in their original setting. Von Mises also observed, if I recall correctly, that the principal attraction of socialism is that invariably, its most ardent advocates secretly all imagine themselves finishing up at the top of the sociopolitical pyramid when, in ironic fact, it is usually the earliest advocates of a socialist revolution who are the first to be rounded up and liquidated by the new regime, since, by succeeding, they have proven themselves to be dangerous subversives.

Over slightly more than two centuries of its existence, socialism has broken itself into a thousand factions, usually due to quarreling over stolen goods exactly like any other gang of robbers. Communalism, communitarianism, mutualism might be thought of as gateways to the total surrender of your personal sovereignty, of your very selfhood. It may be true that sharing what you have with your neighbors doesn't seem like such a bad idea—until the neighbors finally discover that they don't have to work as hard as you do (or at all) to get what you get.

The Pilgrims nearly starved to death under this innocent-seeming arrangement. Too few understand that we celebrate Thanksgiving today because the colonists threw off socialism and returned to individual enterprise.

That's why I fervently support the notion of borders that are open to individuals who wish to escape tyranny and improve their lives and those of their families. It's also why I support the equal right of a free association of individuals called Arizona (I do not refer here to the state, or to the government of the state, but to the people who live and work there because they love it) to resist invaders—mostly spawned, in essence, by drug prohibition—with murderous habits and intentions.

But I digress.

I won't comment here on Marxism, since it has been thoroughly discredited and is only practiced today in American universities, Congress, and the White House. Others, most notably Ayn Rand, have done more than I can to expose the fundamental evil behind the slogan, "From each according to his abilities, to each according to his needs." It's exactly how we all end up in the cannibal pot sooner or later.

Utilitarianism is another early form of socialism, offering "the greatest good for the greatest number" while pursuing the same old collectivist agenda of sacrificing the individual for the sake of the group—or, more frequently, for the sake of the group's leaders. Like any con game, all that any form of socialism needs to grow is a field rich with useful idiots and corruptible fools, each with just a bit of larceny in his heart and a sneaking yen for what his neighbor possesses.

One of the most important things to understand is that two major branches of socialism have been developed over the past couple of centuries. One of them, "left-wing socialism" in the terms employed by libertarian philosopher and lecturer Robert LeFevre, we are all too familiar with, prepared to recognize, and, increasingly, ready to defeat. It is the socialism of Barack Obama, Fidel Castro, Nancy Pelosi, Hugo Chavez, Harry Reid, Mao Tse Tung, and their admirers and followers.

Adolf Hitler was a left-wing socialist.

What's much more difficult, for Americans at least, to identify is the "right-wing socialism" of a George W. Bush. "Progressives" (like "liberal," simply another euphemism for socialist) won't acknowledge it because they find their fraternal-twin relationship with it embarrassing. Conservatives stick their fingers in their ears and chant "I can't hear you!" over and over again, hoping that you'll go away.

But look: no matter what it calls itself, any regime that takes what belongs to you—your rights, your property, your life—in order to achieve some goal that you didn't choose and may not approve of, is sacrificing you for whatever it represents to be something bigger and more important than you are. And that, by definition, is socialism. Rush Limbaugh, Newt Gingrich, Ann Coulter, Sean Hannity, Glenn Beck, G. Gordon Liddy, and Oliver North, are all right-wing socialists.

So was Ronald Reagan.

And any regime that promises it will only do that sort of thing—violate you and use you as a resource—for the duration of some emergency that it has defined and declared, is only promising you that there will be one convenient emergency after another until the end of time.

Or the sun burns out, whichever comes first.

But let's forget about emergencies for a moment and look, instead, at everyday life. What is the proper term for a political regime that fines you annually for owning your home, and then uses this extorted money to forcibly indoctrinate your children, and those of its other victims, so they'll come to believe that such a practice is morally acceptable?

I call it socialism. The public school system—historically, an alien late-comer to the American way of life—is clearly a socialist institution, mindlessly copied from other countries where the lone

232

individual was of no importance and the light of the Constitution was never known to shine, and doomed from the beginning to fail in exactly the same way, and for the same reasons as the late, unlamented Soviet Union.

As I said (or Mirelle Stein said for me) in *Pallas*, there is nothing about the public school system that can be fixed by tinkering with the public school system. The entire structure must be abolished, its buildings emptied of its denizens and then razed to the ground so that not one stone is left standing on another, and salt sown on the ruins.

Thank you, Cato the Elder.

No, I don't care how many fools voted for it—democracy is just another form of collectivism, under which the rights of the supposed minority are routinely sacrificed to the whims of what is represented as a majority—I have a fundamental human right not to be stolen from.

Or enslaved.

And so do you.

Now that the true nature of the public schools is clearer, it becomes easier to examine other examples of right-wing socialism. Why does a nation with a First Amendment in its Constitution have a Federal Communications Commission? Thank that stalwart defender of free enterprise (not), Herbert Hoover who, as a federal bureaucrat, used the First World War as an excuse to seize and nationalize the airwaves.

Why does a nation with a Second Amendment in its Constitution have a Bureau of Alcohol, Tobacco, Firearms, and Explosives, or allow every other faction of government—recently the Environmental Protection Agency (established by Richard Nixon who called privately-held guns an "abomination")—to threaten the individual right to own and carry weapons?

Conservatives scream bloody murder (and rightly so) over Obama's evil "healthcare" scam. Yet they and their corporate symbiotes have benefitted, far beyond our ability to measure or even estimate—and countless millions of ordinary Americans have been stripped of their hard-earned property, their human and Constitutional rights, their very lives—in the name of what is now called "National Security." Back in the 1940s, the catch-phrase was, "Don't you know there's a war on?"

There's always a war on, at least one, on the average, for every generation of Americans ever born. When it isn't a war against "huns" or "nips" or "gooks" it's a war against the right of the individual to medicate himself with anything he wishes in any way he wishes, or it's a war to impose "decency"—as determined by a collection of drunken, crooked, child-buggering old men—on everybody else. Because the important thing, you understand, for the health of the state and the subjugation of everybody else, is to have a war, no matter what it's about.

The clearest indication of what right-wing and left-wing socialism are really all about is the fact that, in the 20th century alone, over a hundred million people were murdered by their own governments, and another hundred million were killed in conflicts between differing brands of socialism. World War II need never have happened (and in any case, America needn't have participated in it) had the winners of the previous war—fought for no discernable reason—not bungled the peace.

In exactly the same way, no matter how conservatives may scream and weep and tear their hair out whenever they're confronted with the unpleasant truth, the attacks on New York and Washington on September 11, 2001, would never have happened had they not been fired by Western interference with the people of the Middle East. Make no mistake: I'm not saying that America or its people are responsible for 9/11, what I'm saying is that their government is, going back at least a dozen administrations.

Decisions and actions supposedly taken for us—whether we wanted them to be or not—squandering our resources and the lives of our children.

Socialism.

And, as Heinlein warned, slavery—in the 20th century form we know as socialism—has begun snaking its way into even the best guarded bastion of individual freedom in the world, the libertarian movement.

Accusing your opponent of being what you, yourself, are is a left-wing tactic so ancient, so threadbare, and so shopworn that it probably predates Saul Alinsky's Neanderthal great-grandfather. And yet left-wing socialists are so dense that they pursue that infantile tactic to this day. In college, four and a half decades ago, I was called a "communist" when I refused to subject myself to military slavery in a war I had not chosen against a people who had done me no harm.

More lately, I have been called a "statist" and a "socialist" myself, because I was, and remain, willing to defend my individual rights against collectivists who have assaulted them—and then attempted to make a "philosophy" out of their pattern of criminal behavior.

The issue, as you may already have anticipated, is "Intellectual Property Rights." The closet collectivists claim that they don't exist, that once whatever you have created is "out there"—in the form of a book, a recording, or a computer file—it's "up for grabs," becoming anybody's property and nobody's property. These parasites usually represent themselves as libertarians, and assert that my insistence on controlling my own creations somehow limits their freedom.

Yet they freely quote Pierre-Joseph Proudhon, a founder of early socialism, famous for declaring "Property is theft," and sneer like a common parlor-pink at anyone who expects to be paid for his effort. I've even seen them quoting the English socialist George Bernard Shaw, infamous racist, eugenicist, genocide, and apologist for Stalinist atrocities.

My view, and that of any working writer, is that what's mine is mine, without regard to how easy it may be to steal (which appears to be their principal "argument") or how difficult it may be to defend. If scavengers like these are free to expropriate the products of my intellect, then, employing different excuses, they can expropriate anything, since everything, a ballpoint pen, a shovel, a tractor, or a uranium mine begins with a thought and is therefore intellectual property.

Everything is intellectual property.

Even more pathetic are those, claiming to be on my side of this issue, who nevertheless urge me, with a surprising degree of passion, not to fight back, apparently because they believe that these thieves represent some kind of unstoppable wave of the future, or perhaps that fighting tyranny is somehow undignified, and I can only damage myself or what I laughingly call my career resisting them. In my time, I've seen unstoppable waves of the future before, and their advice sounds a lot like cowardice and appeasement to me, but I suppose I could be wrong.

That remains to be seen. What I know for sure is that I have been fighting slavery, in one form or another, all of my adult life, since 1962 when I was fifteen years old, just under half a century. Although I may get weary sometimes, and I may get discouraged, and I certainly get disgusted whenever I turn over a rock marked "libertarian" and take a look at what really squirms and crawls and slithers underneath it, as long as I draw breath, my heart beats, and blood pulses through my veins, I will continue to fight against slavery—especially that form we know as socialism—whether it's being advocated by the political left, the political right, or those who falsely claim to be libertarians.

What you do is your choice—that's what it's supposed to be all about.

China Moon

The more fundamental position is the highest ground, allowing the most "perpendicular" attack. If he argues politics, argue ethics—as with punches in a bar-fight, things seldom go beyond this one-two stage. If he argues ethics, argue epistemology (look it up). If he argues epistemology, argue metaphysics. If he argues metaphysics, you're up against Darth Vader and you're in trouble. Switch back to politics and accuse him of being out of touch with everyday reality. Or ask him if he's stopped beating his wife.

—L. NEIL SMITH

'm a novelist by trade, with overwhelming emphasis on science fiction. While many folks believe that "if it's sci-fi it doesn't have to make sense," the truth is, if a science fiction writer doesn't have all his ducks in a row, scientifically and otherwise, his loyal fans will make him think being eaten alive by piranhas is a pleasurable experience.

Over thirty years, I've predicted items like the digital watch, bone-mending electronics, the rise of .40 caliber handguns, the Internet, computer-aided forensics, wall-sized video screens, the laptop computer, and iPads. I even predicted watching movies on your computer.

I'm also a political writer, and sometimes that calls for peering into the future fully as much as writing science fiction does. I have made a number of successful political predictions—the collapse of the Soviet Union, the American embrace of Marxism—and now it's time to make another, one I wholeheartedly hope fails to come true in any respect.

For years—decades, really—I have been saying that there's no good reason to go back to the Moon, or even to pay much attention to Mars.

Aside from some spectacular scenery—which can be enjoyed from orbit, or by means of cameras mounted on unmanned rovers—neither body offers much in the way of attractions: no resources that can improve the average person's existence, no treasure house of mineral wealth that it's worth collecting taxes to extract and bring back home.

The idea of living in one-sixth of Earth's gravity on the Moon, or one-third on Mars is appealing, especially to someone with a bad cardio-vascular medical record, but not the three-gravity ride to get there. And the pioneering days on either world will be arduous and miserable.

Some argue that the Moon represents a necessary and desirable stepping-stone to Mars, but any space scientist who doesn't stand to gain from another Moon program will tell you that going to Mars by way of the Moon is like going from Miami to Houston by way of a shortcut through Moosejaw, Saskatchewan. Add to that the difficulty of going from one deep gravity well, Earth's, that it's difficult and expensive get out of (someone once said it's like climbing a mountain 7000 miles tall), down into another, that of the Moon or Mars, very nearly as deep.

My personal objective, and one I've advised others to pursue, as well, has always been the asteroids: millions of rocks from a few hundred miles in diameter down to a few millimeters, most floating in a broad band between the orbits of Mars and Jupiter. I've always liked islands, and this would be like living on one, with the next asteroid averaging a thousand miles away—only a few minutes by small family rocket.

Asteroids are chock full of resources including plenty of water, and every metal we find useful or valuable. I recall reading that the average nickel-iron asteroid a mile across contains more gold, as a trace element, than the total amount ever mined and refined on Earth in human history. The same for silver, platinum, and so forth. It was iridium that served as the major clue regarding what wiped out the dinosaurs.

Seventy percent of the asteroids, those known as "carbonaceous chondrites," are rich with kerogen, a petroleum-like substance similar to the stuff that turns ordinary western shale into oil shale. Because asteroids are relatively small, everything we want and need is within easy reach of the surface; you don't have to dig deep to get it. With life support measures—a process called terraformation—crops can even be grown there. And, thanks to microgravity which is all such bodies can muster, landing on any of them is essentially the same as docking.

I confess that, as reports keep coming in of discoveries of vast amounts of water on the Red Planet, and the possibility of life forms under the surface (the findings of the original Viking lander are currently being reexamined; great care must be taken to make sure they aren't used by environmental fascists to keep humans from exploring and exploiting the planet), Mars has grown more interesting and enticing. But it turns out there's a better reason to go back to the Moon.

Like my prediction regarding Russia, what follows is made up of bits and pieces. For example, the People's Republic of China has been a nuclear power since the 1960s. Over the past few years, however, she has undertaken an enormous military buildup, especially with regard to her navy. Lately, she's said to be moving troops into North Korea where they can swoop down on South Korea in a heartbeat. Taking South Korea—and, inevitably, Taiwan—would leave Japan isolated and trapped.

Setting aside the question of whether it would be a good thing to do, I can't see anyone in either of the major American parties coming to the aid of South Korea, Taiwan, or even Japan. Their policy—to the extent they have one—is only to fight insanely irrelevant wars against weak, backward cultures. Confronted by someone big and modern and powerful—like China—our glorious leaders will soil their linens.

China has also made a great leap forward in aerospace science and technology, thanks in part to materials and information obtained from the collapsing Russian empire, and apparently buying up parts of a US F-117 stealth fighter somehow shot down over Serbia in 1999 and reverse-engineering it so they'll eventually have swarms of the damn things themselves. What's more, the Chinese can already launch objects into orbit with relative ease, and it's believed that if they get to the Moon, they'll do what America failed to do, build a permanent base there.

This would be bad.

It would be very, very bad.

Remember Luis and Walter Alvarez, who—thanks to their discovery of rare metals found in clay all over the world between the geological layers of the Cretaceous and Tertiary periods—showed the whole wide world how a Manhattan-sized asteroid, falling onto the Yucatan coast, wiped out the dinosaurs and burned every plant above ground on the planet?

Remember Robert A. Heinlein's novel of the revolution, *The Moon Is a Harsh Mistress*, where the inmates of a Lunar prison colony won their independence from Earth by using electrical launchers to drop rocks the size of a railroad boxcar on some of the Earth's major cities?

Did you notice that the US Navy has experimentally launched planes from the deck of an aircraft carrier using more or less the same technology?

The back of the American economy has been broken by political vermin I can't help but regard as traitors (although it could be restored easily enough, virtually overnight, following the precepts in my essay "The Plan"). Its ability to manufacture anything significant has been all but destroyed, through taxation, regulation, and union interference, by many of the same criminals. Whatever advantages of production this country enjoyed in both World Wars are gone. At this point in history, we suffer under the most cowardly and obsequious—and domestically, the most totalitarian—administration in our history.

Forget Iran's nukes. If the Chinese get a lunar monopoly they will rule the Earth. "Confiscate and destroy all privately-owned weapons," they'll demand, "or lose San Diego." "Scrap your entire aerospace industry or we'll flatten Denver." "Give us all your gold or Nashville disappears." "Send us 100,000 female 'guest workers' or say goodbye to Baltimore."

So what happens now?

Well, I'd like to think that the American military is capable of ignoring Presidential trendiness—including the dismantling of NASA which many libertarians cheered, but I never felt quite right about—and has some plan to defend this country from the Chinese or anybody else who wants a piece of us. But then I remember the wars in Korea and Vietnam where incompetence, corruption, and hysterical insanity ruled the day. And I think, too, about Iraq and Afghanistan, where no thought has ever been given to who our real enemies might be, and no hope exists that the application of military force can improve anything.

The frail box-kites and gossamer wings of our nascent civilian spacefleet aren't up to the job yet and won't be for a long, long time. So I'd like very much to think that NASA's extremely conspicuous secret launches earlier this year have something to do with actually defending this country. (What was up with all those dead birds, anyway?) And yet this is an agency that officially believes in the bad science fiction of Global Warm—pardon me, make that "climate change."

Given China's announcement of its brand new shiny anti-carrier missiles, I'd like to think the tactical lasers the Navy has developed will protect the great ships as the Phalanx system did a generation ago.

What would I do?

First, I would eliminate every barrier—taxation, regulations—slowing or preventing the private development of spacecraft, space travel, space stations, and commercial interplanetary colonization. In the long run, this will provide the new guards for our future security.

In the absence of any other immediate action, a decent, rational, intelligent administration (I know that's asking a lot) will retrieve from South Korea, as quickly as possible, the 800,000 World War II vintage Garand rifles and 200,000 M1 Carbines that Barack Obama has been planning to wantonly and profligately destroy, and see them distributed instead, widely and anonymously, throughout the American population.

At the same time, ammunition manufacturers should be encouraged to put the production of .30-06 and .30 Carbine ammunition on the front burner. Its manufacture, distribution, and purchase should be tax-free.

Employing similar incentives, make it cheap and easy to reengineer the old Garands so that they work with 20-round box magazines like the Italian BM-59. (Whether to change the chambering from .30-06 to .308 is something we could debate all day.) These policies alone will send a message to the world that the free people of America plan to stay free.

It can't hurt the ugly situation on the Mexican border, either.

Provided civilization survives the mess it finds itself in at the moment, humanity's future in space is bright. Most people who leave the Earth, either temporarily, to work or vacation, or permanently, for a fresh start somewhere else, won't make the trip riding dangerous and expensive rockets, but by train—or space elevator, if you will—traveling along lines lowered thousands of miles to the planet from space.

A time will come when such constructs will sprout from the equator every few degrees, bringing products and materials from the asteroids, and people will leave the Earth in greater numbers than they are being born. At long last, the threat of humanity's extinction by nuclear war—of having all of our eggs in one basket, so to speak—will be over.

The sad truth today, however, is that decency, rationality, and intelligence, which were always all too scarce in government, are all but non-existent today. What we're seeing is a strangely suicidal senescent culture—as deeply rooted in pompous, empty authority as the British monarchy at the time of the American Revolution—with all of the mythology it has acquired over 250 years (Lincoln was a martyred saint; Roosevelt saved capitalism; gun control reduces crime), beginning to crumble around the edges as a vital new culture of freedom and individual responsibility struggles to arise in its place.

The question: is there enough time left before China owns the Moon?

A Barbarous Relic of the Past

Want a clear indication of what the welfare state is really all about? Note that the barest necessities of life—food, clothing, shelter, transportation, and self-defense—are all taxed.

—L. NEIL SMITH

The average American ends up paying half of what he earns every year to governments at various levels. Aside from federal income and excise taxes, there are state taxes, county taxes, and city taxes of various kinds, not to mention a virtual plague of "special taxing districts."

Property taxes, use taxes, and sales taxes add to a burden that keeps most Americans "in their place," without hope for a better life for themselves or for their children. Criticized by grandiose authorities on economics both here and abroad because they have no savings, nobody ever argues back that, after all is said and done and everything is paid for, the Productive Class have no money left to save.

And if they did, it would be eaten away by capital gains taxes.

Americans have always worked hard to feed, clothe, and house their families, to drive them back and forth to school or church or Little League, to keep them healthy, safe, and secure. Now, thanks largely to the Internet, which allows them to communicate their discontents to one another, they've gotten understandably restive, having half of what they earn—and their entire future in the bargain—stolen by the nonproductive beneficiaries of a runaway government. Accusations coming from the thieves, that this attitude represents some kind of Neanderthal racism on the part of those who only wish to keep the fruits of their labor, only bring America closer to some kind of great explosion.

Politicians should be aware that the American Revolution and the War Between The States both began as tax revolts, as did the 1794 Whiskey Rebellion and before it, to a certain extent, Shays' Rebellion of 1786. It's no wonder at all that tax parasites hate and fear the Tea Party movement. The original Tea Party was all about taxation, too.

Individual observers in the establishment "lamestream" media differ on what they will admit motivates the Tea Party movement. Aside from their usual, reflexive accusations of race prejudice, the most ridiculous attempt to explain it away is that it's all about the federal deficit. I don't believe this for a minute. For better or worse, nobody who lives and works in the real world gives a rusty fuck about the criminally sloppy way the government jiggers its own books. They're much more interested in how they're going to pay this month's bills.

Or make the mortgage payment.

What they do give a damn about are the "four Ps": peace, freedom, progress, and prosperity. (Yes, I know "freedom" doesn't start with a P—"writing" and "arithmetic" don't start with Rs, either.) All four of those values are clearly threatened by legislation like the attempted Obama-Reid-Pelosi takeover of the medical sector, and—more than anything else—that's what sent people out into the streets in the summer of 2009, and brought them to the nation's capital in the summer of 2010. The government's failure to deal with illegal immigration, its high-handed and prissy disdain for people's religious beliefs, and its persistent attempts to disarm, to disautomobile (to coin a term), and to destroy the Productive Class all figure into the phenomenon, as well.

I was just a little kid when my mom and dad first told me about taxation; I was absolutely outraged. How dare anybody threaten to take my money—I was a professional hunter: killing box elder bugs for a penny apiece on my grandmother's back porch was the major source of my income—and inform me I had no choice about it? I'm still outraged, but I wonder about other little kids who drew a different lesson from this chapter of practical reality: if it's okay for the government to threaten people and steal from them, then why shouldn't it be okay for me?

When the average individual finally understands the full extent of what has been stolen from him or her, who can predict what will happen?

Look at it this way: half of everything each of us earns is taken from us by one government or another. This means that our ability to cope with the world around us—to send our children to the doctor or the dentist, to keep our houses warm enough (or cool enough) for them, to make sure they have new shoes occasionally and a broader choice of entertainment and information than broadcast TV or the culture's dying newspapers can provide—or to fulfill our dreams for the future, is slashed in half, just so that some bureaucrat or politician can use your money to keep himself and a string of bimbos wallowing in luxury and think of more ways to deprive you of your life, liberty, and property.

The fat you see, hanging in disgusting rolls off the bodies of the women down at the Department of Motor Vehicles, is the flesh of your children.

As if it weren't enough to subsist on only half of what you earn, everybody you do business with, individuals, companies, is in exactly the same boat. Each of them is paying half, or more, of his income to government. Which means that, when you finally save up enough for that pair of shoes, you'll be paying the shoemaker's taxes, as well as your own.

To review: you only get to keep one-half of the money you have sweated to earn, and that money only goes half as far as it would in a truly free, untaxed economy. We all live on one quarter of the effort we have expended. (In effect, I only get paid for one world out of every four I write.) The rest—an unbelievable three quarters of our earnings—goes to the political sharks and their parasitic pilot fish.

But it gets worse.

Complying with thousands of idiotic and unconstitutional laws and regulations has a cost all its own. Many companies maintain an office, and a gaggle of employees, simply to fill out forms the government demands of them. The person-hours squandered over the past century just completing Form 1040s could probably have built another Great Pyramid or two. Truckers cutting across the corner of a state without buying fuel may be taxed for the fuel they should have bought there. Environmental and "safety" regulations—based on the same quality of science that gave us Global Warming—add to the waste, until the cost of doing business doubles again. We find ourselves living on one-eighth of what we earn, and wondering how the hell to make ends meet, while government takes seven eighths of it away, mostly to use against us.

To confiscate a phrase from the socialist economist John Maynard Keynes (and how could he object: from each according to his ability, to each according to his political pull, as Karl Marx might have said if he'd been more honest), taxation is a barbarous relic of the ancient past.

It almost certainly began 10,000 years ago, when our ancestors made the mistake of giving up the hunter-gatherer life, and settled down to farming. The wandering bands of bullies and thieves they were accustomed to running away from, or fighting off with their hunting tools, could stop wandering, too. They settled down right beside their victims who, stuck on the farm, were no longer free to run away. Nor did the bullies and thieves have to worry any more about facing folks armed with hunting weapons. Farm implements are lousy for self-defense and with agriculture (unlike hunting) there's never any spare time or other resources to make a second set of tools or keep in practice with them.

In due course, the bullies and thieves declared themselves to be kings, princes, barons, lords, supreme gazooties, and so forth; their Productive Class victims became lowly subjects and made to feel they owed this phony-baloney "nobility" everything, including a farmer's bride on their wedding day, or the occasional virgin daughter. Taxes are what we still pay to this day to keep the thieves and bullies (now they mostly call themselves presidents, senators, and congressmen) from stealing everything. Molesting children became the purview of the Church.

The next time you see Betty Battenberg, the Monarch of Airstrip One, or her genetically-depleted halfwit offspring being grandly celebrated on television, remember that she's the Queen only because her ancestors bashed in more heads, and intimidated more helpless, unarmed peasants, than anybody else around. That's all there is to royalty; that's all there ever was. The guillotine was too good for them.

But as usual, I have digressed.

Once upon a time, I ran for the state legislature, entering the race late, against the six-term Speaker of the House. I spent a total of eight dollars on my campaign and got fifteen percent of the vote, a third-party record that stood for at least a decade. My campaign consisted, almost entirely, of reading to audiences from the grocery shopping ads in every Wednesday's newspaper, dividing all the prices by eight, which is what things would cost in an unregulated, untaxed economy.

You should try it. It's educational and lots of fun.

Everybody seemed to love it. In the midst of droning three-minute speeches mumbled by candidates for dogcatcher or tax assessor, what I told them made people sit up, listen, laugh, cheer, even boo and hiss while most of them were transported, if only for a few moments, to a place where the future was brighter and more colorful than they'd ever known. In those moments, my first novel, *The Probability Broach*, was born.

It should be the openly-stated goal of any organization that calls itself libertarian, or claims that it values freedom above all things, to rid civilization of this barbarous relic and abolish all taxes for all time. It will prove difficult, and it may take a long while. But the anti-slavery movement, which finally succeeded in the nineteenth century, was actually started four hundred years earlier by Queen Isabella of Spain in the 1490s, when she was horrified to see the miserable, frightened captives Columbus brought back from the New World.

However long it takes in the end, the economic, scientific, and humanitarian advances that will be engendered, simply by restoring to ourselves the missing seven eighths of what we have earned, will be absolutely staggering. The possibilities certainly stagger me. Our species will never be the same. Humans with thousand-year lifespans—our children, our grandchildren, our great-grandchildren, but possibly you and I, ourselves—will leap for the stars and we will never look back.

We might even get our visiphones and flying cars.

In the short run, ridding ourselves of taxation and regulation will restore the personal and business privacy that the Republicans profess not to believe in, but which is the unquestionable birthright of every American—indeed, of every single individual on the planet. The only political question we'll have left to answer is whether the former employees of the IRS, the EPA, the BATFE, and OSHA should be sentenced to a special prison built for them on Alcatraz, or to a trillion hours of public service, as allowed under the Thirteenth Amendment.

A final thing, for libertarian campaigners and platform writers: when a ravenous carnivore has its claws sunk into your body and its foul predatory breath is blasting hot on your throat, it is not your obligation to find the beast something else—or somebody else—to devour.

The media always want to know what a libertarian tax program would consist of. The one rational and acceptable libertarian tax program is to get rid of every tax we can find enough political power to get rid of, with the ultimate and inexorable objective of ending taxation altogether. Period.

What Would Twelves Hewes Do?

Oh little terr he is a bother, 'cause he'd really never rather
Stand up an' fight a real God-given war.
So we denounces him as heinous, an' intendin' just t'pain us—
An' we're right, 'cause that's exactly what he's for.

Here we go t'all all the strains o' buyin' missile, ships, an' planes
While little terr just builds a bomb or lights a fire.
He's found a way that he can play agin the richer kids, but they
Won't tolerate 'im. Wiseguys just stir up their ire.

—L. NEIL SMITH

Terrorism is used as an accusatory catch-all for behavior that government doesn't like. If the word has any meaning at all (and it seems to have less and less with every day that passes), it is as a category of violent acts, or the threat of violent acts, intended to modify the behavior of governments and populations. It's safe to say that ninety-nine percent of the terrorism in the world is state terrorism; most terrorism is carried out by states against their own people.

According to Amnesty International, in the century just concluded, governments alone—independent of acts of war, which double the figure—purposely murdered more than a hundred million of their own citizens.

In practice, governments are inclined to use the word terrorism to refer to unconventional modes of combat undertaken by groups lacking the resources to fight conventionally. This "asymmetrical warfare" as it's sometimes called, annoys governments, which spend billions on the latest weapons, and more on campaigns to convince taxpayers and voters that such expenses are necessary, only to find themselves challenged—and often humiliated—by interests that don't have billions to spend.

Americans won their freedom this way, as did the people of Vietnam.

Libertarian author and lecturer Robert LeFevre used to tell his seminar classes that a principal goal of terrorism—in those days, the models were the communist Baader-Meinhof gang in Germany (later known as the Red Army Faction), and the murderous Italian Red Brigades—was to force a country's officials to clamp down so stringently on society, in the name of security, that life for the average citizen became intolerable enough to motivate the violent overthrow of the government.

Terrorism—just like total war—is a child of democracy. In previous ages, aristocrats waged war on one another with mercenary or slave armies. Since no one would ever have believed that a kingdom's peasants had anything to do with formulating the policies that had led to war, except for the customary stolen chicken, purloined pig, or ravished daughter, the peasants were pretty much left out of the conflict.

Many, if not all, of those who fought on the side of Independence during the American Revolution would be considered terrorists today by the ruling establishment and their "embedded" media, and they would have been hanged for it, as many were. (I recall seeing a quotation somewhere, maybe from H.L. Mencken, that the easiest way to earn a reputation as a dangerous lunatic is to quote this nation's Founding Fathers.) Note, however, that the first violent actions taken by the weaker side were against property. The Boston Tea Party—George Robert Twelves Hewes, mentioned in the title, above, was its last living survivor—saw tax protesters thinly disguised as Mohawk Indians, dumping hundreds of broken crates of taxed tea into Boston Harbor.

Among the many dubious blessings of democracy, however—or any other form of popular majoritarianism, for that matter—is a widespread misunderstanding by those politically naive enough to believe government's advertisements about itself, that everybody's hand, in the judicial sense, is on the rope. That is, responsibility for a nation's policies are evenly distributed—sort of like Original Sin— to every citizen of that nation, including newborn babies.

To a politician, this handily justifies reducing whole cities and countrysides to ashes, as the forces of Abraham Lincoln, America's original state terrorist, did in the War Between The States, or Harry Truman did to the mostly innocent people of Hiroshima and Nagasaki. To an independent terrorist, it justifies employing deadly violence against helpless victims on airliners, in subways, and in high-rise buildings. Note: given a choice between two gangs of mass-murdering collectivist criminals, there is no reason to choose one over the other.

Now we are presented with a farce: Janet Napolitano, of the unconstitutional (and therefore illegal) Department of Homeland Security, along with other politicians and bureaucrats of her ilk, assert that all dissenters are terrorists—even if these dissenters intend to displace the current regime by purely peaceful political means.

Egged on by despicably anti-freedom pressure groups like the Southern Poverty Law Center, Napolitano has gone so far as to issue official bulletins to police agencies around the country warning officers that bumper stickers, for example, indicating disagreement with current government policies, adherence to the Constitution, or support for anti-socialist entities like talk radio, Ron Paul or the Libertarian Party may represent a deadly danger to officers contacting the drivers of such vehicles. This is an act of state terrorism in and of itself, based on the deadly threat of government force. It merits immediate removal from office and vigorous prosecution under the 14th Amendment.

However, far above any strictly transitory political situation, there is a fact that threatens us and our children and grandchildren with a lifetime in chains unless "we the people" can gain the upper hand. On many occasions, I have tried—without evident success, so far—to convey the all-important truth that the real threat, the real "terror" authorities fear is the inescapable fact that, more and more, on any given day, at any given moment, civilization as a whole is abjectly dependent on the good will of each and every individual in it.

This is increasingly true with the advance of technology across a hundred different fields. A single flipped switch, a shorted circuit, a deliberate spill of chemicals can injure or kill dozens, hundreds, even thousands. There is nothing new about this. In his 1957 novel *Wasp*, libertarian author Eric Frank Russell explained it all in terms that the authority-bound still resent and complain about to this day. It's now being used, with increasing frequency, as an excuse to watch our every step, monitor our every transaction, measure our every breath.

My experience is that it's usually the stupidest people who have the least confidence in human intelligence, and the least trustworthy who do not believe in human integrity. Possibly as a result, more and more, modern societies—or, rather, modern authorities who control them—appear to have lost all respect for the individual, and seem to regard any sign of individuality—let alone of individualism—as some sort of dire threat, which must somehow be contained and managed.

If possible, before it manifests itself.

Contrary to the precepts of socialism of every stripe, left, right, or center, the proper and effective way for any society to deal with this phenomenon is to offer to each individual more for his benevolent participation in it than he must give up in order to be a part of it. Otherwise, what stake do any of us have in helping it survive? And the only system that can accomplish any of that is private capitalism and the strictest possible adherence to the Bill of Rights.

Given all that, let's try to get the following straight, once and for all (fat chance of that): as a military dependent, Cub Scout, Boy Scout, Explorer Scout, Eagle, God & Country awardee, Order of the Arrow, my whole life has been a love affair with America, the best idea for a country, as somebody wise once put it, that anybody ever had.

My entire professional life has also been a kind of love poem to America. True, we've had our lovers' spats. The War in Vietnam was one of those, a bad one. But the problem isn't with America, it's with the slimy toads—back then it was Lyndon Johnson, Robert S. McNamara, Richard Nixon, Henry Kissinger, and Zbigniew Brzezinski—that all too easily insinuated themselves into positions of great power.

They said if I supported Goldwater, we'd wind up in a land war in Asia.

I didn't learn until I was grown about the sleazy things America—or, rather, its long succession of sleazy governments—had done behind my back, some of them before I was born. The broken promise to set the Philippine Islands free, for example, the "helpless" *Lusitania*, Operation Keelhaul, the Tonkin Gulf "Incident," and later on, Ruby Ridge, Waco, Oklahoma City. History was full of such disheartening things.

Among them was the way that the American government under Eisenhower allowed the British government to enlist it in the overthrow of the elected government of Iran in 1953. The issue was oil, and it was not the first time the West had interfered with people's lives in the Middle East—look up the Balfour Declaration—but it was the beginning of a chain of events that have cost uncounted thousands of lives and deprived tens of millions of their self-determination.

By far the worst Western atrocity against the people of the Middle East was a punitive blockade of Iraq, instigated during the Republican administration of George H.W. Bush, and continued under the Democratic administration of Bill Clinton, responding to dictator Saddam Hussein's invasion of neighboring Kuwait, that is said to have resulted in the deaths—from starvation or lack of medicine—of hundreds of thousands of Iraqi kids who had nothing to do with or say about the invasion. Confronted about this atrocity, Clinton's horrible Secretary of State, Madeleine Albright, would say only, "It was worth it."

In the light of that history, George W. Bush's assertion that the World Trade Center and the Pentagon were attacked on September 11, 2001, because "they hate our freedom" is ridiculous and insulting of every single individual on the planet. It was, in fact, the desperate act of a people who are sick and tired of being pushed around. What was crazy and evil about it was that it took no more account of the culpability of political leaders—as opposed to the innocence of those they rule—than was taken by those same leaders who starved half a million Iraqi children, trying to persuade one murderous dictator.

Rather than alter the behavior of American leaders, the hijackers provided further excuse for the Islamophobic bigotry that has polluted Western Civilization for more than 1000 years. And now the enemies that they have made for us are about to arm themselves with nuclear weapons.

Is there anything we can do, or is it too late?

To begin with, let me get this straight: a dozen-and-a-half Saudis seize four aircraft and attack American targets, so we invade Iraq and Afghanistan? The United States government must stop doing the things—like dropping bombs on pregnant widows and ten-year-old goatherds—that make so many Muslims want to kill us, the things that made ordinary individuals dance and cheer in the streets of a dozen Middle Eastern cities when they watched the twin towers burn and fall on television.

We must understand that Islam is at a point in its history comparable to a time when Christianity was dominated by the likes of Savonarola and the Spanish Inquisition. Instead of helping it to mature—possibly by developing better communication with the secular portions of Middle Eastern society—this government has made it vastly worse by providing demagogues and fanatics with an enemy to demonize.

Politicians often say that we must free ourselves from dependence on foreign oil. Favoring unrestricted trade between individuals as I do, I'm not entirely sure of that. But it is at least as important to free ourselves from dependence on energy from the companies that have dominated the field for over a century. There are half a dozen proven energy sources—I don't mean solar or wind—that could be useful in a truly free market. Look up "thermal depolymerization" as just one example.

Finally, at home, all elected politicians, bureaucrats, and police officers should be strictly forbidden, under penalty of law, to utter the demagogic words "terrorist" or "terrorism" in any of their public pronouncements.

And possibly the phrase, "for the children."

If they are forced to find new words, perhaps they can find new ways to interact with those they have injured or who disagree with them.

The Genocide Agenda

Go straight to the heart of the enemy's greatest strength.
Break that and you break him. You can always mop
up the flanks and stragglers later, and they may even
surrender, saving you a lot of effort.

—L. NEIL SMITH

On the grounds—no, let's make that "compound"—of the United Nations in the Big Wormy Apple, stands a sculpture, crafted in 1988 as a calculated affront to everything that its host nation believes in, especially the highest law of the land, the first ten amendments to its Constitution, commonly referred to as the Bill of Rights—and in particular, to the Second Amendment, intended to protect the other nine.

The sculpture in question is an outsized copy of one of the most famous and easily-identifiable handguns ever made, a .357 Magnum Colt Python, recognizable by the barrel, with its vented sight-plane and full-length underlug, a cylinder catch which is pulled back, rather than pushed forward, inward, or upward, the distinctive shape and decoration of the grip, and for its unusual hammer which the accompanying online propaganda says is cocked, but which, in fact, is not.

This so-called "peace sculpture," a gift from the comic-relief nation of Luxembourg, is known as "the Knotted Gun." I'm sure that the sculptor would want his name mentioned. The Python's barrel, which in real life would be a ridiculous eighteen inches long, is tied in an overhand knot, the muzzle pointing up, in representation of a nasty old weapon that has been rendered harmless. In fact, such a gun would be far from harmless, it would blow up upon being fired, injuring or killing the shooter and any close bystanders. The sculptor, in the bucket-headed manner typical of all victim disarmament advocates, has found a way to convert a revolver into a grenade, a sophisticated precision instrument of self-defense into a weapon of indiscriminate destruction.

But here's the point: Colt's Patent Firearms should really sue the sculptor, Luxembourg, and the UN. Quintessentially a civilian weapon, intended for private individuals, the Colt Python's use as a symbol of criminal violence is utter hypocrisy in a world where millions of lives are preserved every year by privately-owned guns, and the vast majority of violence is done—and always has been—with state-issued rifles, by trained killers, usually conscripts wearing state livery.

But they all know this perfectly well. The real target of their pseudo-artistic slander is America, and gun ownership by peasants—you and me—which the world's self-anointed elite in general and the UN thugocracy in particular have always found deplorable. With plenty of American help, the UN has several operations underway aimed specifically at disarming people all over the world, rendering them even more helpless against predatory governments than they are right now.

So much for peace, love, and understanding.

Around the world, Americans may be the last to understand that, when the situation's grim, and the white vehicles and blue helmets of the so-called "peacekeepers" show up on your doorstep, it isn't time to feel relief at being rescued. It's time to hide your wife, your daughter, your sister, even your mother, and whatever valuables you possess.

Don't hide your guns, though, haul them out and get them loaded. The gravest threat to life, liberty, and property in today's world—especially to life—is the UN. It can do absolutely anything it wants to, to whomever it wants to, because it's "the cops of the world."

The UN was conceived in 1939, a brain-child of Franklin Delano Roosevelt and his buddies, who had failed to understand the lesson to be learned from the collapse of its ludicrous predecessor, the League of Nations, that the people of a war-weary planet, fed up to here with self-important bloviating cretins in funny hats ordering them around, were not interested in a world government, or anything even resembling one.

Instead, all the really important people—the equivalents, in 1945, of Barack and Michelle Obama, Bill and Hillary Clinton, Harry Reid, Nancy Pelosi, Barney Frank—got together in one meeting after another, and without so much as a nod at voters and taxpayers forced at gunpoint to support this gaggle of worthless preening parasites, established the UN in its now-crumbling headquarters on the Hudson River.

Its single all-important mission? To succeed where Alexander the Great, Julius Caesar, Napoleon Bonaparte, Vladimir Lenin, Joseph Stalin, and Adolf Hitler had all failed: at the involuntary expense of individuals who actually worked for a living, try to take over the world.

Since the ignominious collapse of the Soviet Union, the new world nerve center for socialism is the UN, which is no less an enemy of everything worthwhile in the western world than Hitler and Stalin were. The UN has been at the very hub of the global warming hoax since the conspiracy began. It has done everything it can to limit American industrial technology and reduce us all to a prehistoric standard of living. It demands the authority to reach into otherwise sovereign countries and extract and punish those who fail to comply with its edicts. The UN admits openly that it wishes to obliterate the American Constitution—especially the Bill of Rights—with a hysterical emphasis on the Second Amendment. And now we're beginning to have a clearer idea what it wants to substitute in place of those ideas and institutions.

It wants you and me and our neighbors to be as helpless as the Nazis wanted Jews to be. It screams for power to control our children and tax us directly. (Talk about "taxation without representation"!) It wants its own army. It struggles ceaselessly to disarm whole populations, exactly the same way the Nazis did, and for exactly the same reasons, rendering them as vulnerable to genocide as the Jews in 1930s Germany. It wishes to render every individual in the world defenseless against criminal butchers. Don't think for a minute that it means to exclude America. It doesn't, and it will tell you so, openly.

The nearest equivalent to what the UN has in mind for all of us is the infamous "Highland Clearances" of the 18th and 19th centuries, when English "landowners" evicted the Scots they had conquered, by the hundreds of thousands, burning whole villages and forcing the Scots to leave their crops rotting in the ground, compelling a people who had been cattlemen for generations to harvest seaweed on the cold and rocky coast—or emigrate to the Americas—so aristocrats could "ride to hounds" and replace their displaced victims on the land with sheep.

"But what," I pretend to hear you ask, "about the United Nations Universal Declaration of Human Rights? Isn't it simply a long overdue 20th-century improvement on the ancient 18th-century American Bill of Rights?"

Only in the sense that it's a cruel hoax. Only in the sense that it isn't anything remotely like our Bill of Rights at all. Only if what you aspire to is to become an absolute dictator. Unlike our Bill of Rights, the so-called Universal Declaration of Human Rights guarantees nothing. It omits many of our most familiar rights—those guaranteed by the Tenth, Ninth, Eighth, Seventh, Sixth, Fifth, Fourth, Third, Second, and First Amendments. Undoubtedly worse, it makes them all subject to approval by the very entity likeliest to suppress them: government.

The Universal Declaration of Human Rights was written specifically to please the heads of UN member states—rather than constituents, voters, or taxpayers—the very sort of monsters who had rounded up and murdered millions of Jews in Germany, farmers in Russia, property owners and people who were literate in China and Cambodia, and so on. The whole idea is to subordinate individual rights to the power of the state, to impose socialism on everybody by inventing "rights"—to the wealth, time, skills, and energy of others—that don't actually exist.

The Universal Declaration of Human Rights fails to protect citizen militias and the individual right to own and carry weapons. In fact it's a major objective of the UN to seize and destroy every privately owned weapon in the world. It fails to protect the people from state-established religion, or from government quartering troops in their homes.

For the same reasons, it forgets to mention search warrants, grand juries, rules against double jeopardy, excessive bail, or seizure of property without compensation. It fails to guarantee a speedy trial, the right to an attorney, a jury trial in the venue where the crime occurred, the right to subpoena witnesses and the right to confront one's accuser.

Under the American Bill of Rights, government exists only with the permission of the people, whom it was specifically created to serve. Under the Universal Declaration of Human Rights, there are no rights, in fact, only political privileges to be granted (or withheld) by governments that people are obligated to obey without question or hesitation. In essence, people exist only with the permission of the government.

The Universal Declaration of Human Rights forbids action on the part of people—as in the American Revolution, for example, the War Between the States, or more recently in Egypt—to secure their rights. It forcibly imposes a perpetual tax-and-spend welfare state on every productive individual anywhere in the world. And finally, in Article XXIX, it says, "These rights and freedoms"—meaning the power of the one-world government to impose itself on us— "may in no case be exercised contrary to the purposes and principles of the United Nations."

And what will the UN do with that power?

Barack Obama, today's leading frontman and mouthpiece for the UN, has done a great deal of talking about change, about hope, and about "remaking America." The truth about what he really has in mind can be discovered in a UN document—enthusiastically supported by most American politicians—called "Agenda 21." It is not obscure. It is not a secret. It is easily available for inspection all over the Internet.

Under this scheme, devised for us in 1992 by humanity's mortal enemies within the UN, every last individual on this continent (and elsewhere, presumably) will be rounded up and forced to live at a vastly reduced standard of living, in "arcologies," vast piles of thousands of apartments, stacked one upon another, as much as a mile high. These grim, gray structures, with their roving patrols and built-in weapons detectors, were colorfully romanticized in the Arnold Schwarzenegger movie *Total Recall*, but if you've ever seen a typical Japanese apartment—Ken Takakura's in the 1989 movie *Black Rain*, for example, or Bruce Willis's "palatial" cubbyhole in *The Fifth Element*,—then you'll have a better idea what's being planned for us.

Life in a shoebox.

Life in a kennel.

Life in a cell.

Refusniks, those who resist this change, will be relegated and confined to the bulldozed ruins of the old towns across America, to starve and die out, perhaps assisted by occasional military training exercises.

With humanity thus contained—quarantined—as if it were some kind of disease (an article of leftist dogma since the 1960s), rather than the pinnacle of evolution that it truly is, under the banner of "saving the Earth," the land will be emptied, cleared of all human artifacts and other traces, ordinary people forbidden ever again to enter the open countryside, and, in keeping with the current environmental fascist insanity, permitted to return to its "natural state."

Except that's never how it really works out.

Instead, the emptied countryside will become a playground for the new socialist elite, the nomenklatura as they were known in bad old Soviet Russia, who will vacation there, perhaps even dwell or retire there in their dachas, in aristocratic splendor that the peasants, locked down together in their dark, dirty, crumbling hundred-story warrens, their brains scientifically numbed by drugs and enervating "entertainment" programs, will never be allowed to see. With the exception, of course, of the many young, attractive, clean-limbed boys and girls the elite select to take with them in the name of "National Service."

Population—reproduction—will be rigidly controlled until the number of people on Earth has been reduced by the 85 or 90 percent the UN and environmentalists have admitted repeatedly they want to see eliminated. Apparently, if you strive to do all of that to Mankind, instead of smaller groups like Jews or Armenians or Chechens—you're a statesman and a benefactor, rather than a mass-murdering monster. Remember that, next time you see a politician or a movie star speaking on behalf of the UN. What they are endorsing by their presence is genocide.

Ironically, in nations foolish enough to sign onto the Universal Declaration of Human Rights, it is forbidden to criticize the document itself or the organization that generated it. Nor does it take a lot of imagination to foresee, in a post-9/11, USA Patriot Act era, how this means that any written, verbal, or electronic criticism of the United States government, the North American Union, or the UN will become an offense punishable by indefinite imprisonment, torture, and death.

Some observers believe the current administration, politicians in both parties, and socialist sugar-daddies like Bill Gates, Warren

Buffet, and George Soros, are wrecking our economy on purpose, trying to provoke open rebellion so that UN military forces can be called in to "restore order." These forces commonly commit atrocities such as looting, rape, and murder, in countries where they're supposed to be peacekeepers. Is there any reason to believe it would be any different here?

Why do we tolerate the presence of this openly declared enemy of liberty and decency on American soil? Without a doubt, that will become one of the most frequently-asked questions about the 21st century, provided humanity survives, and historians remain free to ask it.

I'm no conservative—basically, I'm on my way to the stars, by way of Ceres—but before that happens, I want America back the way I remember it. No, it wasn't perfect, not by a long shot. But it was a hell of a lot better when I was a little kid than it is now. I want an America with no more grand utopian schemes to save an environment that doesn't need saving, to prevent global warming that isn't happening, or to force people to participate in a collectivized medical system that is a hollow farce and a justification for snoopery, robbery, and tyranny.

Everybody in the freedom movement worries constantly—not without justification—about a government, hostile to the very concept of individual liberty, knowing what guns they have and where they keep them. But what about the prescriptions they need to stay alive?

I want an America where the few, pitiful, starving, underpaid bureaucrats that remain—eking out their final days before their positions are abolished forever—have nothing to say about what I eat, what I drink, what I drive, what I keep in my gun cabinet, who I love, how I do it, and even what, in the immortal words of the great George Carlin, I shoot, snort, smoke, or rub into my belly. Maybe it seemed like a good idea at the time, giving them power to interfere in all of these things. Now we know it was a mistake and we must correct it.

I want an America where there are no more hidden agendas—or at least no money to encourage them—like this obscene idea of rounding up the people, forcing them to live in giant hundred-story tenements, while the goody-goods gallop around the empty countryside, shooting peasants. I want an America where the eternally smoldering ruins of the UN building in New York stand as a monument to freedom and a dire warning to collectivists, no matter what rock they choose to hide under.

Look: I'm no great defender of nation-states and borders. But in the world today, sovereign nations act somewhat like the watertight compartments in a ship. When one compartment becomes "flooded" by the cold, dark waters of dictatorship, victim disarmament, starvation, and the mass killings that invariably follow, others can remain warm and dry—free—if their geographical and psychological "bulkheads" remain sound. They act as a refuge for those who manage to escape the "flooded" compartments. All socialists know this, of course. That's why they strive to establish a world government nobody can escape from.

Alone in all the world, we don't have to put up with that crap. Legally, logically, the first ten amendments to the United States Constitution—commonly known as the Bill or Rights—take complete precedence over every other law, including the main body of the United States Constitution itself, lesser statutes and ordinances, as well as over treaties like the UN charter and its phony Universal Declaration of Human Rights. That is the nature of amendments, after all, to supersede everything that has gone before them or was written under a previous authority. It doesn't matter what the UN decrees, or whether the various states or congress go along with it. The Bill of Rights is unassailable.

Be aware, however, that the UN has its tentacles everywhere, with parasitic attachments of various kinds at every level of government in America. The next great Tea Party effort should be to compel all city, county, and state governments to sever every connection with this genocidal organization, and repudiate any agreement ever made with it. Politicians must be forced to disavow it and its criminal ambitions. What good will it do, after all, to bring our own government to heel, only to watch as our peace, freedom, prosperity, and progress are overwhelmed and swept away by the UN and its murderous, evil Agenda 21?

The UN is a political and philosophical cancer, eating away at the heart of everything that was ever good about America. The highest priority of every man, woman, and child who wishes to remain free—not to mention alive—ought to be the United States' withdrawal from the UN, the UN's ejection—forcibly if necessary, or else what's the New York Police Department for?—from United States territory, and, ultimately, the UN's total dismantling and demolition all over the world.

Who needs a corrupt, murderous, freedom-hating UN cluttering the political landscape? Who needs a European Union or a North American Union? What the world truly needs is an International Bill of Rights Union.

Every day, we strive for a future world in which everyone is armed who wants to be, and because of that, there can be no more genocide. At exactly the same time, the UN, in its fanatical totalitarian attempts to disarm everybody, is striving—whether the "useful idiots" who support it know it or not—to make the next genocide happen.

Of course the chronic victim disarmers within the UN, who consist mostly of craven hooligans and bullies, desperately want every human being on Earth to believe otherwise, to distrust the advocates of self-reliance and self-defense, and to behave instead like a warren of frightened rabbits. What terrifies these unelected and unelectable gangsters most is the increasingly real prospect of six billion individuals standing tall, independent, and armed. What the UN needs, for as long as we allow it to continue to exist, is its own Second Amendment. Wouldn't you just love to be there when that idea is introduced?

As a necessary first step, the United States must withdraw from the UN and evict that vile organization from this country with extreme prejudice, once and for all. It has declared war, in writing, in no uncertain terms, on the Bill of Rights which sorely impedes its goals. Its declared interest in "sustainability"—merely a code word for the nightmare it would create under Agenda 21—is enough to condemn it.

All things—even bad ones—come to an end. Grease up that Colt .357 Python sculpture with its barrel tied in a knot, And then go tell those Luxembourgers to bend over, because we're sending it back to them.

Be Ashamed . . . Be Very Ashamed

Politicians, bureaucrats, judges, and cops all see the Constitution in about the same light in which your great-grandmother saw the Sears-Roebuck catalog: a fine useful thing to have around—although its principal application may be somewhat different than its authors intended.

—L. NEIL SMITH

It's very difficult to decide what was more disturbing, half a dozen years ago or more, the news that the United States government was up to some astonishingly ugly business at its naval base down in Guantanamo Bay, Cuba (and a number of other places, as well, it was disclosed), or the news that, for the most part, the American public—along with the whorishly "embedded" American "news" media—seemed to think that what the government was up to at Guantanamo was just peachy.

Prosecuting undeclared and illegal wars (a liberal predilection that conservatives used to rail against before they, themselves, took power) in Afghanistan, Iraq, and elsewhere, the administration of George W. Bush was holding several hundred captives at that base, denying them due process on the ludicrous and self-serving grounds that they were not in the United States (although when it serves the government's purpose, the base is U.S. territory) and, therefore, protections afforded by the Constitution and the Bill of Rights didn't apply.

Nor, insisted Bush's flunkies, did their kidnap victims deserve status under international law as prisoners of war, because they were "illegal combatants," whatever that bit of Orwellian babble meant. I suspect that, under the current rules, George Washington and the Continental Army would have been perceived as "illegal combatants" by King George III. Some kidnapees were held at Guantanamo (and may still be there as far as I know) without charges or legal representation for years.

According to Independent Media-TV and other independent sources, at one time, Guantanamo prisoners were kept in small wire cages, exposed to the hot sun and cold rain, rats, snakes, insects, and scorpions. They were subject to frequent brutal beatings for minor offenses, and systematic humiliation. Devout younger Muslims who had never seen an "unveiled" woman were forced to watch female strippers fondle themselves. Prisoners were told, "We will kill your family and you."

Bound tightly until their circulation was cut off, chained at the neck to a concrete floor, prisoners were interrogated for as long as 15 hours at a time by CIA and British intelligence. They were drugged—on one occasion, a prisoner refused an unidentified injection and was punished by being beaten by the military police "Extreme Reaction Force," using fists, clubs, feet, and knives, while the jackbooted thugs, in full regalia, shouted "Comply! Comply! Do not resist! Do not resist!"

Prisoners were starved when it suited their captors—who made them watch other prisoners eat. They were fed rations ten years out of date. "Recreation," said one inmate, "meant your legs were untied and you walked up and down a strip of gravel. They actually said that 'You have no rights here.' After a while, we stopped asking for human rights—"

"We wanted animal rights."

I don't know to what extent this sort of thing is still going on, not only at Guantanamo, but at secret prisons maintained for the U.S. government in perhaps a dozen foreign countries. Various entertainment television programs (NCIS, for example) have portrayed Guantanamo as a sort of country club. However, having lived through decades of incessant, lying propaganda awkwardly wedged into "entertainment" programming, in support of victim disarmament and other left-wing fetishes, I am disinclined—especially now that the left is back in power and has failed to keep its promise to shut Guantanamo down—to believe anything network television has to say about the issues of the day.

If you want to see more, just put "Guantanamo"+"torture" in your search engine. As long as I've lived, and as cynical as I have become regarding government and the corruptibility of individuals given life-and-death power over others, the stories about Guantanamo disheartened me and made me ill for days. Brought up in the U.S. military, in the shadow of World War II, I "knew" that we were the good guys, and that good guys (like my dad, who had been a prisoner of war himself) don't do this kind of thing. Only communists and Nazis do. It is as painful and sickening to write about as it had been painful and sickening to read.

What I "knew" turned out to be baloney, of course, but that's a story for another day. Why, I asked myself rhetorically, does anybody bother to look for former Nazi death camp personnel anymore, when American doctors have gleefully admitted that they help the military and the "intelligence community" to design the methods used to torture prisoners? There ought to be a special Joseph Mengele medal struck for them.

Since his inauguration, Obama's lawyers have been in court, just like those of the Bush Administration before him, claiming absolute power to hold and abuse its victims—or simply kill them—in clear violation of the Bill of Rights, the Constitution, and international rules of civilized behavior, and to keep it that way by concealing what it is doing from American taxpayers and voters. Looking at coverage on the Web and the Internet, groups like the United Nations and Amnesty International seem oddly helpless to deal with these travesties, which represent the most effectively spiked news story in history.

Be that as it may, every individual connected with these outrages—from the muscle at the bottom doing the dirty work, all the way up to the President—should be removed from office and tried for war crimes. Upon conviction, the members of Guantanamo's "Extreme Reaction Force" should be publicly hanged by the neck until they are dead, to emphasize the fact, established at the Nuremberg War Crimes Tribunals following World War II, that some orders—and certain animalistic impulses we share—must never be yielded to or obeyed, on pain of death.

But even more repulsive than what happened (and may still be happening) at Guantanamo, and ultimately a worse sign for our civilization, are the "patriots" on talk radio and the Internet who not only take the side of the jackbooted thugs, but make fun of their helpless victims. These are exactly the same kind of low, slimy, crawling, cowardly "good Germans" and authoritarian lickspittles who pretended not to smell the stinking chimneys of Buchenwald or Belsen, or to notice the fine gray ash of human flesh settling on their doorsteps.

You know who they are.

Make no mistake, it is perfectly valid to ask why we must believe the stories coming to us, mostly from a handful of prisoners who have been released from Guantanamo. I believe them because, after more than six decades of staying alive and looking around, they sound completely credible to me. More important, what these men say was done to them—and may still be being done to others—is entirely consistent with everything else I've watched this and other governments do over those six decades. I believe them because, like you, I watched what happened at Waco and Ruby Ridge, and listened to the government's lies about it, and because I eventually learned the truth about the *Lusitania*, Pearl Harbor, the Tonkin Gulf "Incident" and especially Operation Keelhaul.

Look it up.

I believe because, from Paleolithic times, this is what government has been all about. It's all that government is about, or ever will be.

Torture can be defined as the use of pain—or the anticipation of pain—either to elicit some specific behavior from a victim under the perpetrator's control, or merely for the sadistic pleasure of the perpetrator. Any definition of torture must include "psychological duress," such as playing loud, obnoxious music for hours on end to helpless captives, at least partly in order to deprive them of sleep. Another possible form of torture is humiliation, either sexual or religious, or degrading an individual by depriving him of dignity or self-possession.

Ironically, physical torture is actually unnecessary. Experience has demonstrated that, if you have the time, sleep-deprivation alone will produce desired results. What's more—despite the protestations of its advocates—information obtained in that way can't usually be trusted. It isn't very complicated: what wouldn't you say in order to avoid another crank of the phone generator wired to your gonads, or to get them to stop hanging you from your wrists tied behind your back—especially if you could figure out what your captors wanted to hear?

I'm frequently asked, discussing this subject, whether I would torture a prisoner in order to save the life of somebody I love. The memory is decades old, but I seem to recall Matt Helm, in the very first novel about him, torturing a woman to death with a pocket knife in order to find out what she'd done with his daughter. My answer to the question is: absolutely. Nor do I doubt that American soldiers and other operatives have been torturing prisoners since the Revolution. But there's a difference between a hypothetical situation deliberately contrived so that principles and reason can't function—Ayn Rand called it a "lifeboat case"—or a "field expedient" that should lead to a court martial, and torturing prisoners as a matter of government policy.

If I had to save a friend or member of my family this way, I'd do it, then accept whatever retribution the universe chose to inflict on me.

Despite what government and the round-heeled media would have you believe, torture is neither difficult to recognize nor to define. Any five-year-old can tell you exactly what it is, and that it's wrong. Unless, of course, you don't want what you're doing to be defined as torture.

Only adults can be sufficiently self-deceiving to deny the obvious truth, or to expect others to swallow what they're serving up without examination. The same Republicans who complained so bitterly about Bill Clinton's obfuscations over what the meaning of the word "is" is, apparently have no more shame at the end of the day than he does. Sometime in the future, the same measures will be used on them, and the same weasel-words will be used by their enemies to explain it all away.

A civilization can't countenance this sort of thing for long without unintended evil consequences. Here at home, the cops seem to be going crazy, shooting unarmed individuals, often dozens of times, brutalizing those who simply wish to know why they've been stopped or what they're being charged with. Their latest hobby seems to be beating people up and jailing them for recording their activities on camera.

Everything that is best within us, everything that makes us most human, also makes us vulnerable to the evil art of the torturer.

In his splendid BBC television series *The Ascent of Man*, mathematician and philosopher Jacob Bronowski related the story of Galileo, who was in trouble with the Catholic Church because he had made a religiously incorrect discovery with his telescope. Commanded by the Inquisition to recant, Galileo was arrested and taken to a dungeon where he was shown the instruments of torture laid out neatly before his horrified gaze.

Unlike some hypothetical dull-witted peasant, Bronowski suggested, who would have to be burned, whipped, broken, blinded, disemboweled, and flayed to pieces before complying, Galileo, cursed with the vulnerability of intelligence, could imagine—he probably couldn't keep himself from imagining—what those tools would do to his flesh, and what it would be like to spend the rest of his life a helpless cripple.

There should be special punishment for using intelligence against itself.

So Galileo recanted. The Sun, the stars, and the planets all whirl around the Earth, he admitted, exactly as Ptolemy had decreed. Galileo retired under permanent house arrest, and eventually died. (On his deathbed he is said to have recanted his recantation.) Three hundred fifty years later, the Church had the brass gall to pardon him. One of the greatest intellects in human history had been forced to waste most of his time and talent defending his basic human right to use his mind.

Who knows what we're doing to history today?

The punishment for torture should be death by public hanging.

Free As The Air?

*It is moral weakness, rather than villainy, that accounts
for most of the evil in the universe—and feeble-hearted
allies, far rather than your most powerful enemies, who
are likeliest to do you an injury you cannot recover from.*

—L. NEIL SMITH

I received an e-mail message today about a proposed Constitutional amendment that would compel our elected representatives to be fully subject to the same laws citizens and taxpayers are all expected to obey.

This would include Social Security, in which the Congress and the Senate have never been forced to participate, Obamacare, which is what caused the issue to be raised now, and myriads of other statutes and regulations to which politicians have made themselves happily immune. There's even a part of the Constitution, Article I, Section 6, that keeps them from being punished for anything political they do while in office.

While I heartily agree with and greatly admire the spirit in which this proposed new amendment was written, I also believe that, while amendments are being proposed, there are a few higher priorities to address.

When I was a member of the national Libertarian Party platform committee in 1977, meeting in San Francisco, I wrote and introduced a plank attempting to warn my fellow libertarians that the then-new security measures being imposed in the country's airports—they were shockingly mild by today's ugly standards—would inevitably spread out from there like a cancer, eventually transforming America into a full-blown police state, which is exactly where we find ourselves today.

I was laughed at and shouted down by a collection of characters and movement icons as legendary and illustrious as they could possibly be. Over the thirty-four years that have passed since then, not one of these legendary and illustrious characters has come forth to say, "You were right, Neil, we were wrong." But I was right: if you want to know what America will be like tomorrow, look at what airports are like now.

Today's news is filled with horrifying stories of people—women, children, diapered babies, little old ladies in wheelchairs—being groped and explored obscenely by dull-witted, slovenly placeholders, many of them with criminal backgrounds including sex offenders, who couldn't even meet the eligibility standards of the Bureau of Alcohol, Tobacco, Firearms, and Explosives, formerly the most incompetent, corrupt, and least scrupulous bottom-of-the-barrel agency in the government.

Now they're Number Two.

But we knew that.

The great libertarian teacher and writer Robert LeFevre was famous for having remarked, among other things, that government is a disease masquerading as its own cure—a quote often erroneously attributed to me. Today, the thoroughly unconstitutional Transportation Safety Administration, as well as the equally illegal Department of Homeland Security of which it is a part, are in fact the very terrorists they pretend to be protecting us from. And they are only a small fraction of the vast standing army—a crooked, increasingly brutal, occupying army—of which America's Founding Fathers were so terribly wary and afraid.

These are the same kind of "humanitarians" who would scramble military fighters and shoot down a hijacked commercial airliner full of innocent passengers, rather than allow these victims Constitutional access to the means of defending themselves. Some observers believe that's what actually happened to United Airlines Flight 93, one of the four aircraft seized on 9/11, which crashed into a farmer's field near Shanksville, Pennsylvania—but that the "public servants" who authorized this outrage and atrocity are ashamed to admit what they did.

Is it true? Given all their other lies, from the sinking of the *Lusitania* to Iraq's WMDs, how would we ever be able to tell? It is instructive in this connection—and sobering—to remember that not one single individual in the government lost his or her job as a consequence of having utterly failed to predict or prevent the 9/11 attacks. Yet today, even as they tighten their death-grip on the Constitution, their terrorist-under-every-bed cant increasingly rings as hollow as the Yellow Peril of the 1890s or the Red Scare of the 1920s. There is a lot of money and power to be had by frightening people.

And now they are attempting to expand their operations to railway stations and bus terminals, as part of an all-out push—or should I say *putsch?*—to impose totalitarian discipline on what was once the freest country in the history of the world. Here and there, with increasing frequency, government minions are stopping cars illegally, searching people without probable cause, and even stealing money from them.

The infamous "no-fly list" of individuals whom the government has decided—for no reason that they are required to reveal—won't be allowed to board an airplane is unprecedentedly heinous and tyrannical, a page straight out of the Hitlerian or Stalinist playbook. Those who created the list, compiled it, and apply it belong in prison. Instead they remain free to advocate that the same procedure be applied to bus and train travel, to buying a firearm, and, eventually, to using the Internet.

But we all know that. We see it in the news, online, every day. We also know they want to silence their critics by seizing control of the Internet, something which, at all costs, must never be allowed to happen.

September 11, 2001, if we choose to believe the official story, could have been stopped before it ever started by a single individual aboard each aircraft, armed with a .22 caliber revolver. Nor would the 9/11 hijackers simply have equipped themselves with better weapons. As plummeting crime rates in concealed-carry locales clearly demonstrate, criminals only act when they feel that they enjoy an overwhelming advantage.

In my 1980 novel *The Probability Broach*, and again in *The Venus Belt*, published in the same year, I discuss alternative methods of assuring passenger safety in the air while respecting the individual's absolute right to self-defense and the means of self-defense. This is neither brain surgery nor rocket science. Rendering innocent people harmless is just the same as rendering them helpless, which is morally unacceptable.

The monstrosity of 9/11 occurred, in fact, because the government supplied the perpetrators with that advantage, illegally forbidding American citizens to fly properly protected (please, don't bring up those useless lumps known as "Air Marshals")—a policy we now call victim disarmament—and convincing the whorish media and a gullible public that the Second Amendment right to own and carry weapons, and the many social benefits it confers, somehow doesn't apply at 40,000 feet.

What can be done about it, short of violent revolution? Many individuals believe it's too late and that nothing can be done. But a simple fact that no one can dispute—a feature of reality that people need to stop evading and face squarely and courageously—is that if you continue to fly, your compliance is helping to take freedom away from your friends, family, neighbors, your countrymen and women.

I've often reflected that when you suffer blinding migraines, what you need, in the long run, is a CAT-scan or something like it, and perhaps surgery. But there's nothing wrong with taking an aspirin in the short run. Today, those blinding pains are in another part of our body politic, the part being brutally groped by the filthy hands of tyranny.

America was once the freest country in the history of the world, offering unprecedented peace, progress, prosperity, and above all, freedom to a new Productive Class. And it was freedom, of course, that let all the rest of it happen, that made all of us wealthy and secure, compared to the inhabitants of the rest of the globe, in a wonderful historical period when everyone wondered what marvel would be invented next.

With freedom, you can do anything. All things are possible. Without freedom, very little is possible except barbarism and death. Today, by comparison to the times of our great-grandfathers, we all languish in the debtors' prison that our country has become, bound down by the chains that should have been used to bind the government down.

For a long-run solution to this and many other problems currently plaguing the former land of the free and home of the brave, it is necessary to pay attention to Thomas Hobbes, an author unsympathetic to freedom, who I'm not generally accustomed to quoting, but who was pitch perfect when he declared in *Leviathan*, that "... covenants, without the sword, are but words...of no strength to secure a man at all."

America's Founding Fathers made a deadly error—or perhaps the Hamiltonian Federalists got what they actually wanted—when they failed to write a penalty clause into the Bill of Rights. If, for the past 220 years, we had been arresting, indicting, trying, convicting, and punishing politicians, bureaucrats, and policemen who violate or evade its provisions, we might have a completely different country today. A free country, technologically centuries ahead of where we are now.

Instead, our ancestors allowed the Founders to write the precise opposite into the Constitution, an immunity clause, Article I, Section 6, which has permitted what was so hard-won in the Revolution through bloodshed, gunpowder, and steel, to be gnawed away at and finally destroyed.

Our highest priority today must be to write that long overdue penalty clause ourselves, to make it, along with the Bill of Rights, the highest law of the land, and then to repeal Article I, Section 6. Supreme Court justices must be held to higher standards or replaced. Police departments must be reduced in numbers and demilitarized. After 49 years of political activism on my part, this is the only path I can see clearly, short of another bloody Revolution, to getting a free country for ourselves and for our children and grandchildren to live in.

The following proposed amendment has been criticized because it doesn't call for capital punishment, which may be a fair observation. A second clause, repealing Article I, Section 6, could be added. Whether it was ever ratified or not, if this proposal were circulating widely enough on the Internet, it might just give the many enemies of individual liberty some occasion to pause and to reflect on possible consequences:

> Any official, appointed or elected, at any level of government, who attempts, through legislative act or other means, to nullify, evade, or avoid the provisions of the first ten amendments to this Constitution, or of the Thirteenth Amendment, forbidding involuntary servitude of any kind, shall be summarily removed from office, and, upon conviction, deprived of all pay and benefits including pension, and sentenced to imprisonment for life.

But with regard to commercial air travel, right now and for the foreseeable future, the proper palliative is obvious. The airlines must be forced to choose between respecting the Bill of Rights or going bankrupt. They may choose the latter course, and then go whimpering to the government for subsidy, but government's means are limited. There isn't that much real money left to steal, and to print more would be suicidal.

Our policy must be *boycott*. I repeat: as long as you continue to fly, you are helping to take freedom away from your friends, family, neighbors, and your countrymen. Until the Bill of Rights is enforced in the air as it should be on the ground, don't buy, don't fly, don't comply.

Period.

If you're not willing to do what is necessary to restore freedom to the skies, then just stand there, spread your legs, and enjoy the grope.

It's your only alternative.

Ultimate Authority

Lies can be custom-tailored; truth comes straight off the
rack—one size fits all.

—CATHY L.Z. SMITH

An enormous amount of fluff has been floated by all sides of every issue over the concept of the United States Constitution as a "social contract."

Most pertinent, in all likelihood, to those individuals who call themselves libertarians, are the curious notions, stated in a little pamphlet, still in print, called No Treason: the Constitution of No Authority, of a 19th-century abolitionist lawyer with a splendidly sprawling beard, as well as the splendidly sprawling name of Lysander Spooner.

It was Spooner's contention that, under the principles of English common law established over the previous thousand years or so, if the Constitution, which was ratified in 1789, was any kind of contract at all—social or otherwise—then it could be binding only upon those fifty-odd individuals who had actually signed it, certainly not upon anyone who had not done so, and especially those who hadn't been born yet.

The Constitution, then, by Spooner's time, possessed or conveyed no authority, and it was no treason (a serious consideration at a time in history when pennies bore the inscription "Our Nation's Flag—Should Anyone Attempt to Haul It Down, Shoot Him on the Spot") to say so.

It's more than a little difficult to get past Spooner's argument, especially in a civilization in which "government is instituted among men, deriving its just powers from the consent of the governed." It may be the most important principle we live by, the only difference between rape and sex, after all, being consent. The late philosopher Robert LeFevre believed that this "consent of the governed" should be unanimous, or at least super-majoritarian in nature. Thanks to him, that's the idea my first novel, *The Probability Broach*, was founded on.

So if the Constitution isn't—and can't be—a social contract, what is it? It is a charter—a blueprint, if you will—controlling the activity of government in this country. (Interestingly, those who participate in various ways as members of the government, are legally required to take a binding oath to uphold and defend the Constitution, making their consent to it explicit.) I have long contended that it is an operating system, little different in its intended function from C/PM, DOS, Windows, Unix, or Linux, demonstrating about the same reliability, but to be altered or disregarded with many of the same consequences.

Most importantly, it's the one and only source from which those who exercise power in this country legally derive any claim to possess authority. Their faithful adherence to it ought to be the first—and possibly the only—qualification for obtaining and holding public office.

Unlike any other government on the planet, this one was handed a list by its founders—Article I, Section 8 of the Constitution—of all the things it can or must do. It's a short list, very specific. Anything else that government does, it does without Constitutional sanction, in violation of the law. Various experts differ as to how much government would be left if this one item were enforced. Whether it's a third, a quarter, or, as I suspect, five percent, it isn't much.

There is also a list (tacked on as an afterthought, which should have told us something) of things government can't do. It's the first ten amendments to the Constitution, commonly (but erroneously) called the Bill of Rights. There are certain things it's vital to know about it.

First and foremost, those ten amendments recognize the prior existence of rights. Most emphatically, they do not create or bestow them. They do attempt to guarantee or protect a number of them, basic rights that all human beings possess, simply by virtue of having been born. Which is to say, every man, woman, and child has unalienable individual, civil, Constitutional, and human rights that spring from our very existence, and not from any government document, doctrine, or dogma.

It should be noted that, since the Bill of Rights is a series of limits on government power, and not of rights we're "allowed" to exercise, there is no age limit involved. Children have exactly the same right to be free from molestation by agents of the government as adults. Which means, among other things, that they have a right to the means of self-defense, and to be free from the authoritarian socialist school system spying on their Facebook postings.

Second and foremost (yeah, I know) the Bill of Rights was never written for us, but for them—power-hungry clowns unhappy with the loose-knit gaggle of small republics that America consisted of under the Articles of Confederation, and who wanted a strong central state, instead. At the risk of repeating myself, the Bill of Rights is not a list of things we're allowed to do. As human beings, we are free to do any damn thing we want, and the word "allow" doesn't come into it at all, as long as it doesn't damage anybody else's right to do the same thing.

Third and foremost, there is no provision whatever, within the Constitution, for suspension of the Bill of Rights or any other part of the document. That's the only place such a provision could be, and it isn't there. And, since it is the highest law of the land, no lesser legislation can create such a provision. The Constitution stands, no matter what "emergency" or any other excuse is cited. Any member of the government who attempts to override or ignore the Constitution has not only violated his sworn oath of office, he is a criminal.

Other creatures have natural defenses they can use to preserve their lives. Lions have claws and teeth. Gazelles run swiftly. Prairie dogs duck down into their burrows. A human being's natural defenses are his rights, providing him with the freedom to employ his other faculties, his eyes, ears, hands, and brain to get him out of trouble. In any emergency, people's rights are their means of survival and are more important, not less, than at other times. Nor does it make sense to surrender our own judgment to "experts" who, for many reasons, are in no way qualified—and probably not particularly inclined—to make rational and efficacious survival decisions for us. It is certain laws that ought to be suspended during an emergency, not people's rights.

Fourth and foremost, some of the enemies of freedom will tell you, now and again, that your rights and mine, while possibly protected by the narrow and parochial Constitution, are nevertheless up for grabs under various treaties the government has made with other nations. Setting aside the question of whether the government should be allowed to do that (how many folks would be all that dismayed to see creatures like Madeleine Albright or Hillary Clinton propped up against a wall somewhere and shot for treason?), they couldn't be more completely wrong.

They will cite you a portion of the Constitution, Article VI, Section 2, that says treaties have the same clout as the Constitution itself. But here's the thing: that clause doesn't mention amendments. And amendments, by their very nature, take precedence over everything that went before them or is based on what went before them. So when Hillary tells us the UN will have our guns, now, thank you very much, we'll say, no it won't, the Second Amendment trumps any treaty you can write or sign, and, by the way, you're under arrest, under Title 18, Sections 241 and 242, for trying to violate our rights "under color of law."

Ironically, there are certain "progressive" locales—the city and county of Denver, Colorado, comes to mind—that claim their status under "home rule" allows them to violate the rights of their citizenry with impunity. And there are plenty of lunatics, cretins, and crooks— the Colorado Supreme Court comes to mind, as well—who, for one crazy, stupid, or corrupt reason or another, will back them.

But there can be no "home rule" when it comes to the Bill of Rights. That same clause, Article VI, Section 2, mandates that where the supreme law of the land—meaning, as we have seen, the Bill of Rights, not the Constitution itself, nor lesser laws, nor treaties—is concerned, "the Judges in every State shall be bound thereby, any Thing in the Constitution or Laws of any State to the Contrary notwithstanding."

It is judges, in the end, not bureaucrats or cops, who enforce the law.

Fifth and foremost (I'll bet you thought we were through with all that), there is an excellent reason why those in power should be interested in seeing the Bill of Rights as a series of laws that must be enforced, not simply rules to be gotten around, somehow. The first ten amendments were an absolute condition, imposed on the Federalists by the Anti-Federalists, on which ratification of the remainder of the Constitution depended. If you blow one, Mr. President, Mr. Governor, Mr. Mayor, then you break the deal, the Constitution is over with, and the whole house of cards comes crashing down. And since your authority is contingent upon the Constitution, you're out of power and out of luck.

These are the rules to which you, by your own actions, have been bound. They're your rules, Mr. President, Mr. Governor, Mr. Mayor, not mine, but by all that's sacred to anybody, you will abide by them.

For those of you who've never held a job in the private sector, let me make it very plain. No more Second Amendment (just to choose a single example), no more Bill of Rights. No Bill of Rights, no more Constitution. No Constitution, no more Mr. President, Mr. Governor, Mr. Mayor. No more you. It may be the legal equivalent of Windows Vista, but you won't like living in a country without an operating system.

With the rest of us.

Lysenko's Revenge

It isn't the fact that people go on and on reinventing the wheel that I mind so much, as their idiotic insistence on reinventing it square.

—L. NEIL SMITH

Once upon a time, one Trofim Denisovich Lysenko—and I should add that I owe this insight to my good friend and cherished colleague Albert Perez—was a peasant lad who attended a local university and quickly rose to become the supreme galootie of Russian agriculture, all because of a theory of his that clicked with certain aspects of Marxism.

A theory that—like Marxism itself—was completely bogus.

And wasn't really Lysenko's to begin with.

It seems that, about the time of the American Revolution, a bright young fellow with the elaborate moniker Jean-Baptiste Pierre Antoine de Monet, Chevalier de la Marck, a poor but proud French aristocrat—and one of the world's original thinkers about evolution—decided (I don't know why) that the process occurred through the inheritance of characteristics that were acquired by one's ancestors. In short (no pun intended) if you chopped off the tails of a sufficient number of generations of rats, baby rats would eventually be born without any tails.

The proper way to achieve this effect, of course, is to find and breed rats born naturally without tails, or selectively breed rats with smaller and smaller tails, until you have a family of rats that have no tail, the rodent equivalent of a Manx. (I've always said that "Manx!" is the noise a cat makes when you cut its tail off, but I was kidding.)

The Lamarckian theory of evolution by the inheritance of acquired characteristics was thoroughly disproven by the later work of Gregor Mendel and a great many others. In its time, however, it was widely considered to be leading-edge, favored even by Charles Darwin himself as an explanation for what he was seeing in the field. Comrade Lysenko appears to have come along a couple of centuries later and revived Lamarck, in the process vehemently denouncing Mendel and every legitimate geneticist who followed the good abbot as hopelessly bourgeoisie (for which read "Productive Class") and therefore counter-revolutionary.

Mendel himself was safely dead, beyond the reach of the Grand Inquisition or its modern offspring the OGPU. And in the ordinary course of events, a pseudoscientist like Lysenko would have been ignored as a psychopath or a charlatan. But this was Sovietized Russia, under the bloodstained thumb of Joseph "Stalin" Djugashvili, god-emperor himself of psychopaths and charlatans. The prophet Karl Marx had written that, having lived a sufficient number of generations under the "dictatorship of the proletariat," a new kind of human being would emerge—later known as "New Soviet Man"—who would automatically live his life for the sake of others, giving to them according to his abilities, letting them receive according to their needs.

This might be possible (although it would ultimately result in the extinction of our species; what other organism would accept such a suicidal philosophy?), if acquired traits—that is, traits forced on unwilling individuals at bayonet-point—were inheritable. The trouble was that they are not. As Ayn Rand pointed out, no matter how many generations of communists passed, individuals were still born and grew up demanding to be free. Mendel and his intellectual heirs—indeed the entire field of scientific genetics—became anti-Soviet heresy, punishable by arrest, exile, and death. More than one of Russia's foremost scientists was shot, or starved or worked to death in Siberia. Hundreds paid the penalty for their allegiance to the truth.

As with good and evil, in which any compromise is also evil, in any compromise between science and politics, science will inevitably lose. Supported by transparent fraud and naked brutality, Lysenkoism nevertheless reigned supreme within the Union of Soviet Socialist Republics from the 1920s until 1964, stunting the growth of real science, holding back progress, and through the repeated failure of Lysenko's crackpot Lamarckian agricultural theories, starving millions to death for decades. And regrettably—as we are beginning to see here in the West—this is exactly the kind of catastrophe that can happen to any culture, at any time that science and politics get mixed together.

It can start, for example, with skyrocketing fuel prices—the direct result of idiotic foreign policy, taxes and regulations, and the suppression of new technologies, bolstered by a surrealistic desire to create a "green" economy—and what then become advertised as energy shortages. In reality, it's the Developed World's equivalent of a Cambodian forced march and will eventually produce the same results.

Look: a company in any other branch of industry wants you to buy as much of their product as you can, in part so that they are able to manufacture a greater volume, lowering their costs and passing savings on to their customer who will be motivated to buy even more. This is a familiar part of the happy cycle of profit and progress under real capitalism.

As Robert LeFevre pointed out long ago, only an industry that is run by government, or to government standards, refers to its customers as "pigs" for "buying too much." And only in a government-run economy are individuals, desperate just to obtain the necessities of life, forced to stand in long lines for hours to purchase shoddy and over-priced products.

Exactly as no shortage of food on this planet is responsible for people in the Third World or anywhere else not having enough to eat, no lack of resources is responsible for what are advertised as energy shortages.

In the Third World, governments—corrupt politicos and military dictators looking to starve their enemies or simply for their piece of the action—stand between food producers and consumers. In the First World, similar obstructions are augmented by the established energy companies desperate to keep efficient, innovative competitors out of the market. They endorse solar and wind power, of course, because they're trivial and impractical; historians of the future will laugh at them. But suppressed technologies like catalytic fusion and thermal depolymerization constitute a real threat—except that they have to get past ranks of bureaucratic and political gatekeepers, dedicated to defending the interests—and the vast fortunes—of energy's Old Guard.

But I have digressed.

"Manmade Global Warming" is a collection of ideas that have been thoroughly discredited by real science for years. Yet you would never know it by observing the behavior of politicians, media personalities, and certain corrupt academics and scientists. There is not now, nor has there ever been, any scientifically respectable evidence for global warming. Just like Lysenkoism, it is a complete and total fabrication, a hoax, deliberately perpetrated for prestige, power, and material gain.

The field is rich, but three facts alone are sufficient to dismiss it out of hand. Recently, when the Earth was indeed warming slightly, Mars and Jupiter were enjoying the same relatively balmy weather. I could be wrong, of course, but to the best of my knowledge, there are no farting cows or SUVs on either of those planets. Earth's climate seems to be more closely linked—and not unreasonably—to what's happening with the Sun, than to anything our species does or doesn't do.

Then, too, there's the intriguing truth that high levels of carbon dioxide actually follow periods of atmospheric warming, by roughly 900 years, not the other way around as advertised. Be that as it may, carbon dioxide, far from being an enemy of the Earth as ludicrously claimed by those who wish to make an Original Sin of exhaling, is the staff of life for plants. High levels of the stuff have produced the lushest periods in geological history. And plants, in turn, make oxygen.

Finally, Global Warming's most "respectable" proponents, at the University of East Anglia, Pennsylvania State University, and NASA, have been caught cherry-picking evidence or simply fabricating it altogether.

Of course it hasn't helped the poor warmistas that the winters lately have been colder, record-breakingly so, forcing humiliating cancellations of their tax-supported confabs. Nor that the northern and southern icecaps have been growing thicker and more extensive, rather than otherwise. Nor that as many (if not more) glaciers are growing as retreating. Nor that there have been fewer, not more, hurricanes. And worst of all, that the carbon credit exchange they'd all hoped to make trillions from collapsed and died an ignominious death.

No polar bears were drowned in the composition of the paragraph above.

Yet Global Warming (now known euphemistically as "Climate Change" in the same spirit-of-the-catbox that "liberal" became "progressive") continues to eke out a strictly political life because, exactly as Lysenkoism served Stalinism by backing up Marx's flawed biological conceits, Global Warming serves today's collectivists—in particular the United Nations and their vicious Agenda 21—by offering them an endless supply of justifications to seize absolute control, not merely of the means of production as Marx had aspired to do, but of each moment, breath, thought, word, footstep, gesture, and every other aspect of the lives of the unfortunate individuals within their malign reach.

To be absolutely certain that there be no opposition to their vile putsch, dissenters—honest meteorologists and other scientists who dismiss Global Warming as the crock it happens to be—have found themselves intimidated, denied funding and tenure, even fired. Here and there you'll even see demands in astonishingly high places that all "climate change deniers" (how much more appropriate it would be, simply to call them "heretics") should be prosecuted, imprisoned, or even executed. Somewhere, the ghosts of Stalin and Lysenko are having a huge laugh together, along with Savonarola, Torquemada, Himmler, and Mengele.

And now we see exactly the same methods being applied to promote another con-game called "socialized medicine." The reputation for failure that this bonnet-bee has acquired since it was first rolled out in Prussia in the 1880s should be enough. And yet its advocates appear to be motivated more by a species of religious faith than by evidence and reason. Anyone who objects to having this monstrosity foisted on them by naked force is denounced by its proponents—moral and intellectual bankrupts unable to construct any rational, coherent arguments in its favor—as "brownshirts," "racists," or "Nazis," when in fact it is their jackboots that we are feeling on our necks.

There's really only one cure for this societal disease, and that is a Constitutional amendment which, once and for all, will mandate a formal separation of science—especially medicine—and state, in effect, denying government funds to all forms of scientific (as well as anti-scientific) endeavor. We must leave technical progress to the market, instead, which once made us the most productive, prosperous, and progressive nation in the history of humanity. Government funding of science has always been a corrupting influence, skewing the pursuit of knowledge in directions it wouldn't have taken without political pressure.

Naturally, this will lead to calls for the abolition of corporate taxes (which are not paid by corporations in any case, but passed on to individuals like you and me, through prices that are higher than they would be otherwise) so that there will be sufficient capital for companies—and individuals—to invest in genuine scientific endeavor.

It's long past time that we rid ourselves of "Lysenkoism American Style." We must scrap every article of legislation inspired by the discredited theory of Global Warming, and for the most part, by environmentalism in general. We must remove the corrupt politicians and bureaucrats guilty of having rammed it all down our throats. We must prosecute the academic hoaxsters behind the lie of "climate change."

While we're at it, we should give the United Nations and all of its little tentacles 24 hours to get the hell off the North American Continent.

And then we can get on with the important business—clearly beyond the average Marxist's comprehension—of living in a free society.

The Plan

THE PROBLEM

The United States of America are in trouble. To some, it is a horrible surprise. Many others have helplessly watched it coming for years.

At the most fundamental levels, with regard to its continued national and cultural existence, in both economic and philosophical terms, this country is in vastly worse danger at this moment than it was during the so-called Great Depression or the War Between the States. More and more, it appears that the destruction of the American economy and the civilization it supports was a deliberately calculated act.

No fewer than fifteen decades of federal government usurpation and mismanagement—culminating in the most openly rapacious and criminal administrations in its history—have brought the nation to this point. Of the ruling parties, the Democrats are arguably the worst offenders in this regard, relentlessly expanding the power and scope of government, invariably at the expense of the personal freedom and individual enterprise this country was supposed to have been all about.

The War Century was largely a Democratic century.

While Republicans properly criticize the many shortcomings of the Democrats, they systematically and hypocritically overlook or ignore their own part in the destruction of a civilization that once stood as the brightest hope for all Mankind. Both have conspired together to block any third party that might have set America on a different course, one more consistent with the dreams and aspirations of its Founders.

In any event, this essay is about what needs to be done, without regard to who might actually do it, Democrat, Republican, or anybody else, with the warning and understanding that if it doesn't get done, America is doomed, the rest of the world will inexorably follow, and our species is about to plunge into a long, dark night that may never end.

THE SOLUTION

It may come as an annoyance to individuals who think of themselves as "nuts and bolts" problem-solvers that in the field of practical economics, expectations can be just as important as actualities. To them, I'm sure that sounds indistinguishable from the very cynical observation that in politics, perception is more important than reality.

But the fact is that people in an economic context have to be able to plan, and to do that, they have to make guesses about a future which, at best, is always murky, and which, muddled by half-witted, ham-fisted, off-and-on government interference, becomes impossible to predict.

America is in a Depression, and more loans, to the banks or from the banks, more money-printing—more debt—aren't going to get it out. Make no mistake about who is responsible for what happened. For decades, both parties spent vastly more than the government took in, creating debt—with interest—that had be paid by printing paper money and generating credit where there was no real wealth to back it up.

The mortal blow to America's future came when lending institutions were forced by Congress, first under the Carter Administration, and then again under the Clinton Administration, to make home loans to individuals they knew perfectly well would be unable to pay them back. Naturally, as defaults and foreclosures started to pile up, the banks began to fail, which caused a cascade—an avalanche—of other failures.

It didn't help that by then the country was embroiled in two illegal, expensive, and irrational wars in the Middle East, initiated for the most cynical of reasons, using the atrocity of 9/11 as an excuse.

In any case, the financial collapse was in no way the fault of capitalism or the market system, as the opportunistic left which bears the real guilt—and its whorish media—presently claims, but of a command-and-control system which, no less than that of the late, unlamented Soviets, was doomed to collapse of its own unbearable weight.

The current administration has done nothing right and everything wrong; increasing numbers of individuals think it isn't any accident. What's actually needed is a stability of expectations, and an end to the lethal drain on the country's resources that government, in fact, represents.

TAXES

The first, most important thing that anyone in charge should do is declare a universal tax amnesty. All past debts to government at any level will be null and void. That alone would be sufficient to stop the plunge, trigger growth, and start businesses and industry hiring again.

Any government shortfalls caused by this policy should be dealt with, not by more deficit spending, but by serious reductions in government activity, by downsizing personnel, and by liquidation of assets.

And that's just for practice. The next step, to be announced at the same time as the amnesty—aimed at restoring predictability to the market while infusing it with cash (or, rather, allowing it to infuse itself), without government loans or further inflation—must be a total moratorium on every form of taxation, for a period of at least one year, so that the economy can get back on its feet and recover from the damage the last several administrations have done to it.

Once again, when politicians and bureaucrats whimper, demanding to know who will "pay" for such a "program," they will be informed that they will. Government will do less. And it holds millions of acres of land and tens of thousands of buildings that can be auctioned off (once the original owners have been made whole), endless parking lots covered with vehicles, hangars full of aircraft, harbors full of boats and ships, vast warehouses stuffed with hardware and supplies that were obtained with stolen money and should be returned to the free market.

If all else fails, there are at least a hundred—or perhaps a thousand—times as many public employees as there ought to be. Some can be let go, as well. The recovering market should absorb them with ease.

During the tax moratorium, the details can be worked out on an innovative new two-tier system—in reality, simply another interim measure—under which no taxes of any kind may be levied against any object or activity protected by the Bill of Rights (establishing long overdue parity with the First Amendment protection afforded to churches and religion) or against any of the five fundamental human requirements of life, food, clothing, shelter, transportation, and self-defense.

Healthcare would be included under self-defense; a separate effort would be called for to establish a formal, Constitutional separation of medicine and state, exactly as there needs to be for science and state.

Another essential change is the permanent and total abolition of taxes on so-called "capital gains." Americans are always criticized, the world over, for not putting enough money in savings. The primary reason is basically Marxoid-inspired legislation against "unearned income."

Likewise, so-called "corporate taxation" is just another cynical shot at sucking the Productive Class dry—mostly with their own idiotic approval. No corporation pays taxes, they pass them on to their customers, doubling the price of goods and services. Abolishing corporate taxation would, in and of itself, create an historic economic boom that will change the course of American—and world—history.

So-called "limited liability" must end, as well, along with the pernicious legal fiction that the corporation is a person, pulling a long overdue emergency brake on the size, wealth, influence, and power of corporations, and forcing their owners—the stockholders who used to be in control—to take full responsibility for whatever companies do.

The ultimate goal, of course, must be the total elimination of all taxation. Abolitionists who struggled for three hundred fifty years to put an end to chattel slavery faced no more daunting a task. One of the problems this supposedly revolutionary country has always suffered is that its government—no different from the stagnant European satrapies it should have differentiated itself from in this regard—is financed by extortion and theft, the pervasive threat to beat non-compliers up, kidnap, or kill them. At the most charitable, it's a rotten example for teaching children proper behavior. It makes one wonder whether facing the slings and arrows of no government at all might be a better choice than paying government to protect us from itself.

HONEST MONEY

Along with freeing America from taxation, the nation must be free of government-issued fiat money, as well, allowing the market system to create, all by itself, many kinds of money from commodities with an intrinsic value, and imposing no coercive standard on anyone of any kind.

Money is, above and beyond everything, a medium of communication, conveying the vital datum known as "price"—how much of a thing should be made, what should it be sold for—the lack of which killed the Soviet Union and spells ultimate death for any command-and-control economy. A government monopoly on money is censorship. And inflation—printing too much paper money or generating "air credit"—is a lie.

REGULATION

At the same time, as taxes are being cut and abolished, something must be done about the mind-boggling, back-breaking burden of laws and regulations at all levels of government, federal, state, county, and municipal. Speed is of the essence if decades of damage inflicted by Democrats and Republicans is to be repaired—yet, some estimate that there are in excess of fifteen million regulations at just the federal level.

Individuals must be free—they must be encouraged, in fact—to make what would amount to criminal charges against regulations and regulators on Constitutional, as well as other grounds. Government must be compelled to defend itself—and each and every item of regulation—in purely Constitutional terms, or to abandon the given regulation altogether. In the end, a thorough sweep of regulations must be made, employing Article I, Section 8—which explicitly enumerates the very few acceptable functions of government—as a broom.

JUSTICE

This plan would not be complete without mentioning certain items of "housekeeping" that must be done before this nation can begin to heal.

Foremost among those items is to bring a halt to the criminal mischief committed by the last two administrations under the guise of economic "stimulus." This "policy" must be brought to a halt now, and any unspent money returned to the general fund. Political cronies who were the actual beneficiaries of this giveaway scheme must be stripped of all their embezzled fortunes while the politicians responsible are removed from office and prosecuted for having violated their oath of office.

Other measures are called for if we are to get this recovery right and prevent our grandchildren from having to do it all over again. No lawyers, for example, should ever be permitted in the legislature or in any other lawmaking body. Their self-serving presence there today represents a massive conflict of interest that must be swiftly resolved.

The Founding Fathers' worst, most calamitous mistake must be corrected by giving the Bill of Rights a penalty clause with real teeth.

It might go something like this:

> "Any official, appointed or elected, at any level of government, who attempts, through legislative act or other means, to nullify, evade, or avoid the provisions of the first ten amendments to this Constitution, or of the Thirteenth Amendment, forbidding involuntary servitude of any kind, shall be summarily removed from office, and, upon conviction, deprived of all pay and benefits, including pension, and sentenced to imprisonment for life."

The medieval doctrine of Sovereign Immunity—the vile notion that the King can do no wrong—must be dispensed with, once and for all.

Consistent with that, this nation can never heal fully until the criminals actually responsible for atrocities like the Philadelphia MOVE bombing, Ruby Ridge, Waco, and perhaps even the Oklahoma City bombing (to mention only four of many) are hunted down and brought to justice.

And at the end of the reform period, a greater Moratorium, against all further legislation of any kind for 100 years, must be appended to the Constitution. A notable single exception would be made for bills of repeal.

No discussion of economic reform and recovery can be considered complete without finally addressing two clusters of issues that have always impinged directly on this nation's economic health and well-being.

TRADE

The first, international trade, is relatively easy to dispose of. In a country that is truly free—not one that merely says it is, or pretends to be—any decision about what to trade, or with whom, or for how much, does not rest with government, which can have nothing legitimate whatever to say with regard to "acts of capitalism between consenting adults," but with individual consumers, businessmen, and entrepreneurs.

Tariffs, a form of taxation that has been with us since America's beginning, have distorted markets, drained resources, made ill-gotten fortunes for the politically connected, and caused the War Between the States. There are many who argue that tariffs also cause international wars.

Businesses that try to use tariffs against foreign competitors are picking our pockets by denying us the benefits of free trade. They don't deserve to be protected by the law. And any "agreement" longer than half a page is not about free trade, no matter what it calls itself.

RATIONAL DEFENSE

Finally, there is the matter of foreign policy and war.

Throughout America's history, its government has managed to supply at least one war for each generation of old men to send young men off to fight for them, just as they were sent off in their youth to fight for their generation of old men. The cycle is insane and must be stopped.

Elsewhere, I have listed America's major conflicts and examined each to see if it could be called a "just war." The vast majority fail to pass the examination. Only the Revolution, the Mexican War, and the War Between the States pass muster. All the rest were irrational, fought to enrich some group or enhance their power, and could have been avoided altogether, along with the death and destruction they caused.

"Why those three wars in particular?" I pretend to hear you ask.

Well, pretty obviously, if there hadn't been a Revolution, there wouldn't be any United States of America. I have friends—mostly British—who think our War of Independence was unnecessary, but I doubt we'd have made the centuries-spanning leap, technologically, economically, and especially in terms of the philosophy of individual liberty, that we made had we remained a part of that mercantilist empire.

America had no choice about the Mexican War, which was declared by Mexico against the United States because it had annexed Texas—the independence of which politicians in Mexico insanely refused to recognize despite their defeat by Sam Houston at the Battle of San Jacinto and the utter humiliation of General Antonio Lopez de Santa Anna. Mexico deserved what she got, her whimperings to the contrary notwithstanding.

Finally, there is the matter of the War Between the States, commonly, but incorrectly, known as the Civil War. From a Northern point of view, it was as unnecessary as any other war the United States has involved itself in. (Contrary to Lincolnian propaganda and popular, public school belief, it had nothing whatever to do with black chattel slavery—if it had, then why do we have photographs of the Capitol dome being rebuilt throughout the war—by slaves?) But for the South, there was no alternative. While Southerners represented only a quarter of the U.S. population, through tariffs imposed by the North they were already paying 80 percent of the taxes. Lincoln and his orcs promised to triple the tariff, reducing all Southerners to serfdom.

And yes, I include the so-called "good war" as unnecessary. In fact it was an observation of my father—a gallant Air Corps veteran, former prisoner of war, and 30-year career Air Force officer—about the strange coincidence of a war for each generation, that made me think about the other wars Americans have fought to no good purpose.

It is impossible to estimate the degree to which all these wars, especially in the 20th century, distorted our history and retarded its progress. The trillions spent prosecuting them, the resulting waste of resources consumed and destroyed, the loss of human potential would be paralyzing, were we not thoroughly numbed to it by close historical acquaintance.

Just a single sobering thought: the genius who might have cured cancer died, instead, as a nineteen-year-old private or seaman in World War I, World War II, Korea, Vietnam, Iraq, the Balkans, or in Afghanistan.

And for what? The government and its useful idiots say it was for freedom. But not a single American's freedom was ever endangered by any of these enemies. And not one of these wars prevented what happened on 9/11/2001.

No, for once I have not digressed. If America is ever to recover from this economic crisis, its leaders will have to give up their addiction to war, even though it is, indeed, the very "health of the state."

Two solutions come to mind. The first is what I call the "You Go First Amendment" under which (1) the War Powers Act is repealed so that no President can ever start a war again without a Congressional declaration of war, and (2) all those voting for such a declaration will immediately join the (now former) President who requested it, in uniform, on the prospective battlefield, ahead of anybody else in the military.

Finally, because taxation is the fuel of war, military spending, as we have experienced it since World War II, has to stop. If the country needs to be defended, let it be done as the Founding Fathers intended, by a network of well-armed, well-trained, and well-supplied volunteer militias—preferably organized and prepared at the county level—among whom the technical means to defend America must be distributed.

Freed of being the "cops of the world," we will prosper as never before.

THE FUTURE

As to how we get from here to there, I believe showing people what "there" is like may motivate them to work to change "here." That was the idea behind my novel *The Probability Broach*, the only shortcoming of which is that so far it hasn't reached a sufficiently wide audience.

Of course it may, if things continue to get worse.

What happens next is entirely up to you. Every politician in the country, in every party and at every level of government, must be made familiar with "The Plan." None of them—not even the Libertarians or Tea Party Republicans—are going to want to take the steps outlined here. They will attempt to pat you on the head or react hysterically. They will call you names—like "radical" or "extremist"—and threaten you. If you're reading this, you have already been identified by the unconstitutional Department of Homeland Security as a domestic terrorist.

It is up to you to hold fast through that period.

Then slowly, timidly, as these ideas start to spread, some will adopt portions of what's offered here, ultimately claiming it as their own.

Let them.

We will know the truth.

L. NEIL SMITH

Fort Collins, Colorado

March 2011

Index